THE JUDGE IN A DEMOCRACY

THE JUDGE IN A DEMOCRACY

Aharon Barak

PRINCETON UNIVERSITY PRESS   PRINCETON AND OXFORD

Library of Congress Cataloging-in-Publication Data
Barak, Aharon.
The judge in a democracy / Aharon Barak.
p. cm.
Includes index.
ISBN-13: 978-0-691-12017-1 (hardcover : alk. paper)
ISBN-10: 0-691-12017-X (hardcover : alk. paper)
1. Judges. 2. Judicial process. 3. Law—Interpretation and construction.
4. Judicial power. 5. Judges—Israel. 6. Judicial power—Israel.
7. Judge-made law—Israel. 8. Courts—Israel. 9. Israel.
Bet ha-mishpaòt ha-'elyon. 1. Title.
K2146.B37 2006
347'.014—dc22
2005028578

British Library Cataloging-in-Publication Data is available

This book has been composed in Galliard

Printed on acid-free paper.

pup.princeton.edu

Printed in the United States of America

1 3 5 7 9 10 8 6 4 2

Contents

Introduction

I am not a philosopher. I am not a political scientist. I am a judge—a judge in the highest court of my country's legal system. So I ask myself a question that many supreme court judges—and, in fact, all judges on all courts in modern democracies[1]—ask themselves: What is my role as a judge? Certainly it is my role, and the role of every judge, to decide the dispute before me. Certainly it is my role, as a member of my nation's highest court, to determine the law by which the dispute before me should be decided. Certainly it is my role to decide cases according to the law of my legal system. But is that all that can be said about my role? Are there criteria for assessing the quality of my work as a judge? Certainly no such assessment should be based on the aesthetic quality of my writing.[2] Nor should the criterion be the number of sources I cite in my decisions. But then what would be a meaningful criterion? What is my role, and do I even have a role beyond merely deciding the dispute before me according to the law? These questions occupy me daily as I enter the courtroom and take my seat on the bench. In my twenty-six years of service on the Supreme Court of Israel, I have written thousands of opinions. But am I a "good" judge?

[1] *See generally* Michael Kirby, "Judging: Reflections on the Moment of Decision," 18 *Austl. B. Rev.* 4 (1999); Beverley M. McLachlin, "The Charter: A New Role for the Judiciary?" 29 *Alta. L. Rev.* 540 (1991); Beverley M. McLachlin, "The Role of the Court in the Post-Charter Era: Policy-Maker or Adjudicator?" 39 *U. N.B. L.J.* 43 (1990); Georghios M. Pikis, "The Constitutional Position and Role of the Judge in a Civil Society," *Commonwealth Jud. J.*, Dec. 2000, at 7.

[2] Although aesthetics are important, as Richard Posner's discussion of Justice Cardozo indicates. *See* Richard A. Posner, *Cardozo: A Study in Reputation* 10, 42, 143 (1990).

This question is important not merely to judges who want to assess their performance, but to the system as a whole. The answer determines the criteria for developing the law and provides a basis for formulating a system of interpretation of all legal texts. Establishing criteria for judging judges is particularly important in view of the frequent attempts to dress up political problems in legal garb and place them before the court. De Tocqueville 170 years ago characterized this tendency to legalize political questions as a quirk of the United States.[3] Today, however, this phenomenon is common in modern democracies.[4] How are we judges to deal with political problems that have taken on a legal character?

The questions I wish to consider are not new. They are as old as judging itself, and they have accompanied various legal systems in their progressions throughout history. Sometimes they can be found at the center of public debate. Sometimes they are marginalized. The time has come to reconsider these questions. There are four main reasons for their timeliness.

First, democracy is celebrating its victories over Nazism and Fascism in World War II and over communism at the end of the twentieth century. Our age is the age of democracy.[5] New countries have joined the community of democracies. Many of them wish to reexamine the nature of modern democracy,[6] which is not based solely on the rule of people through their representatives (formal democracy) but also on the separation of powers, the independence of the judiciary, the rule of law, and human rights (substantive democracy). A key historical lesson of the Holocaust is that the people, through their representatives, can destroy democracy and

---

[3] Alexis de Tocqueville, *Democracy in America* 97 (Harvey C. Mansfield and Delba Winthrop eds.-trans., 2000) (1835).

[4] *See, e.g.*, McLachlin, "The Role of the Court," *supra* p. ix, note 1 at 49–50.

[5] See Richard H. Pildes, "The Supreme Court 2003 Term—Foreword: The Constitutionalization of Democratic Politics," 118 *Harv. L. Rev.* 28, 29 (2004) ("This Is the Age of Democracy"). *See also* Fareed Zakaria, *The Future of Freedom: Illiberal Democracy at Home and Abroad* 13 (2003).

[6] *See generally* Bruce Ackerman, *The Future of Liberal Revolution* (1992); Herman Schwartz, *The Struggle for Constitutional Justice in Post-Communist Europe* (2000); Ruti G. Teitel, *Transitional Justice* (2000); *Transition to Democracy in Latin America: The Role of the Judiciary* (Irwin P. Totsky ed., 1993).

human rights. Since the Holocaust, all of us have learned that human rights are the core of substantive democracy. The last few decades have been revolutionary, as we have learned the hard way that without protection for human rights, there can be no democracy and no justification for democracy. The protection of human rights—the rights of every individual and every minority group—cannot be left only in the hands of the legislature and the executive, which, by their nature, reflect majority opinion. Consequently, the question of the role of the judicial branch in a democracy arises.

Second, democracy today faces the emerging threat of terrorism. Passive democracy has been transformed into defensive democracy. All of us are concerned that it not become democracy run rampant. As judges, we are aware of the tension between the need to protect the state and the rights of the individual. This ever-present tension intensifies and becomes more pronounced in times of national emergency. What is the role of the judge in these special situations?[7]

Third, since World War II there has been a better understanding of the nature of judging.[8] Legal realism, positivism, the natural law movement, the legal process movement, critical legal studies, and the movements to integrate other intellectual disciplines into law have provided new tools for understanding the complexity of the judicial role. I find much truth in all of these approaches. Nonetheless, like the human condition, legal reality is too complex to be adequately captured by any one of these schools of thought. In my opinion, it is time for what I call an eclectic reexamination of the various theories about the judicial role. This reexamination is timely now, as globalization exposes us to ideals and thoughts that transcend national boundaries and legal systems.[9]

Finally, a survey of the de facto status of the judicial branches in the various democracies shows that since the end of World War II, the importance of the judiciary relative to the other branches of the

[7] *See infra* p. 283.
[8] *See generally* Brian Bix, *Jurisprudence: Theory and Context* (3d ed. 2003). *See also* Duncan Kennedy, *A Critique of Adjudication (fin de siècle)* (1977); William Lucy, *Understanding and Explaining Adjudication* (1999).
[9] *See generally* William Twining, *Globalisation and Legal Theory* (2000).

state has increased.[10] We are witnessing a strong trend toward "the constitutionalization of democratic politics."[11] People increasingly turn to the judiciary, hoping it can solve pressing social problems. Several questions therefore arise: Is this enhanced judicial status appropriate? Have judges taken on too much power? Has the separation of powers become blurred? Indeed, some claim that in recent years, the gap has widened between the practices and public expectations of democratic courts, on the one hand, and the intellectual-normative principles that are supposed to guide the courts on the other. This gap is dangerous, because over time, it will likely undermine public confidence in judges. Some now argue that judges are too active and that the constitution should be taken away from the courts.[12] Others argue that they are too self-restrained. These criticisms come from all corners of society. In recent years, for example, accusations that the U.S. Supreme Court is too activist have swelled.[13] Such allegations should be evaluated within the framework of a court's role in a democracy. A reexamination is therefore needed, and conclusions must be drawn, both about what can be demanded of judges and about what can be expected from the normative frameworks within which they operate.

---

[10] See The Power of Judges: A Comparative Study of Courts and Democracy (Carlo Guarnieri and Patrizia Pederzolil eds., C.A. Thomas (English ed.), 2002); Alec Stone Sweet, The Judicial Construction of Europe (2004); Ran Hirshl, "Restituting the Judicialization of Politics: Bush v. Gore as a Global Trend," 15 Can. J.L & Jons 191 (2002); Ran Hirshl, Towards Juristocracy: The Origin and Consequences of the New Constitution (2004); Tim Koopmans, Courts and Political Institutions: A Comparative View (2003). As to the Hungarian experience after the fall of communism, see Constitutional Judiciary in a New Democracy: The Hungarian Constitutional Court (László Sólyon and Georg Brunner eds., 2000); Richard Hodder-Williams, Judges and Politics in the Contemporary Age (1996).

[11] Richard Pildes, "The Supreme Court 2003 Term—Foreword: The Constitutionalization of Democratic Politics," 118 Harv. L. Rev. 28, 31 (2004).

[12] See Mark Tushnet, Taking the Constitution Away from the Courts (1994). See also Mark Tushnet, The New Constitutional Order (2003). Compare also Larry D. Kramer, The People Themselves: Popular Constitutionalism and Judicial Review (2004).

[13] See, e.g., Larry D. Kramer, "The Supreme Court, 2000 Term—Foreword: We the Court," 115 Harv. L. Rev. 4, 130–58 (2001).

These questions do not arise in the "easy cases"[14] in which there is only one answer to the legal problem and the judge has no choice but to choose it. Such cases do not generally reach the highest court at all. But how am I to decide the "hard cases,"[15] the cases in which the legal problem has more than one legal answer? These are the cases that find their way to the highest court, and I have discretion[16] in resolving them.[17] My decision may be legitimate, but how do I know if it is the proper one? What must I do in order to fulfill my role? What *is* my role?

One might try to dismiss my question with the philosophical argument that there are no "hard cases", and that judicial discretion in this sense does not exist. This answer is far from satisfactory. Even Professor Ronald Dworkin, proponent of the theory that every legal problem has only one correct answer,[18] merely says that there are better and worse judicial decisions.[19] He propounds a complete theory describing how Judge Hercules should make the better decision in "hard cases." Is Hercules the proper model by which we should judge?[20] Whatever the philosophical answer may

---

[14] With respect to the easy cases, *see* Aharon Barak, *Judicial Discretion* 36–39 (Yadin Kaufmann trans., 1989).

[15] I define a "hard case" as a case in which a judge has the power to choose between two alternatives, both of which are lawful. The power to choose is judicial discretion. This discretion is not a psychological concept. It reflects a normative situation. It expresses the legal community's position on the distinction between lawful and nonlawful. *See* Barak, *supra* p. xiii, note 14 at 20. *See also* Tom Bingham, *The Business of Judging: Selected Essays and Speeches* 35 (2000); Kenneth Davis, *Discretionary Justice* (1969).

[16] On discretion generally, *see* *The Uses of Discretion* (Keith Hawkins ed., 1992); D.J. Galligan, *Discretionary Powers: A Legal Study of Official Discretion* (1986).

[17] *See generally* Marisa Iglesias Vila, *Facing Judicial Discretion: Legal Knowledge and Right Answers Revisited* (2001).

[18] *See* Ronald Dworkin, *Taking Rights Seriously* 81 (1977); Ronald Dworkin, "Judicial Discretion," 60 *J. Phil.* 624, 624–25 (1963).

[19] Ronald Dworkin, "Pragmatism, Right Answers, and True Banality," in *Pragmatism in Law and Society* 359, 367 (Michael Brint and William Weaver eds., 1991). *See also* Bingham, *supra* p. xiii, note 15 at 25.

[20] On Dworkin's Hercules, *see* Ronald Dworkin, *Law's Empire* 239–40 (1986). On other models, *see* *Judges in Contemporary Democracy: An International Conversation* (Robert Badinter and Stephen Breyer eds., 2004).

be, the reality is that the large majority of judges think, as I do, that in some cases they do have a choice.[21] This thought is not an expression of judicial delusions of grandeur, nor is it the result of judicial imperialism. It reflects the uncertainty inherent in law. The source of this uncertainty is the uncertainty of language, the limitations of the creator of the legal text, and the uncertainty of interpretive rules.[22] Of course, the power to choose— judicial discretion—is never absolute. It is always subject to procedural limitations (such as fairness) and substantive limitations (such as reasonability, coherency, consistency, and rationality). But what should the judge do when the scales are balanced? In such cases, it is not that their decisions legitimate their rulings, but rather that their decisions are based on a legitimacy that precedes the rulings. Their judicial discretion is an expression of this legitimacy. How, then, should judicial discretion be exercised? When does exercising judicial discretion advance the role of a judge, and when does it depart from the proper path? What is the proper path?

I reject the contention that the judge merely states the law and does not create it. It is a fictitious, even childish approach.[23] Montesquieu's theory that the judge is "no more . . . than the mouth that produces the words of the law"[24] is similarly discredited. I suspect that most judges believe that, in addition to stating the law, they sometimes create law. Regarding the common law, this is certainly true: no common law system is the same today as it was fifty years ago, and judges are responsible for these changes. This change involves creation. The same is true of the interpretation of a legal

---

[21] *See* Alan Paterson, *The Law Lords* 190–95 (1982).

[22] *See* Brian Bix, *Law, Language and Legal Determinacy* (1993).

[23] *See* Bora Laskin, "The Role and Functions of Final Appellate Courts: The Supreme Court of Canada," 53 *Can. B. Rev.* 469, 477–80 (1975); Anthony Lester, "English Judges as Law Makers," 1993 *Pub. L.* 269, 269 (quoting Reid, *infra*, at 22); Lord Reid, "The Judge as Law Maker," 12 *J. Soc'y Pub. Tchrs. L.* 22 (1973); Tom Bingham, "The Judge as Lawmaker: An English Perspective," in *The Struggle for Simplicity in the Law: Essays for Lord Cook of Thorndon* 3 (Paul Rishworth ed., 1997).

[24] Montesquieu, *The Spirit of the Laws* 209 (Thomas Nugent trans., Univ. Cal. Press 1977) (1750).

text. The meaning of the law before and after a judicial decision is not the same. Before the ruling, there were, in the hard cases, several possible solutions. After the ruling, the law is what the ruling says it is. The meaning of the law has changed. New law has been created. What is my role, as a judge, in this creative process?

When I refer to the role of the judge, I do not mean to suggest that the judge has a political agenda. As a judge, I have no political agenda. I do not engage in party politics or in politics of any other kind. My concern is with judicial policy, that is, with formulating a systematic and principled approach to exercising my discretion. I ask whether judges, who set precedent for other courts, have (or should have) a judicial policy with regard to the way we exercise our discretion. I wish to examine the judicial philosophy underlying our role as judges in our democracies.[25]

Different judges have varying answers to the question that I am posing.[26] These differences stem from variances in education, personalities, responses to the world around us, and outlooks on the world in which we live. This is only natural. Each judge is a distinct world unto himself, and we would not wish it otherwise. Ideological pluralism, not ideological uniformity, is the hallmark of judges in democratic legal systems. Diverse judges reflect—but do not represent—the different opinions that exist in their societies. But I think many of us agree that the question I have posed is central to our function as judges, even if we disagree about its answer. Our judicial policy and our judicial philosophy are fundamental to us, since they guide us in our most difficult hours. Every judge has difficult hours. They mold us and give us self-confidence. They inform us that our strength as judges is in understanding our limitations. They teach us

---

[25] Justice Cardozo performed similar examinations—with great success—in his books, particularly in Benjamin N. Cardozo, *The Nature of the Judicial Process* (1921). *See* Posner, *supra* p. ix, 2 at 32 (noting that Cardozo's nonjudicial writings are a contribution to jurisprudence, but adding that "they are not only that. They are also a judge's effort to articulate his methods of judging"). *The Nature of the Judicial Process* is the first systemic effort by a judge to explain how judges reason and to articulate a judicial philosophy.

[26] For the views of leading English judges, see Bingham, *supra* p. xiii, note 15; Johan Steyn, *Democracy Through Law: Selected Speeches and Judgments* (2004).

that, more than we have answers to the difficult legal problems that confront us, we have questions regarding the path we should take. They make us understand that, like all human beings, we err, and we must have the courage to admit our mistakes. And they lead us to the judicial philosophy that is proper for us, for there is nothing more practical than good judicial philosophy.

My purpose in this book is to suggest answers to the questions I have posed. I wish to present my views on the role of a court and its judges in a democracy. My aim is to describe the judicial policy and judicial philosophy that guide me. I do not naively claim that my position reflects an absolute truth. Democratic countries differ from one another, and what is good and proper for one may not be good and proper for another.[27]

My proposed judicial philosophy applies only to the judge in democracies. I do not address societies that are not democratic.[28] The democratic nature of a regime shapes the role of all branches of the state. It also directly affects the judiciary. Furthermore, the character of the regime affects the interpretive system that the judge should adopt. A judge should not advance the intent of an undemocratic legislator. He or she must avoid giving expression to undemocratic fundamental values. Indeed, my entire theory about the role of the judge and the means he or she employs is grounded in the character of a democratic regime. With a regime change, the view of the judge's role and the way it is exercised also change. Moreover, I am examining my role as a judge in a modern democracy—that is, as a judge at the beginning of the twenty-first century. I do not think that

---

[27] *See* Ruth Gavison, "The Role of Courts in Rifted Democracies," 33 *Isr. L. Rev.* 216 (1999).

[28] For discussions of this topic, see Ingo Müller, *Hitler's Justice: The Courts of the Third Reich* (Deborah Lucas Schneider trans., 1991) (1987); and Michael Stolleis, *The Law Under the Swastika: Studies in Legal History in Nazi Germany* (Thomas Dunlap trans., 1998) (1994). South Africa is an additional example. For a discussion of the functioning of its judges during apartheid, their behavior, and the way they should have behaved, see David Dyzenhaus, *Hard Cases in Wicked Legal Systems: South African Law in the Perspective of Legal Philosophy* (1991); David Dyzenhaus, *Judging the Judges, Judging Ourselves: Truth, Reconciliation and the Apartheid Legal Order* (1998).

it would have been possible to formulate a judicial philosophy like my own a hundred years ago or more.[29] And my philosophy will inevitably no longer be valid in a hundred years' time. Indeed, any perspective on the judicial role is a function of place and time. It is influenced by its environment. It is relative and incomplete. It changes periodically. Therefore, recognition and realization of the judicial role will vary with different democracies at different times.

Although I focus mainly on courts of legal systems that belong to the common law family, such as the United States, England, Canada, Australia, and a number of mixed jurisdictions, such as South Africa, Scotland, Cyprus, and Israel, I think that what I have to say also applies substantially to other legal systems, such as the Roman-Germanic family, including France, Italy, Germany, Austria, and the family of Scandinavian systems. I believe that my approach is also valid for legal systems that have emerged from the family of socialist systems, such as Russia, Hungary,[30] Poland, and the Czech Republic.[31]

After this introduction, in Part 1 of this book I lay the foundation for the two central elements of the judicial role beyond actually deciding the dispute, as I see them.[32]

One element is bridging the gap between law and society. I regard the judge as a partner in creating law. As a partner, the judge must maintain the coherence of the legal system as a whole. Each particular creation of laws has general implications. The development of a specific common law doctrine radiates into the entire legal system. The interpretation of a single statute affects the interpretation of all

---

[29] Of course, many aspects of my approach are not unique to contemporary life. The need to bridge the gap between law and society, for example, is not unique to the present. In the past, too, this was understood to be central to the role of judging.

[30] See generally *Constitutional Judiciary in a New Democracy: The Hungarian Constitutional Court* (László Sólyom and Georg Brunner *eds.* 2000).

[31] See generally Schwartz, *supra* p. x, note 6; Teitel, *supra* p. x, note 6.

[32] Of course, courts have other roles. *See* Helen Hershkoff, "State Courts and the 'Passive Virtues': Rethinking the Judicial Function," 114 *Harv. L. Rev.* 1833, 1852–76 (2001) (surveying U.S. state court practices such as issuing advisory opinions, deciding political questions, and engaging in judicial administration).

statutes. A legal system is not a confederation of laws. Legal rules and principles together constitute a system of law whose different parts are tightly linked. The judge is a partner in creating this system of law. The extent of this partnership varies with the type of law being created. In creating common law, the judge is a senior partner. In creating enacted law, the judge is a junior partner. Nonetheless, he or she is a partner, and not merely an agent who carries out the orders of his or her principal.

The second major task of the judge is to protect the constitution and democracy. In my opinion, every branch of government, including the judiciary, must use the power granted it to protect the constitution and democracy. The judiciary and each of its judges must safeguard both formal democracy, as expressed in legislative supremacy and proper elections, and substantive democracy, as expressed in the concepts of separation of power, the rule of law, fundamental principles, independence of the judiciary, and human rights.

The judge is charged with both jobs simultaneously, and in most cases they are complementary.[33] But during various periods of history, one of them has taken precedence over the other. I think that in light of the increasing recognition of judicial review of the constitutionality of statutes since World War II and of the inclusion of human rights provisions in new constitutions, the second role, preserving democracy, has grown in importance. This is certainly the case in the current age of defensive democracy, although the second role has always existed, particularly in the field of private law. Of course, these two roles are not unique to the judiciary. Every branch of government in a constitutional democracy must protect that institution and work to bridge the gap between law and society. The individual branches of government are partners in fulfilling

---

[33] It can be argued that there is a discrepancy between these two roles. According to this view, bridging the gap between law and society requires the judge to give expression to modern developments, whereas in protecting the constitution and democracy, the judge must protect *against* modern developments. *See* Antonin Scalia, "Modernity and the Constitution," in *Constitutional Justice Under Old Constitutions* 313, 315 (Eivind Smith ed., 1995). This outlook is unacceptable. The two roles require a recognition of modern developments while giving expression to principles and fundamentals, and not to passing vogues.

these roles.[34] I emphasize the role of the judiciary to point out that the judiciary shares responsibility for these tasks, and I wish to examine the methods that the judiciary employs to carry them out.

I conclude Part 1 by considering a critique of this view and the responses to it.

In Part 2, I explore the means by which the court can fulfill its role. These means are bounded. Judges have only a few basic materials with which to build legal structures. I begin by considering the preconditions for carrying out the complex role of the judge, including judicial impartiality and objectivity, acting within the social consensus and the maintenance of public confidence in the judiciary. I then focus on constitutional and statutory interpretation as instruments for realizing the judicial role by presenting purposive interpretation as the proper system of interpretation. I then discuss the means available to a judge within the common law. Furthermore, I analyze the theory of balancing as a complex and sensitive judicial tool. I also discuss a number of tools and concepts that help judges fulfill their role, including justiciability, standing, comparative law, and the writing of the judgment.

In Part 3, I discuss the reciprocal relationship between the court and other branches of the state in a democracy. I consider the relationships among the judiciary, the legislature, and the executive. This relationship is perpetually tense because each branch constitutes a separate but interconnected part of the state. This tension should be based on each branch's respect for the other branches and a recognition of their centrality. The court must engage in a dialogue with the legislature and executive. In this context, I analyze the scope of judicial review over legislative (statutory and non-statutory) and administrative activity. I look into the role of reasonableness and proportionality in those matters.

In Part 4, I evaluate the role of the judge in a democracy. I concentrate on the general distinction between activism and self-restraint. In particular, I discuss the role of the judge when a democracy is

[34] *See* Lorraine E. Weinrib, "Canada's *Charter of Rights*: Paradigm Lost?" 6 *Rev. Const. Stud.* 119, 124 (2002).

fighting terror, which is one of the most important problems that courts in democracies face today. In this context, I develop the concept of a defensive democracy, with the court at its center, as a response to the phenomenon of modern terrorism. In this area, regrettably, Israeli courts have acquired a certain expertise. Numerous legal problems related to a defensive democracy's battle with terrorism reach the doors of Israeli courts.

In the concluding segment, I make some final observations about the theory, the practice, and the future of the role of the judge in a democracy.

It goes without saying that the opinions expressed in this book are my personal opinions. They do not reflect the opinions of the Supreme Court of Israel. As is evident from the decisions I cite, in some cases my view reflects Israeli case law, while in other cases I write a minority opinion.

In this book, I cite many opinions that I have written—perhaps more than is customary. I have done so to indicate that I have put my theoretical viewpoints to the test of judicial reality by applying them in actual opinions. In some instances, my views have become binding case law. In others, they were merely obiter dicta. In still others, they were in minority opinions.

This book is a substantial expansion of an article that originally appeared in the *Harvard Law Review*.[35] I am grateful to the editors of the *Harvard Law Review* for their thoughtful and thorough work on the original manuscript. Chapter 10 was published in 80 *Tul. L. Rev* (2005–2006). A substantial part of Chapter 16 was published in the *University of Miami Law Review*.[36]

This book could not have been completed without the generous help of a number of individuals who provided thought-provoking and constructive comments. Their ideas enrich the debate about these issues. I am grateful to Rosie Abella, Bruce Ackerman, Akhil Amar, Dorit Beinisch, Stephen Breyer, Robert Burt, Guido Calabresi,

---

[35] Aharon Barak, "Foreword: The Role of a Supreme Court in a Democracy," 116 *Harv. L. Rev.* 16 (2002)

[36] Aharon Barak, "The Role of a Supereme Court in a Democracy, and the Fight Against Terrorism," 58 *U. Miam. L. Rev.* 125 (2003).

Mishael Cheshin, Alan Dershowitz, Owen Fiss, Paul Gewirtz, Richard Goldstein, Gershon Gontovnik, Leonard Hoffman, Frank Iacobucci, Jeffrey Jowell, Paul Kahn, Michael Kirby, Roy Kreitner, Pnina Lahav, Anthony Lester, Beverley McLachlin, Yigal Mersel, Jon Newman, Boaz Okon, Georghios Pikis, Richard Pildes, Robert Post, Judith Resnik, Johan Steyn, Cass Sunstein, Laurence Tribe, Lorraine Weinrib, Stephen Wizner, Harry Woolf, Gustavo Zagrebelsky, and Yitzhak Zamir. I also wish to thank Jonathan Davidson, Sari Bashi, and Efrat Hakak for their translation and editing work.

Part One

THE ROLE OF THE JUDGE

CHAPTER ONE

Bridging the Gap between Law and Society

LAW AND SOCIETY

The law regulates relationships between people. It reflects the values of society. The role of the judge is to understand the purpose of law in society and to help the law achieve its purpose. But the law of a society is a living organism.[1] It is based on a factual and social reality that is constantly changing.[2] Sometimes the change is drastic and easily identifiable. Sometimes the change is minor and gradual, and cannot be noticed without the proper distance and perspective. Law's connection to this fluid reality implies that it too is always changing. Sometimes a change in the law precedes societal change and is even intended to stimulate it. In most cases, however, a change in the law is the result of a change in social reality. Indeed, when social reality changes, the law must change too. Just as change in social reality is the law of life,[3] responsiveness to change in social reality is the life of the law.

These changes in the law, caused by changes in society, are sometimes appropriate and sufficient. The legal norm is flexible enough to reflect the change in reality naturally, without the need to change the norm and without creating a rift between law and reality. For example, the legal prohibition against possessing weapons works well, without the need for change, whether the weapon is an antique pistol

---

[1] *See* Brian Dickson, "A Life in the Law: The Process of Judging," 63 *Sask. L. Rev.* 373, 388 (2000).

[2] *See* Benjamin N. Cardozo, *The Paradoxes of Legal Science* 10–11 (Greenwood Press 1970) (1928).

[3] *See* William H. Rehnquist, "The Changing Role of the Supreme Court," 14 *Fla. St. U. L. Rev.*, 1.

or a sophisticated missile. Often, however, the legal norm is not flexible enough, and it fails to adapt to the new reality. A gap has formed between law and society. We need a new norm. For example, the norm that the owner of a carriage owes a duty of care to a pedestrian may be flexible enough to solve the problem of the duty of care that an automobile owner owes to a pedestrian. However, it is not flexible enough to solve the problem of industrialization, urbanization, and thousands of cars traveling on the streets, a situation in which proving negligence becomes more and more difficult. We need a change in law to move from negligence-based liability to strict liability in the context of an insurance regime. When changes occur in social reality, many of the old legal norms fail to adapt. The tort of negligence, which can generally deal with various changes in conventional risks, will likely prove insufficient to address an atomic risk. We would need a formal change in the norm itself.

The life of law is not just logic or experience.[4] The life of law is renewal based on experience and logic, which adapt law to the new social reality. Indeed, there are always changes in law, caused by changes in society. The history of law is also the history of adapting law to life's changing needs. The legislative branch bears the primary role in making conscious changes in the law. It has the power to change the legislation that it itself created. It has the power to create new legal tools that can encompass the new social reality and even determine its nature and character. In the field of legislation, the legislature is the senior partner. The role of the judge is secondary and limited.

CHANGES IN LEGISLATION
AND IN ITS INTERPRETATION

The judge has an important role in the legislative project: The judge interprets statutes. Statutes cannot be applied unless they are interpreted. The judge may give a statute a new meaning, a dynamic

---

[4] For a different view, see Oliver Wendell Holmes, *The Common Law* 1 (1881): "The life of law has not been logic: it has been experience."

meaning, that seeks to bridge the gap between law and life's changing reality without changing the statute itself. The statute remains as it was, but its meaning changes, because the court has given it a new meaning that suits new social needs. The court fulfills its role as the junior partner in the legislative project. It realizes the judicial role by bridging the gap between law and life. I noted as much in a case that addressed, among other things, the question of whether Israel's civil procedure regulations recognized a class action lawsuit against the state. In answering in the affirmative, I noted:

> We are concerned with the existing law, which must be given a new meaning. This is the classic role of the court. In doing so, it realizes one of its primary roles in a democracy, bridging the gap between law and life. The case before us is a simple example of the many situations in which an old tool does not fit a new reality, and the tool therefore must be given a new meaning, in order to address society's changing needs. It is no different from the many other situations in which courts today are prepared to give a dynamic meaning to old provisions, in order to adapt them to new needs.[5]

Here is an additional example: Israeli tort law is based on the Tort Ordinance, passed at the end of the period of the British Mandate in Palestine (1947). According to the Ordinance, if an act of negligence causes a person's death, his dependents are entitled to compensation from the tortfeasor. The Tort Ordinance defines dependents to include "husband, wife, parents, and children." This provision was taken from the English statute, passed in 1846. There is no doubt that the British mandatory legislature intended to refer to a husband and wife who were lawfully married. However, what of the common law wife who has lived with her common law husband for many years and even given birth to a daughter with him? The common law husband becomes the victim of a deadly work-related accident; is the common law wife entitled to damages from the tortfeasor for loss of her dependency? When

---

[5] L.C.A 3126/00, *State of Israel v. A.S.T. Project Management and Manpower, Ltd.*, 47(3) P.D. 241, 286.

the question came before the Israeli Supreme Court, at a time when the phenomenon of common law marriages was prevalent, the Court answered in the affirmative. In my opinion, I wrote:

> I am prepared to assume that the phrase "wife" in the 1846 English statute refers to a married woman. However, that does not mean that it is the meaning that an English court would give it today. It certainly does not mean that it is the meaning that we, in the State of Israel, would give the phrase "Husband, Wife." Much water has flowed through the English Thames and the Israeli Jordan since 1846. As judges in Israel, our duty is to give the phrase "Husband, Wife" the meaning assigned to it in Israeli society, and not in English Victorian society of the mid-nineteenth century . . . that is mandated by our interpretive rules.[6]

Here is an additional example from public law: The Defense Regulations (State of Emergency) enacted in 1945 by the British government continue to apply in Israel. Among other things, these regulations establish military censorship of publications in Israel. The military censor is authorized to ban publications that it deems likely to harm state security, public security, or the public peace. The Supreme Court has given this provision a dynamic interpretation, based on the fundamental principles of Israeli law. In my opinion, I noted that

> The meaning that should be given to the Defense Regulations in the State of Israel is not identical to the meaning that they might have taken on during the period of the Mandate. Today, the Defense Regulations are part of the laws of a democratic state. They must be interpreted against the background of the fundamental principles of the Israeli legal system.[7]

We held that the military censor may prevent publication only if the uncensored publication would create a near certainty of grave harm to state security, public security, or public peace.

---

[6] C.A. 2000/97, *Lindoran v. Kranit–Accident Victim Compensation Fund*, 55(1) P.D. 12.
[7] H.C. 680/88, *Schnitzer v. Chief Military Censor*, 42(4) P.D. 617, 628.

Characteristic of these examples and many others is the change that has taken place in the law without any change occurring in the language of the legislation. Such a change is made possible by the change in the court's interpretation. It is made possible by the court's recognition of its role to bridge the gap created between the old statute and the new social reality. The court did not say, "Adapting the law to the new reality is not my role. It is the role of the legislature. If the legislature does not do anything, it bears the responsibility." The court viewed it as its own responsibility—complementary to the responsibility of the legislature—to give the old law a new meaning that suited the social needs of modern Israel.

Statutory interpretation will facilitate the statute's adaptation to changes in the conditions of existence only if the system of interpretation allows for that. Such a system is the system of purposive interpretation.[8] It is predicated on giving a dynamic interpretation to the statute, to allow it to fulfill its design. In one case, I addressed the way in which dynamic interpretation works:

> The meaning that should be given to a phrase in a statute is not fixed for eternity. The statute is part of life, and life changes. Understanding of the statute changes with changes in reality. The language of the statute remains as it was, but the meaning changes along with "changing life conditions" . . . the statute integrates into the new reality. This is how an old statute speaks to the modern person. This is the source of the interpretive approach that "the statute always speaks" . . . interpretation is a regenerative process. Old language should be filled with modern content, in order to minimize the gap between law and life. It is therefore correct to say, as Radbruch does, that the interpreter may understand the statute better than the author of the statute, and that the statute is always wiser than its creator . . . the statute is a living creature; its interpretation must be dynamic. It must be understood in a way that integrates and advances modern reality.[9]

[8] *Infra* p. 125.
[9] C.A. 2000/97, *supra* p. 6, note 6 at 32. The reference is to Gustav Radbruch, "Legal Philosophy," in *The Legal Philosophies of Lask, Radbruch, and Dabin* 141 (20th Century Legal Philosophy Series, Vol. IV, Kurt Wilk trans., 1950).

Of course, it is not always possible to bridge the gap between law and life by giving a new and modern meaning to an old statute. Sometimes the judge lacks the power to bridge the gap between the old language of the statute and society's new reality. In such a case the judge must set aside his work tools. The judge may not act against the law. He can only hope that the legislature will do its job and repeal the old statute. The judge, as a faithful interpreter, cannot achieve such a result. For example, the court could not entirely repeal the military censorship of publications or, for that matter, civilian censorship of plays and movies, also created by the British mandatory regime. Such repeal required legislative intervention. Indeed, following a decision by the Supreme Court restricting civilian censorship, the legislature repealed censorship of plays. Censorship of movies, like military censorship, still exists. The judge lacks the power to deliver that change.

In this context, Guido Calabresi's proposition[10] is noteworthy. He suggested that courts should be able to repeal legislation that has become obsolete. Of course, Calabresi's proposition cannot be implemented unless the legislature explicitly authorizes courts to repeal obsolete legislation. I personally do not think that is the proper solution to a painful problem. The right way is not to rely on judges to repeal obsolete laws but rather for the legislature to do so. Indeed, the Israeli legislature occasionally collects pieces of old legislation that are no longer necessary and repeals them. That is the right way to proceed.

CHANGES IN SOCIETY AFFECTING
THE CONSTITUTIONALITY OF STATUTES

Social changes sometimes lead to a situation in which a statute passed in the context of a certain reality and that was constitutional at the time of its enactment becomes unconstitutional in light of a

---

[10] Guido Calabresi, *A Common Law for the Age of Statutes* (1982).

new social reality. Of course, the court will do everything it can to give the old statute a new meaning, in order to preserve its constitutionality. The limitations of interpretation, however, do not always allow that to happen. Where interpretation fails to give an old law a new meaning, the question may arise as to whether, in light of the social changes, the old statute is constitutional. Even though the court is not authorized to give a new meaning to an old statute, if such meaning deviates from the system's rules of interpretation, the court may declare the old statute, with the old meaning, unconstitutional. As an example, in 1986 the United States Supreme Court held that a statute criminalizing consensual homosexual relations between adults was constitutional.[11] Twenty years passed. The United States Supreme Court overturned its prior holding.[12] It held that the Constitution bars legislation criminalizing consensual sexual relations between adults. The difference between the two decisions did not reflect a constitutional change that took place during that period. Rather, the change that occurred was in American society, which learned to recognize the nature of homosexual relationships and was prepared to treat them with tolerance.[13] Justice D. Dorner of the Israeli Supreme Court discussed this social change in a case that raised the issue of employee benefits for same-sex partners:

In the past, intimate relations between members of the same sex— relations considered to be a sin by monotheistic religions—were a criminal offense . . . this treatment has gradually changed. Legal scholars have criticized the definition of a homosexual relationship as criminal and discrimination against homosexuals in all areas of life . . . movements fighting for equal rights for homosexuals have sprung up. Today, the trend—which began in the 1970s—is to a liberal

[11] *Bowers v. Hardwick*, 478 U.S. 186 (1986).
[12] *Lawrence v. Texas*, 123 S. Ct. 2472 (2003).
[13] Robert Post, "Foreword: Fashioning the Legal Constitution: Culture, Courts, and Law," 117 *Harv. L. Rev.* 4 (2003).

treatment of a person's sexual tendencies, which are viewed as a private matter. . . . Israeli law concerning homosexuals reflects the social changes that have taken place over the years.[14]

CHANGES IN THE COMMON LAW

The court may not repeal an obsolete statute. It may, however, repeal a common law holding that has become obsolete. It may change even a non-obsolete precedent if it does not suit today's social needs. Indeed, judges created the common law. In doing so, they sought to provide a solution to the social needs of their time. As these needs change, judges must consider whether it is appropriate to change the judicial precedent itself, by expanding or restricting the existing case law or overturning an old precedent.[15] Sometimes the new social reality necessitates creating new case law to resolve problems that did not arise at all in the past, where the goal of the new case law is to bridge the gap between law and the new social reality. Justice Agranat expressed this idea well:

> Where a judge is presented with a set of facts based in new life conditions, for which the current law was not designed, the judge should review anew the logical premise on which the case law, created in a different background, is based. The goal is to adapt the case law to the new conditions, either by expanding or restricting it, or, where there is no other way, completely to abandon the logical premise which served as the basis for the existing law and to replace it with a different legal norm—even if the legal norm was previously unknown.[16]

Within the common law project, the judge is the senior partner. The judge creates the common law and bears responsibility for making sure that it fulfills its role properly. The legislature is the

---

[14] H.C. 721/94, *El Al Israeli Airlines v. Danielovitz*, 45(5) P.D. 749, 779 (English translation available at www.court.gov.il).
[15] *See infra* p. 158.
[16] C.A. 150/50, *Kaufman v. Margines*, 6 P.D. 1005, 1034.

junior partner, the outside observer, who generally intervenes only when asked to correct a particular issue or replace the entire legal regime from a common law regime to a statutory regime.

CHANGE AND STABILITY

The Dilemma of Change

The need for change presents the judge with a difficult dilemma, because change sometimes harms security, certainty, and stability. The judge must balance the need for change with the need for stability. Professor Roscoe Pound expressed this well more than eighty years ago: "Hence all thinking about law has struggled to reconcile the conflicting demands of the need of stability and of the need of change. Law must be stable and yet it cannot stand still."[17]

Stability without change is degeneration. Change without stability is anarchy. The role of a judge is to help bridge the gap between the needs of society and the law without allowing the legal system to degenerate or collapse into anarchy. The judge must ensure stability with change, and change with stability. Like the eagle in the sky, which maintains its stability only when it is moving, so too is the law stable only when it is moving. Achieving this goal is very difficult. The life of the law is complex. It is not mere logic. It is not mere experience. It is both logic and experience together. The progress of case law throughout history must be cautious. The decision is not between stability or change. It is a question of the speed of the change. The decision is not between rigidity or flexibility. It is a question of the degree of flexibility. The judge must take into account a complex array of considerations. I will discuss three such considerations that apply in the development of the law. A judge must consider (1) the coherence of the system in which he operates, (2) the powers and limitations of the institution of the judiciary as defined within that system, and (3) the way in which his role is perceived.

---

[17] Roscoe Pound, *Interpretations of Legal History* 1 (1923).

Considerations of System

The development of law, be it common law or enacted law, must maintain normative coherence within the legal system.[18] It must reflect the fundamental values of the legal system. Every ruling must be integrated into the framework of that system. As Professor Lon Fuller explained:

> Those responsible for creating and administering a body of legal rules will always be confronted by a *problem of system*. The rules applied to the decision of individual controversies cannot simply be isolated exercises of judicial wisdom. They must be brought into, and maintained in, some systematic interrelationship; they must display some coherent internal structure.[19]

Indeed, a judge who develops the law does not perform an individual act, isolated from an existing normative system. The judge acts within the context of the system, and his ruling must integrate into it. For this reason, judges must ensure that the change is organic and the development gradual and natural.[20] Change generally should occur by evolution, not revolution.[21] We are mostly concerned with continuity, not discontinuity. Judicial activity, according to the attractive analogy of Professor Ronald Dworkin, is like several co-authors taking turns in writing a book, one after another.[22] Judges no longer on the bench wrote the earlier chapters. We must now write the continuation of the work. We must ground ourselves in the past while

---

[18] *See* Barak, *supra* p. xiii, note 14 at 152; Neil MacCormick, *Legal Reasoning and Legal Theory* (1993).

[19] Lon L. Fuller, *Anatomy of the Law* 94 (1968).

[20] *See S. Pac. Co. v. Jensen*, 244 U.S. 205, 221 (1917) (Holmes, J., dissenting); Roscoe Pound, *The Formative Era of American Law* 45 (1938); Henry J. Friendly, "Reactions of a Lawyer—Newly Become Judge," 71 *Yale L.J.* 218, 223 (1961).

[21] *See* Roger J. Traynor, "The Limits of Judicial Creativity," 29 *Hastings L.J.* 1025, 1031–32 (1978) ("The greatest judges of the common law have proceeded in this way, moving not by fits and starts, but at the pace of the tortoise that steadily advances though it carries the past on its back").

[22] *See* Ronald Dworkin, "Law as Interpretation," 60 *Tex. L. Rev.* 527 (1982) (likening judges to collaborators in a vast "chain novel").

ensuring historical continuity. The chapters that we are writing become, after they are written, chapters from the past. New chapters, the creations of new judges, will be written in the future.

Likewise, we must ensure consistency.[23] In similar cases we must act similarly unless there is a proper reason for distinguishing the cases. This rule does not bar departure from existing precedent, but it does ensure that departure from precedent is proper, that it reflects reason and not fiat,[24] and that it is done for proper reasons of legal policy,[25] so that the contribution the change makes to future law outweighs any harm caused by changing the old law, including the instability and resultant uncertainty inherent in change.[26]

Institutional Considerations

In bridging the gap between law and society, the judge must take into account the institutional limitations of the judiciary.[27] Admittedly, judicial lawmaking, mostly through interpretation, is central to the role of a court. But that role is incidental to deciding disputes. This is the striking difference between judge-made law and enacted law. Without a dispute there is no judicial lawmaking.[28] By nature, then,

---

[23] *See* Barak, *supra* p. xiii, note 14 at 166–67.

[24] *See* Lon L. Fuller, "Reason and Fiat in Case Law," 59 *Harv. L. Rev.* 376 (1946).

[25] *See* John Bell, *Policy Arguments in Judicial Decisions* (1983).

[26] *See infra* p. 160.

[27] *See* Barak, *supra* p. xiii, note 14 at 172; Jon O. Newman, "Between Legal Realism and Neutral Principles: The Legitimacy of Institutional Values," 72 *Cal. L. Rev.* 200 (1984); Lon L. Fuller, "The Forms and Limits of Adjudication," 92 *Harv. L. Rev.* 353 (1978).

[28] The dispute may be of a private nature or of a public nature; it may be concrete or abstract; it may involve only situations where there is a "case and controversy" (as in the United States) or it may do without it (as in Germany); it may be—as in the Canadian reference—of an advisory nature. But there must always be a dispute. Regarding the different possibilities, see Allan-Randolph Brewer Carías, *Judicial Review in Comparative Law* (1989); C. Neal Tate and T. Vallinder, *The Global Expansion of Judicial Power* (1995).

judges create law sporadically, not systematically.[29] The changes they make to law are partial, limited, and reactive. The issues brought before a court are to some extent randomly selected. Many years may pass before a problem that troubles the public enters a judicial forum. A court's control over the matters it hears is negative in nature, permitting only dismissal of what the court does not want to consider. Consequently, a judge cannot plan a strategy of bridging the gap between law and society. The changes he makes to the law are partial and limited. When a comprehensive and immediate change is needed in an entire branch of law, the legislature ought to make it. Moreover, one cannot bridge the gap between society and law without having reliable information about society. The court does not always have the information about social facts that might justify a change in the law. Our laws of evidence usually look backward (adjudicative facts), providing a (partial) answer to the question of "what happened."[30] They usually do not look forward (legislative facts), and they do not provide an answer to the question of "what should happen." Moreover, the means at a judge's disposal are limited. The court may, in developing the common law in its legal system, impose a new duty of care in torts. It may also use the existing remedies, such as injunctions[31] and damages, to solve new problems. But it cannot, for example, impose taxes or establish a licensing regime.

Finally, the nature of the legal policy underlying existing law should be a factor in the judge's willingness to change the law. For example, a judge is generally qualified to consider the legal policy underlying human rights protections. Naturally, he has little difficulty evaluating legal policy that can be derived from logic, a sense of justice, or existing law (enacted or case law). By contrast, a judge should beware of evaluating complex, polycentric[32] questions of

---

[29] *See* Henry Friendly, "The Courts and Social Policy: Substance and Procedure," 33 *U. Miami L. Rev.* 21, 22 (1978).

[30] *See* Antonio Lamer, "Canada's Legal Revolution: Judging in the Age of the Charter of Rights," 28 *Isr. L. Rev.* 579 (1994).

[31] *See* Owen Fiss, *The Civil Right Injunction* (1978).

[32] *See* Hanne Peterson and Henrik Zahle, *Legal Polycentricity: Consequences of Pluralism in Law* (1995).

economic or social policy that require specialized expertise and knowledge and that may rely on assumptions concerning issues with which he is unfamiliar. I am aware of the difficulties in making this distinction. I mean to say only that a judge should be sensitive to this type of consideration. I feel much more comfortable holding that one economic plan is discriminatory compared to another than I do holding that one economic plan falls within the range of reasonableness while another does not.

Considerations of the Perception of the Judicial Role

Judicial lawmaking that bridges the gap between law and society must be consistent not only with society's basic values but also with society's fundamental perception of the role of the judiciary.[33] The power of a judge to bridge the gap between law and society in a society that, like Montesquieu,[34] sees the judge merely as the mouthpiece of the legislature is different from the judge's power in a society that views comprehensive judicial lawmaking as legitimate. Society's perception of the judicial role, however, is fluid. Not only is judicial activity influenced by it, it also influences that perception.

In common law systems, bridging the gap between law and society appears to be a central role of the judiciary. By their nature, common law systems view the judge as a senior partner in lawmaking. But does this perception apply beyond the confines of the

---

[33] See Barak, *supra* p. xiii, note 14 at 192; M.D.A. Freeman, "Standards of Adjudication, Judicial Law-Making and Prospective Overruling," 26 *Current Legal Probs.* 166, 181 (1973) ("Every institution embodies some degree of consensus about how it is to operate. To understand the judicial role and apprise the legitimacy of judicial creativity one must explore the shared expectations which define the role of judge"); Paul Weiler, "Two Models of Judicial Decision-Making," 46 *Can. B. Rev.* 406, 407–08 (1968). On the difference between the perception of the judicial role of the English judge and the American judge, see Louis L. Jaffe, *English and American Judges as Lawmakers* (1969); Richard Posner, *Law and Legal Theory in England and America* (1996). *See also* Robert Stevens, *The English Judges: Their Role in the Changing Constitution* (2002).

[34] Montesquieu, *supra* p. xiv, note 24.

common law? And, in common law systems, is it possible to regard the judge as someone who ought to bridge the gap between law and society in the sphere of legislation?[35] Certainly the main actor in this bridging is the legislature. Its democratic nature (in the sense that the legislature is elected by the people), the tools at its disposal, and the ways in which it receives information about different policies and different alternatives all make the legislature chiefly responsible for bridging the gap between law and society.

But can the judge be recognized as a junior partner in such a bridging because of his role as the interpreter of legislation? The answer to this question is not at all simple. The question is whether to accept a model of partnership—albeit a limited partnership—or a model of agency.[36] In the agency model,[37] the judge is an agent of the legislature. He must act according to its instructions, just as a junior officer is bound to carry out the orders of his superior officer.[38] There are many problems with this approach. To my mind, a judge is not an agent who receives orders and the legislature is not a principal that gives orders to its agent.[39] The two are branches of the state with different roles; one is legislator and the other is

[35] On this question, see Guido Calabresi, *A Common Law for the Age of Statutes* 2 (1982).

[36] These are not the only models, and they certainly do not apply to all issues that arise. I address them because they are relevant to the two roles of a judge in a democracy that I focus on here. For an extensive discussion of these two models, see Ronald A. Cass, *The Rule of Law in America* 46–97 (2001). Cass claims that the prevailing model in American law is the "weak agency model," in which the judge acts as a translator. *See id.* at 49, 92–97. I disagree. *See also* Kennedy, *supra* p. xi, note 8; Lucy, *supra* p. xi, note 8.

[37] *See* Richard A. Posner, *The Federal Courts: Crisis and Reform* 286–87 (1985); Frank H. Easterbrook, "The Supreme Court, 1983 Term—Foreword: The Court and the Economic System," 98 *Harv. L. Rev.* 4, 60 (1984); John F. Manning, "Deriving Rules of Statutory Interpretation from the Constitution," 101 *Colum. L. Rev.* 1648, 1648 note 1 (2001).

[38] For this analogy, see Richard A. Posner, *The Problems of Jurisprudence* 269 (1990).

[39] *See* Michael C. Dorf, "The Supreme Court, 1997 Term—Foreword: The Limits of Socratic Deliberation," 112 *Harv. L. Rev.* 4, 19 (1988) (noting an alternative to textualism "in which courts play a vital role as partners with, rather than mere servants of, the legislature"); William N. Eskridge, Jr., "Spinning Legislative

interpreter. Indeed, legislatures create statutes that are supposed to bridge the gap between law and society. In bridging this gap, the legislature is the senior partner, for it created the statute. But the statute itself cannot be implemented without being interpreted. The task of interpreting belongs to the judge. Through his interpretation, a judge must give effect to the purpose of the law and ensure that the law in fact bridges the gap between law and society. The judge is a partner in the legislature's creation and implementation of statutes, even if this partnership is a limited one.[40]

Regarding the judge merely as an agent is too narrow an approach. That point of view isolates a particular statute and sees it as an island. But a statute is not an island. It is part of a legislative enterprise that is many years old. Moreover, legislation, together with the common law, forms part of the legal system. All parts of the law are linked. Whoever interprets one statute interprets all the statutes. Whoever enforces one statute enforces the whole legal system. Normative harmony must exist among the different parts of the legal system. An interpretation of an individual statute, such as a new common law rule, must be integrated into the system. The judge is responsible for all of this. He must interpret the individual

---

Supremacy," 78 *Geo. L.J.* 319, 322 (1989); Daniel A. Farber, "Statutory Interpretation and Legislative Supremacy," 78 *Geo. L.J.* 281, 284 (1989); Richard J. Pierce, Jr., "The Role of the Judiciary in Implementing an Agency Theory of Government," 64 *N.Y.U. L. Rev.* 1239, 1239 (1989) (stating that all branches are "the agent of the people").

[40] *See* Dworkin, *supra* p. xiii, note 20 at 313 ("[Hercules, the hypothetical ideal judge] will treat Congress as an author earlier than himself in the chain of law, though an author with special powers and responsibilities different from his own, and he will see his own role as fundamentally the creative one of a partner continuing to develop, in what he believes is the best way, the statutory scheme Congress began"); William D. Popkin, *Statutes in Court: The History and Theory of Statutory Interpretation* 155 (1999) (viewing judges "as collaborators in the interpretive process, albeit as junior partners"); Douglas Payne, "The Intention of the Legislature in the Interpretation of Statutes," 9 *Current Legal Probs.* 96, 105 (1956) ("The proper office of a judge in statutory interpretation is not, I suggest, the lowly mechanical one implied by orthodox doctrine, but that of a junior partner in the legislative process, a partner empowered and expected within certain limits to exercise a proper discretion as to what the detailed law should be").

statute consistently with the whole system and ensure that the interpretation succeeds in bridging the gap between law and life. From this perspective, the judge's role in creating common law (as a senior partner) is similar to the judge's role in interpreting legislation (as a junior partner).[41] In both cases the judge works in the interstices of legislation.[42] Of course, he has a different degree of freedom in each situation, but his role is primarily the same: to bridge the gap between law and society. A judge must therefore consider the elements discussed above—the need to guarantee stability through change and to take systemic and institutional considerations into account—in bridging the gap between law and society, both by creating common law and by interpreting legislation. This approach directly affects the formation of a proper system of interpretation. It should be a system that bridges law and society's needs. It should be a system that ensures dynamic interpretation,[43] giving a statute a meaning compatible with social life in the present and, as far as can be anticipated, in the future, too.

The judge's role is to be the bridge between the law and life. He must not ignore this role. Nevertheless, the public must not expect the judge to bridge every gap between law and life. Many limitations, both substantive and procedural, are placed on the judge. His discretion is limited. He functions within a given social and legal framework. The court's ability to link life and law, therefore, is limited by its very nature. It is not wise to harbor expectations that cannot possibly be met. In this regard, we should avoid staking

---

[41] See David A. Strauss, "Common Law Constitutional Interpretation," 63 *U. Chi. L. Rev.* 877, 879 (1996). Justice Scalia's approach is different. See Antonin Scalia, *A Matter of Interpretation: Federal Courts and the Law* 3–14 (1997). According to his view, there is a profound difference between the activity of a judge in interpreting legislation and the activity of a judge in the enterprise of the common law. *See id.* Although I agree that such a difference exists, I do not believe it is as acute as Justice Scalia describes.

[42] See S. Pac. Co. v. Jensen, 244 U.S. 205, 221 (1917) (Holmes, J., dissenting) ("I recognize without hesitation that judges do and must legislate, but they can do so only interstitially . . ."). *See also* Bell, *supra* p. 13, note 25 at 17–20 (1983) (outlining a model of the judge as an "interstitial legislator").

[43] See William N. Eskridge, Jr., *Dynamic Statutory Interpretation* 9 (1994).

out extreme positions. We should not accept the claim, often raised, that the court should not be expected to make necessary changes in order to bridge the gap between law and life.[44] But at the same time, neither should we accept the claim that the judge is all-powerful and that his will alone determines the existence or nonexistence of the change.[45] Reality is infinitely more complex. Sometimes it is possible to bridge the gap between law and life's changing reality through legitimate judicial actions; at other times such a bridge cannot possibly be constructed. On this matter as on many others, one must be realistic[46] and understand both the judicial power and its limitations.

[44] *See* Gerald Rosenberg, *The Hollow Hope* (1991).
[45] *See* Gary Peller, "The Metaphysics of American Law," 73 *Cal. L. Rev.* 1151 (1985).
[46] *See* Mark Kozlowski, *The Myth of the Imperial Judiciary: Why the Right Is Wrong about the Courts* (2003).

CHAPTER TWO

Protecting the Constitution and Democracy

THE STRUGGLE FOR DEMOCRACY

The second role of the judge in a democracy is to protect the constitution[1] and democracy itself.[2] Legal systems with formal constitutions impose this task on judges, but judges also play this role in legal systems with no formal constitution. Israeli judges have regarded it as their role to protect Israeli democracy since the founding of the state,[3] even before the adoption of a formal constitution.[4] In England, notwithstanding the absence of a written constitution, judges have protected democratic ideals for many years.[5] Indeed, if we wish to preserve democracy, we cannot take its existence

---

[1] See *Hunter v. Southam*, [1984] 2 S.C.R. 145, 155 (Can.) ("The judiciary is the guardian of the constitutions."); Jutta Limbach, "The Role of the Federal Constitution Court," 53 *SMU L. Rev.* 429 (2000).

[2] See *The Role of Courts in Society* (Shimon Shetreet ed., 1988).

[3] See Aharon Barak, "Constitutional Law Without a Constitution: The Role of the Judiciary", in *The Role of Courts in Society, supra* p. 20, note 2 at 448; Zeev Segal, "A Constitution Without a Constitution: The Israeli Experience and the American Impact", 21 *Cap. U. L. Rev.* 1, 3 (1992).

[4] In C.A. 6821/93, *United Mizrahi Bank Ltd. v. Migdal Cooperative Village*, 49(4) P.D. 221, the Israeli Supreme Court held that the two Basic Laws passed in 1992, Basic Law: Human Dignity and Basic Law: Freedom of Occupation, are the supreme law of the land and constitute part of Israel's constitution. *Mizrahi Bank* subjects any new statute to judicial review under these Basic Laws. I called this development a "constitutional revolution."

[5] See Stanley de Smith et al., *Judicial Review of Administrative Action* 159–62 (1995); John Laws, "The Constitution: Morals and Rights," *Pub. L.* 622 (1996); John Laws, "Is the High Court the Guardian of Fundamental Constitutional Rights?" *Pub. L.* 59, 60 (1993); John Laws, "Law and Democracy", *Pub. L.* 72, 81 (1995); Harry Woolf, "Droit Public—English Style," *Pub. L.* 57, 67 (1995); Harry Woolf, "The Additional Responsibility of the Judiciary in the New

for granted. We must fight for it. This is certainly the case for new democracies,[6] but it is also true of the old and well-established ones. The assumption that "it cannot happen to us" can no longer be accepted. Anything can happen. If democracy was perverted and destroyed in the Germany of Kant, Beethoven, and Goethe, it can happen anywhere. If we do not protect democracy, democracy will not protect us. I do not know whether the judges in Germany could have prevented Hitler from coming to power in the 1930s. But I do know that a lesson of the Holocaust and of World War II is the need to enact democratic constitutions and ensure that they are put into effect by judges whose main task is to protect democracy. It was this awareness that, in the post–World War II era, helped promote the idea of judicial review of legislative action[7] and made human rights central. It led to the recognition of defensive democracy[8] and even militant

---

Millenium", in *The Clifford Chance Millennium Lectures: The Coming Together of the Common Law and the Civil Law* 133,135 (Basil Markesinis ed., 2000). *See also R. v. Sec'y of State for Home Affairs* ex parte *Leech,* 1994 Q.B. 198 (Eng. C.A.); *R. v. Sec'y of State for Home Dep't ex parte Simms,* 3 W.L.R. 328, 340 (A.C. 1999) (Can.); Stevens, *supra* p. 15, note 33.

[6] *See* sources cited *supra* p. 10, note 6.

[7] *See* Mauro Cappelletti, *Judicial Review in the Contemporary World* 45 (1971); *Constitutionalism and Democracy: Transitions in the Contemporary World* (Douglas Greenberg et al. eds., 1993); *The Global Expansion of Judicial Power* (C. Neal Tate and Torbjörn Vallinder eds., 1995); Marina Angel, "Constitutional Judicial Review of Legislation: A Comparative Law Symposium," 56 *Temp. L.Q.* 287 (1983).

[8] *See* E.A. 1/65, *Yardor v. Chairman of Central Elections Committee for Sixth Knesset,* 19(3) P.D. 365. This case addressed the question of whether the court could proscribe a party that denied the existence of the "State of Israel" from participating in the electoral process. This question arose because the relevant legislation did not include any express provision on the matter. The court held that such a party could not participate in the electoral process. For the majority, Justice Sussman wrote:

> The said basic *supra-legal* rules are merely, in this matter, the right of the organized society in the State to protect itself. Whether we call these rules "natural law" to indicate that they are the law of the State by virtue of its nature . . . or whether we call them by another name, I agree with the opinion that the experience of life requires us not to repeat the same mistake to which we were all witness. . . . As for myself, with regard to Israel, I am prepared to satisfy myself with "defensive democracy," and we have tools to protect the existence of the State, even if we do not find them set out in the Elections Law. (*Id.* at 390.)

democracy.[9] And it shaped my belief that the main role of the judge in a democracy is to maintain and protect the constitution and democracy. As I noted in one of my opinions:

> The struggle for the law is unceasing. The need to watch over the rule of law exists at all times. Trees that we have nurtured for many years may be uprooted with one stroke of the axe. We must never relax the protection of the rule of law. All of us—all branches of government, all parties and factions, all institutions—must protect our young democracy. This protective role is conferred on the judiciary as a whole, and on the Supreme Court in particular. Once again we, the judges of this generation, are charged with watching over our basic values and protecting them against those who challenge them.[10]

The protection of democracy is, I believe, a priority for many judges in modern democracies. Judicial protection of democracy in general and of human rights in particular is a characteristic of most developing democracies.[11] This phenomenon is largely a result of the events of World War II and the Holocaust. Legal scholars often explain this phenomenon as an increase in judicial power relative to other powers in society.[12] This change, however, is merely a side effect. The purpose of this modern development is not to increase

---

[9] In contemporary Germany, the militant democracy (*streitbare Demokratie*) is one of the foundations of the constitutional structure. *See* David P. Currie, *The Constitution of the Federal Republic of Germany* 213 (1994); Donald P. Kommers, *The Constitutional Jurisprudence of the Federal Republic of Germany* 37, 217 (2d ed. 1997). The phrase "militant democracy" was coined by Karl Lowenstein in the context of the fall of the Weimar Republic: *see* Karl Lowenstein, "Militant Democracy and Fundamental Rights" I, II, 31 *Am. Pol. Sci. Rev.* 417, 638 (1937). About militant democracy, see *A Militant Democracy* (Andràs Sajò ed., 2004).

[10] H.C. 5364/94, *Velner v. Chairman of the Israeli Labor Party*, 49(1) P.D. 758, 808 (internal citations omitted).

[11] *See* Michael Kirby, "Australian Law—After 11 September 2001," 21 *Austl. B. Rev.* 21 (2001); Sir Anthony Mason, "A Bill of Rights for Australia?," 5 *Austl. B. Rev.* 79, 80 (1989); Beverley McLachlin, *The Role of the Supreme Court in the New Democracy* 13–15 (2001) (unpublished manuscript, on file with the Harvard Law School Library).

[12] *See The Global Expansion of Judicial Power*, *supra* p. 13, note 28 at 1–5.

the power of the court in a democracy but rather to increase the protection of democracy and human rights. An increase in judicial power is an inevitable result, because judicial power is one of many factors in the democratic balance.

Each branch of the government must protect the constitution and democracy. The legislature must do so by enacting legislation and exercising its other powers. The executive (the president in a presidential democracy and the government in a parliamentary democracy) must do so by actualizing democracy in all its actions. And every judge in the state, particularly the judges of the supreme court, must also give effect to democracy. They must educate the people in the democratic spirit, because judges are also educators. To do so, judges must educate the public about the law and the role of the judiciary.[13] In this regard, a court should function as an educational institution whose judges are teachers participating, as Eugene Rostow put it, "in a vital national seminar."[14] Judges must give expression to democracy in its richest sense in their rulings, so that the public will understand it.

WHAT IS DEMOCRACY?

The Essence of Democracy

What is democracy? According to my approach, democracy is a rich and complex normative concept.[15] It rests on two bases. The first is the sovereignty of the people. This sovereignty is exercised in free elections, held on a regular basis, in which the people choose their representatives, who in turn represent their views. This aspect of democracy is manifested in majority rule and in the centrality of the legislative body through which the people's representatives act.

[13] See Marna S. Tucker, "The Judge's Role in Educating the Public About the Law," 31 Cath. U. L. Rev. 201, 205 (1981).
[14] Eugene V. Rostow, "The Democratic Character of Judicial Review," 66 Harv. L. Rev. 193, 208 (1952).
[15] See Carlos Santiago Nino, The Constitution of Deliberative Democracy 8 (1996).

This is a formal aspect of democracy. It is of central importance, since without it the regime is not democratic. Of course, different democratic regimes vary regarding the level of representativeness of the elected officials and the connection between them and the people. It is not uncommon to find a democratic regime in which the representatives in the legislative body represent the minority of the populace. Indeed, the formal aspect of democracy raises perplexing and difficult problems, whose examination is beyond the scope of this book.

The second aspect of democracy is reflected in the rule of values (other than the value of majority rule) that characterize democracy. The most important of these values are separation of powers, the rule of law, judicial independence, human rights, and basic principles that reflect yet other values (such as morality and justice), social objectives (such as the public peace and security), and appropriate ways of behavior (reasonableness, good faith). This aspect of democracy is the rule of democratic values. This is a substantive aspect of democracy. It too is of central importance. Without it, a regime is not democratic.

Both aspects, the formal and the substantive, are necessary for democracy.[16] They are "nuclear characteristics." I discussed them in one case, holding that "these characteristics are based . . . upon the recognition of the sovereignty of the people manifested in free and egalitarian elections; recognition of the nucleus of human rights, among them dignity and equality, the existence of separation of powers, the rule of law, and an independent judiciary."[17] A regime in which the citizens is not sovereign and the legislative and executive branches do not represent it is not a democratic regime. A regime devoid of the separation of powers, the rule of law, the independence of judges, human rights, and fundamental values reflecting ethical values, social objectives, and appropriate ways of behavior is not

---

[16] *See* Robert Post, "Democracy, Popular Sovereignty, and Judicial Review," 86 *Cal. L. Rev.* 429 (1998). *See also Democracy's Valve* (Ian Shapiro and Casiano Hacker-Cordon eds., 1999); Ian Shapiro, *The State of Democratic Theory* (2003).
[17] E.A. 11280/02 *The Central Elections Committee for Sixteenth Knesset v. Tibi*, 57(4) P.D. 1, 21 (Barak, P.).

a democratic regime. Indeed, a regime in which the majority denies the minority human rights is not a democratic regime.

Democracy's world is rich and multifaceted. Democracy should not be viewed from a one-dimensional vantage point. Democracy is multidimensional. It is based both on the centrality of laws and on democratic values, and, at their center, human rights. Indeed, democracy is based on every individual's enjoyment of rights, of which even the majority cannot deny him simply because the power of the majority is in its hands. As Dworkin wrote,

> true democracy is not just *statistical* democracy, in which anything a majority or plurality wants is legitimate for that reason, but *communal* democracy, in which majority decision is legitimate only if it is a majority within a community of equals. That means not only that everyone must be allowed to participate in politics as an equal, through the vote and through freedom of speech and protest, but that political decisions must treat everyone with equal concern and respect, that each individual person must be guaranteed fundamental civil and political rights no combination of other citizens can take away, no matter how numerous they are or how much they despise his or her race or morals or way of life.[18]

It can be argued that only the formal aspect defines democracy itself, whereas the substantive aspect defines the quality of the democracy—whether it is a worthy one or not. According to this approach, a regime in which the people rule through their representatives (formal democracy) is a democratic regime as long as it maintains equality in the right to vote. This is not my view of democracy, and it is not my view of the judicial role. I am of the opinion that democracy has its own internal morality, without which the regime is no longer democratic. I explained this idea in one case in the following way:

> [D]emocracy is not only majority rule. Democracy is also the rule of basic values and human rights as they have taken form in the constitution. Democracy is a delicate balance between majority rule and

---

[18] *See* Ronald Dworkin, *A Bill of Rights for Britain* 35–36 (1990).

society's basic values, which rule the majority. Indeed, democracy is
not only "formal" democracy (which is concerned with the election
process by which the majority rules). Democracy is also "substantive"
democracy (which is concerned with defense of the rights of a person
as an individual). . . . When the majority denies the minority human
rights, it harms democracy . . . take majority rule away from constitutional democracy, and you have struck at its very essence. Take the
rule of basic values away from constitutional democracy, and you
have struck at its very existence.[19]

Democracy, then, is based on the simultaneous existence of both
the rule of the majority and the rule of values that characterize
democracy. This dual nature should not lead to the assumption that
any flaw in one of these aspects denies the regime its democratic
character. We are dealing with a spectrum of situations that runs
from the existence of the mere heart of democracy—the minimal
existence of the different aspects that ensure the existence of a democratic regime—at one end to the maximal existence of those
aspects, at the other. Therefore, there are "better" and "stronger"
democracies and "worse" and "weaker" democracies. However,
there is a certain minimum that must be observed, without which a
regime is no longer democratic. A delicate balance must be maintained, therefore, between the two aspects of democracy, in a way
that protects the nucleus of each one of its aspects. This balance will
be based inherently on the restrictions placed both on majority rule
and on the rule of fundamental values of democracy. Furthermore,
it is not uncommon to find conflict between the different substantive values of democracy. This situation is likely to exist also within
the framework of a single characteristic of democracy, internally.
Thus, for example, there are internal conflicts between different
human rights. The solution to all these conflicts is the use of the
tool of balancing (horizontal and vertical), which I explain below.[20]

---

[19] C.A. 6821/92, *United Mizrahi Bank Ltd. v. Migdal Cooperative Village*, 49(4)
P.D. 221, 423.
[20] *See infra* p. 170.

Formal Democracy and Legislative Supremacy

FORMAL DEMOCRACY AND ELECTIONS

Everyone agrees that a democracy requires the rule of the people, which is usually[21] effectuated through electing representatives in a legislative body. Therefore, frequent elections are necessary to keep these representatives accountable to their constituents.[22] Elections must be fair, both substantively and procedurally. Substantive fairness means, *inter alia*, equality. "Equality of chances, equality of results, equality of starting point, equality of resource allocation, equality of needs, etc."[23] Procedural fairness means, *inter alia*, that the rules according to which elections are held must be clear and set in advance.[24] It would be wrong to change them in the middle of the elections. Properly held elections combine the supreme democratic interest in popular representation with the democratic interest in realizing the individual's right to participate in elections (either as a candidate or as a voter). This is why it is so important that everyone be given the right to vote.

Some human rights, such as freedom of political expression, derive from, *inter alia*, the need to ensure the proper functioning of the systems through which the people choose their representatives. These human rights are so important that the High Court of Australia was prepared to grant them constitutional status, even though they are not mentioned expressly in the Australian Constitution. The court regarded them as implied constitutional

[21] But not always. There are examples of aspects of direct democracy: *see* Gregory A. Fossedal, *Direct Democracy in Switzerland* (2002); Kris Kobach, *The Referendum: Direct Democracy in Switzerland* (1993).

[22] *See* Robert A. Dahl, *On Democracy* 95–96 (1998).

[23] H.C. 7111/95, *Center for Local Government v. Knesset*, 50(3) P.D. 485, 502 (Cheshin, J.).

[24] For an example of the problems that result when the rules are unclear, *see Bush v. Gore*, 531 U.S. 98 (2000).

rights.[25] As Justice Brennan of the Australian High Court observed:

> Once it is recognized that a representative democracy is constitutionally prescribed, the freedom of discussion which is essential to sustain it is as firmly entrenched in the Constitution as the system of government which the Constitution expressly ordains.[26]

This approach is a proper one. It reflects the role of the judge in giving effect to democracy.[27]

DEMOCRATIC ELECTIONS AND NONDEMOCRATIC PARTIES

The question arises whether, in a democracy, it is possible to limit the right of a party to participate in elections where the goals of that party are to negate democracy itself. This question has arisen in a number of legal systems.[28] Courts in Australia,[29] Germany,[30] and Spain[31] confronted this question. The European Court of Human Rights also ruled on this issue.[32] The Israeli experience has been interesting.[33] In Israel, the question that arose was whether it is possible to prevent the participation of a candidate who denies the existence of Israel as a democratic and Jewish state. That question must

---

[25] See *Kruger v. Commonwealth* (1997) 190 C.L.R. 1, 112–21 (Austl.); *Levy v. Victoria* (1997) 189 C.L.R. 579; *Lange v. Austl. Broad. Corp.* (1997) 189 C.L.R. 520; *Stephens v. W. Austl. Newspapers Ltd.* (1994) 182 C.L.R. 211; *Theophanous v. Herald & Weekly Times Ltd.* (1994) 182 C.L.R. 104; *Austl. Capital Television Party Ltd. v. Commonwealth* (1992) 177 C.L.R. 106; *Nationwide News Party Ltd. v. Wills* (1992) 177 C.L.R. 1.

[26] *Nationwide News Party*, 177 C.L.R. at 48.

[27] On the role of the judiciary in elections, see Pildes, *supra* p. xii, note 11.

[28] See Gregory H. Fox and Georg Nolte, "Intolerant Democracies," in *Democratic Governance and International Law* 389 (G.H. Fox and B.R. Roth eds., 2000); P. Franz, "Unconstitutional and Outlawed Political Parties: A German-American Comparison," 5 *B.C. Int'l and Comp. L. Rev.* 51 (1982).

[29] See *Australian Communist Party v. Commonwealth*, 83 C.L.R. 1 (1951).

[30] See 2 BVerfGE 1(1952); 5 BVerfGE 85 (1956).

[31] See S.T.C. 5/2004.

[32] See *Refah Partisi v. Turkey* (2002) 35 E.H.R. 56.

[33] See Mordechai Kremnitzer, "Disqualification of Lists and Parties: The Israeli Case," in *A Militant Democracy, supra* p. 22, note 9 at 157.

be addressed both as a social-theoretical issue and as a practical-legal problem.

As a theoretical matter, we must overcome a political-philosophical difficulty. I discussed that difficulty in the *Neiman* case:

> The difficulty arises from the dilemma—or, if you prefer, the paradox—whether disqualifying antidemocratic lists from participating in the elections is consistent with democracy itself or whether in doing so, democracy itself does something antidemocratic. This is an old question, which Plato discussed in asking whether absolute freedom leads to slavery and whether democracy, by granting the freedom to choose, leads to despotism . . . neither philosophers nor political scientists agree on the issue. Some say that the nature of democracy is to allow complete freedom of expression, in all situations and of all opinions, including those likely to negate democracy itself . . . others think—and they are in the majority—that the internal logic of democracy gives it the right to disqualify lists that negate democracy itself from participating in the democratic process.[34]

In the *Tibi* case, I added that

> this dilemma arises from the existing tension, within democracy, between two opposing views. On the one hand is the view that democracy is based on the free market of ideas, and that every party or candidate list—including one that seeks to negate or harm democracy—may express its opinion and compete, on an egalitarian basis, in elections that determine the face of society. In this view, disallowing antidemocratic lists participation in elections is inconsistent with democracy itself. It would seem to be opposed to the basic idea of there being an "open market" of ideas. Furthermore, disqualifying antidemocratic lists from participation will generally raise the specter of misusing majority power to suppress the political power of the minority. It may also appear as a panacea that, rather than treating the problem at its root, suppresses it from being aired, thus radicalizing the activities of the antidemocratic lists. On the other hand, there is the consideration that democracy is entitled to protect itself from those who seek to destroy it. Democracy

[34] E.A. 2/84, *Neiman v. Chairman of Cent. Elections Comm. for Eleventh Knesset*, 39(2) P.D. 225, 321 (English translation available at www.court.gov.il)

has the right to disqualify lists that negate democracy itself from participating in the democratic process. Democracy need not commit suicide
in order to demonstrate its vitality. Furthermore, one who rejects or
seeks to change democracy's fundamental values cannot ask to participate in democracy in the name of those very rules he rejects.[35]

Within that dilemma, my opinion is that democracy may and must
defend itself from those who seek to destroy it. Democracy cannot
remain neutral toward political parties that seek to eradicate it. This is
the militant democracy that has been written about in Germany.[36] This
is the defensive democracy that was discussed in Israel.[37] In my view,

> Democracy is entitled to defend itself from those who seek to use it in
> order to destroy its very existence. True, democracy must be tolerant of
> the intolerant. But in its tolerance, democracy need not allow its eradi-
> cation. That is the principle of "militant democracy" or "non-tolerant
> democracy" or, in the words of Justice Sussman, "defensive democracy."[38]

The same applies to the character of Israel as a Jewish state.
Israel was founded as the state of the Jewish people. The reason
for the existence of the State of Israel is its existence as a Jewish state.
That character is central to its existence, and it is "an 'axiom' of the
state."[39] It is a "fundamental principle of our law and our system."[40]
We therefore cannot allow a list or an individual seeking to negate
this reason and this foundation to participate in elections.

As a practical-legal matter, the question arises as to how the court
decides when to deny a candidate list the possibility of participating in
the democratic process because it has the goal of negating the
existence of the state as democratic. In the *Neiman* case,[41] the majority held that in the absence of an explicit provision on the issue,

---

[35] E.A. 11280/02, *Chairman of Cent. Elections Comm. for Sixteenth Knesset
v. Tibi*, 57(4) P.D. 1, 14.
[36] *See supra* p. 000.
[37] E.A. 1/65, *Yardor v. Chairman of Cent. Elections Comm. for Sixth Knesset*,
19(1) P.D. 365, 390.
[38] L.C.A. 7504/95, *Yassin v. Party Registrar*, 50(2) P.D. 45, 62.
[39] E.A. 11280/02, *supra* p. 30, note 35 at 21.
[40] L.C.A. 7504/95, *supra* p. 30, note 38 at 63.
[41] E.A. 2/84, *supra* p. 29, note 34.

an antidemocratic list cannot be denied the right to participate in elections. I took a different view in my opinion in that case. My opinion was—and it remains to this day—that a list can be prevented from participating in elections because its goals are to negate democracy, even in the absence of an explicit statutory provision, if there is a reasonable possibility that the list's participation in elections will harm the democratic character of the state. In any event, the difficulty posed by the absence of an explicit provision has been resolved. The Basic Law: The Knesset has been amended to add a provision that a candidate list or individual whose goals or actions explicitly or implicitly include "negating the existence of the State of Israel as a Jewish and democratic state" may not be a candidate in Knesset elections.[42]

The Supreme Court must now interpret and apply this provision. The Supreme Court is not just as a body that exercises judicial review over the decisions of the Central Elections Committee. The Supreme Court is part of the decision-making process itself, because a decision by the Central Elections Committee disqualifying a candidate from participating in elections "is subject to the approval of the Supreme Court."[43]

In its rulings, the Court has emphasized that the provisions of Section 7A of the Basic Law: The Knesset should be implemented "with an approach that takes into consideration the significant weight accorded to our perspectives on fundamental liberties."[44] Therefore, a number of criteria have been established to ensure that the power to disqualify is narrowly interpreted:

First, the reference to a candidate list's goals is a reference to its "dominant characteristics, which are central to the list's aspirations or

---

[42] Sec. 7Aa.(1) of the Basic Law: The Knesset.

[43] Sec. 7Ab. of the Basic Law: The Knesset. *See also* E.A. 11280/02, *supra* p. 30, note 35 at 28. For a similar provision, see Art. 21(2) of the German Constitution ("Parties that, by reason of their aims or the behaviour of their adherents, seek to undermine or abolish the free democratic basic order or to endanger the existence of the Federal Republic of Germany shall be unconstitutional. The Federal Court shall rule on the question of unconstitutionality").

[44] E.A. 1/88, *Neiman v. Chairman of Cent. Elections Comm. for Twelfth Knesset,* 42 (4) P.D. 177 at 187 (Shamgar, P.).

activities" . . . Second, the dominant and primary goals of the list . . .
are those deduced from its explicit declarations which stem directly
from the conclusions that unequivocallyarise . . . ;Third, it is not
enough for these goals to be theoretical. It must be shown that a candidate list "acts to realize its goals and turn them from an idea into
reality . . . there must be "activity on the ground" that is intended to
carry out the goals of the list into practice. Such activity must be
repetitive. Sporadic activity does not suffice. The activity must be
severe and extreme in the force of its expression . . . indeed, democracy does not take action against those who do not take action
against it. This is defensive democracy, which does not prevent a candidate list from participating in elections just because of the list's
goals, but rather defends against actions taken against it. Finally, the
evidence establishing the goals and actions leading to preventing the
participation of the candidate list or candidate for Knesset elections
must be "persuasive, clear, and unequivocal."[45]

LEGISLATIVE SUPREMACY

The rule of the people implies legislative supremacy.[46] This conceptualization, however, is imprecise because supremacy belongs to
the constitution and not to the legislature. Nonetheless, judges
must respect the role of the legislature. Legislative supremacy tends
to restrict the legislative power of the executive to those situations
in which the primary arrangements are determined by primary
legislation.[47] A respect for the legislative role should influence the
formulation of a proper system of interpretation, which would recognize the intent of the legislature as an important factor in the
interpretation of legislation.[48] Indeed, the people create a statute
through their representatives in the legislature. The statute is
designed to carry out a public policy that the legislature wishes to

[45] E.A. 11280/02, *supra* p. 130, note 35 at 18.
[46] On legislative supremacy, *see* William Eskridge, "Spinning Legislative
Supremacy," 78 *Geo. L.J.* 319 (1989).
[47] *See infra* p. 227.
[48] *See infra* p. 140.

effect on behalf of its constituents. This policy should be taken seriously and should be given expression in the interpretation of the legislation.

Substantive Democracy

Democracy is not satisfied merely by abiding by proper elections and legislative supremacy. Democracy has its own internal morality based on the dignity and equality of all human beings. Thus, in addition to formal requirements (elections and the rule of the majority), there are also substantive requirements. These are reflected in the supremacy of such underlying democratic values and principles as separation of powers, the rule of law, and independence of the judiciary. They are based on such fundamental values as tolerance,[49] good faith, justice, reasonableness, and public order. Above all, democracy cannot exist without the protection of individual human rights—rights so essential that they must be insulated from the power of the majority.[50] As Justice Iacobucci of the Canadian Supreme Court observed, "[t]he concept of democracy is broader than the notion of majority rule, fundamental as that may be."[51] Democracy is not just the law of rules and legislative supremacy; it is a multidimensional concept. It requires recognition of both the power of the majority and the limitations on that power. It is based on legislative supremacy and on the supremacy of values, principles, and human rights.[52] When there is internal conflict, the formal and substantive elements of democracy must be balanced to protect the essence of each of these aspects. In this balance, the system must place limits on both legislative supremacy and the supremacy of human rights.

[49] *See* Ronald Dworkin, *A Bill of Rights for Britain* 35–36 (1990).
[50] *See* Woolf, *supra* p. 20, note 5 at 68–69; McLachlin, *supra* p. 22, note 11 at 6.
[51] Vriend v. Alberta, [1998] 1 S.C.R. 493, 566 (Can.).
[52] *See* Robert Post, "Democracy, Popular Sovereignty, and Judicial Review," 86 *Cal. L. Rev.* 429 (1998) (distinguishing between democracy as a substantive value and popular sovereignty as a mechanism for decision making).

To maintain democracy—and to ensure a delicate balance between its elements[53]—a formal constitution is preferable. To operate effectively, a constitution should enjoy normative supremacy, should not be as easily amendable as a normal statute, and should give judges the power to review the constitutionality of legislation. Without a formal constitution, there is no legal limit on legislative supremacy, and the supremacy of human rights can exist only by the grace of the majority's self-restraint. A constitution, however, imposes legal limitations on the legislature and guarantees that human rights are protected not only by the self-restraint of the majority but also by constitutional control over the majority. Hence the need for a formal constitution.

The need for judicial review, like the need for a formal constitution, is less intense when one can rely on the self-restraint of the majority. This is apparently the situation in the United Kingdom. The Human Rights Act, an ordinary statute, allows judges to hold legislation incompatible with it, without authorizing them to void the incompatible legislation.[54] I hope that this arrangement will work well in the United Kingdom and that it will guarantee the proper combination of parliamentary supremacy and human rights.[55] Personally, however, I am skeptical. In difficult situations, such as terrorist attacks or other emergencies, this self-restraint is unlikely to suffice. In any event, what is good and proper for the United Kingdom—which in any case is subject to the jurisdiction of the European Convention on Human Rights—is not necessarily good and proper for other countries, such

---

[53] This is not, of course, the only reason. For other reasons, see Walter F. Murphy, "Constitutions, Constitutionalism, and Democracy," in *Constitutionalism and Democracy: Transitions in the Contemporary World, supra* p. 21, note 7 at 3, 8–12; Cass R. Sunstein, "Constitutionalism and Secession," 58 *U. Chi. L. Rev.* 633, 636–43 (1991).

[54] *See* Art. 4(2) of the Human Rights Act 1998 ("If the court is satisfied that the provision is incompatible with a Convention right, it may make a declaration of that incompatibility"). *See Human Rights Law and Practice* 38 (Anthony Lester and David Pennick eds., 2d ed., 2004).

[55] *See* Irvine, "Sovereignty in Comparative Perspective: Constitutionalism in Britain and America," 76 *N.Y.U. L. Rev.* 1, 18–19 (2001). *But see* Dworkin, *supra* p. 33, note 49.

as Israel. Therefore, while a written constitution and judicial review are not necessary conditions for the existence of democracy, they are important conditions that should be preferred.[56]

THE SEPARATION OF POWERS

The Separation of Powers as the Backbone of Democracy

Substantive democracy is based on the separation of powers.[57] It is "the backbone of [the] constitutional system."[58] When a single branch creates the statutes, administers them, and adjudicates disputes arising from them, arbitrary government results, freedom suffers, and real democracy does not exist. Indeed, as I have written:

> [T]he separation of powers is not a value in itself. It is not designed to ensure efficiency. The purpose of separation of powers is to strengthen freedom and prevent the concentration of power in the hands of one governmental actor in a manner likely to harm the freedom of the individual.[59]

The words of Justice Brandeis, writing about the principle of separation of powers, are well known:

> The purpose was, not to avoid friction, but, by means of the inevitable friction incident to the distribution of the governmental powers among three departments, to save the people from autocracy.[60]

The ensuring of liberty is vital to democracy. Thus, the separation of powers is central to an understanding of democracy. There

---

[56] *See* Dieter Grimm, "Constitutional Adjudication and Democracy," 33 *Isr. L. Rev.* 193, 199 (1999).

[57] *See* 1 Laurence H. Tribe, *American Constitutional Law* (3d ed. 2000), § 2-1 through 2-10 (discussing the separation of powers); Andràs Sajò, *Limiting Government: An Introduction to Constitutionalism* 69 (1999).

[58] *Cooper v. Canada*, [1996] 3 S.C.R. 854, 867.

[59] H.C. 3267/97, *Rubinstein v. Minister of Def.*, 52(5) P.D. 481, 512; [1998–9] IsrLR 139.

[60] *See Myers v. United States*, 272 U.S. 52, 293 (1926).

is no democracy without proper separation of powers. Separation of powers is the backbone of democracy. The modern understanding of the separation of powers is based on a "trinity of branches" whose status stems from the constitution. Each one of the three branches is limited in its authority and its powers. None of them is omnipotent. The legislative branch, the executive branch, and the judiciary branch have no authority beyond that granted them in and by the constitution.

The three branches of government are of equal status. The power of all three stems from the constitution, whose power stems in turn from the people. Each of the branches has its unique character. This character does not create three latifundia that have no connection between them. The importance of the principle of separation of powers is in the very connection between the branches and in the limitations[61] they place on each other. Thus, for example, the legislature can change the rules of the game, but it must do so within the framework of the constitution. The binding interpretation of the constitution is granted not to the legislative branch but rather to the courts. The court is authorized to interpret the constitution, but it is not authorized to create a constitution, to amend a constitution,[62] or to enact a statute. Indeed, the three branches are equal; each has its own unique character, and their equality is reflected even in those characters. Each one's unique character is balanced out by the others'. In this way the internal harmony of the system is ensured. No branch has total power. The branches are connected and intertwined with each other. Indeed, the modern principle of separation of powers is based on the concept of reciprocal relations between the different branches of power such that each branch checks and balances the other branches. The meaning of this modern principle is threefold: first, each branch of government has a function that is its major function. Its nucleus should not be impinged upon. Second, each branch should perform

---

[61] *See* Sajò, *supra* p. 35, note 57.
[62] *See Responding to Imperfection: The Theory and Practice of Constitutional Amendment* (Sanford Levinson ed., 1995).

its function according to its outlook and its discretion. Third, balancing and review between the three branches is needed. We briefly
discuss each of these elements.

The Relationship between a Branch and Its Functions

The first foundation of the modern perspective of the separation of
powers is that there is a recognized distinction between the different branches such that each branch of government has a function
that serves as its central and primary function. The primary function
of the legislative branch is to legislate (to create statutes, in their
functional meaning); legislate (to create statutes, in their the primary function of the executive branch is to execute the laws; the
primary function of the judiciary branch is to judge (in other
words, to resolve disputes by determining the facts, interpreting
the law, filling in gaps, and/or developing the common law).
This approach recognizes that the separation of powers is not pure
and that, in addition to its primary function, each branch of
government performs some functions that belong to the other
branches, so long as they are intimately related to the branch's
primary function.

The principle of separation of powers requires that derogating
from the primary function assigned to a branch and transferring it
to another branch will not adversely affect the core of the function.
For example, it is not a problem for a parliament to engage in judging in order to take disciplinary action against its members. Such
action does not significantly derogate from the authority of the
judicial branch, and the derogation itself is in the service of issues
that belong to members of parliament. Even when the parliament
removes the immunity of one of its members, a power common to
many parliaments,[63] it does not violate the separation of powers.
Another example is when the judiciary executes the judgments it

[63] *See* Merilie Crespo Allen, *Parliamentary Immunity in the Members States of the
European Union and in the European Parliament* (1999).

has handed down. This executive power of the judiciary does not violate the separation of powers. Executing a judicial decision is intimately connected to the giving of the decision. Similarly, judicial lawmaking does not create a constitutional problem because it derives from the act of judging itself. The principle of *stare decisis* does not violate separation of powers.

Disciplinary adjudication within an executive branch does not pose a serious problem for the separation of powers because it is intimately related to the discipline of the civil service. Similarly, we would not violate the separation of powers by determining that decisions by the executive branch that severely restrict individual freedom require judicial approval before taking effect. Even though doing so makes the judicial branch part of the process of execution, such intervention is justified by the severe restriction on the individual freedom which the courts must protect. On the other hand, making that process of judicial approval routine would unduly violate the separation of powers. The fact that the judiciary has the authority to review the constitutionality of executive action does not mean that it has the authority, as a general matter, to pre-approve administrative action as a condition of it taking effect. Judicial review is one thing; intervention in agency action is another.

A more serious problem is created by the authority of the executive branch to legislate. This legislation (regulations, orders) is of broad scope and in terms of sheer quantity, it exceeds that of the parliament. This state of affairs infringes on the separation of powers. In order to reduce the scope of the violation, administrative legislation should be subject to the approval of the parliament. An additional problem occurs when the parliament transfers "preliminary" decisions affecting national life to the executive branch. Such decisions should remain within the jurisdiction of the legislature.

In determining the ties between a particular function and the branch responsible for its realization, one must remain flexible and take into account the needs of a modern democracy. A "monist" approach to authority should be prevented. While it is important to recognize the interweaving between the authorities, we must take care not to impinge on the essence of every one of the authorities.

Nonintervention in the Exercise of Discretion

The second foundation of the principle of separation of powers is that every branch of government must fulfill the functions given to it according to its own perspective and discretion, without intervention from the other branches. Therefore, the court will not invalidate a decision by the executive branch that falls within the zone of reasonableness, just because the court would have chosen a different reasonable option. The choice between reasonable options is the function of the executive branch, and there is no room for judicial intervention in that decision. According to the principle of separation of powers, if the executive branch operates within the framework of its authority, the judiciary will not intervene and will not change that decision. The authority to execute belongs to the executive branch, not the judiciary. The judiciary may not replace the discretion of the executive on how to implement with its own judicial discretion. The same is true if the parliament passes a statute that meets the requirements of the constitution. A court may not invalidate such a statute simply because it does not agree with it or because the judges would have passed a better piece of legislation had they been given the opportunity. The task of legislating belongs to the legislative branch, and the judiciary may not replace the legislature's legislative discretion with its own discretion. Similarly, the legislative branch may not replace the discretion of the executive branch in carrying out its assigned function of execution. If the parliament is dissatisfied with the way the government exercises its authority, it may vote—in a parliamentary system—no confidence in the government and replace it. The parliament may not, without violating the principle of separation of powers, co-opt the executive branch's authority to execute. Indeed, the judiciary would violate the principle of separation of powers if it were to try to dictate how the executive branch exercises its authority. The executive branch in turn would violate the principle of the separation of powers if it were to try to influence the content of decisions within the authority of the judiciary.

Checks and Balances

THE SEPARATION OF POWERS AND CHECKS AND BALANCES

The third foundation of the principle of separation of powers is the need for checks and balances between the three branches. In the absence of checks and balances, a branch is likely to accumulate power in a way that is harmful to democracy itself. "The separation of powers does not mean the creation of a barrier that absolutely blocks any connection or contact between the branches, but rather is expressed through the existence of a de facto balance between the authorities of the branches, which provides for independence through defined and reciprocal checks."[64] Similarly, in one case I wrote that

> an enlightened democratic regime is a regime of the separation of powers. This separation does not mean every branch exists in isolation, without taking the other branches into account. Such a perspective would wreak significant harm to the foundations of democracy itself, because it would create a dictatorship of each branch within its own sphere. The opposite is true: Separation of powers means reciprocal checks and balances between the different branches. It does not mean walls between the branches but rather bridges which balance and check.[65]

BALANCES

In discussing the separation of powers, we would do well to distinguish between "balances" and "checks." Balance refers to interdependence among the different branches. In a parliamentary system, for example, the confidence of the legislature is required for the government to retain power. The legislature "hires" and "fires" the

---

[64] H.C. 306/81, Flatto-Sharon v. Knesset Committee, 45(4) P.D. 118, 141. (Shamgar, P.)
[65] H.C. 73/85, *"Kach" Party v. Knesset Chairman*, 39(3) P.D. 141, 158.

government. The appointment of a governmental minister requires the approval of the legislature. Both the judicial and executive branches need the budget that the legislature approves. In a number of countries, the approval of the legislative branch is required in order for certain appointments within the executive branch to take effect. In a number of countries, judges are appointed by the executive branch (Canada) or the legislative branch (judges of the Constitutional Court in Germany) or through the cooperation of the executive and legislative branches (the United States). In Israel, the President—who is external to all three branches of government—formally appoints judges according to the choices made by a judicial appointment committee. The committee is composed of two ministers (one of whom is the Minister of Justice), two members of parliament, three Supreme Court judges (including the president of the Supreme Court), and two members of the Israeli Bar Association. The members are chosen by the bodies they "represent."

CHECKS

What if a branch of government acts illegally? What if a branch deviates from the authority which the constitution grants it? What if a branch makes illegal use of its constitutionally assigned authority? The solution to these problems lies in the concept of checks that one branch has over another. In this context, it is important to emphasize the authority of the judiciary to exercise judicial review over the other branches. Indeed, the principle of separation of powers does not mean that each branch may deviate from its authority or exercise it illegally without the other branches being allowed to intervene. Separation of powers means that each branch is independent within its zone, so long as it acts according to the law. It is not a license for the branches to violate the law. But who decides when a branch acts with authorization and according to the law? Does separation of powers mean that each branch determines the scope of its authority and the legality of its actions? The clear answer in every democracy is that each branch of government is authorized and obligated to interpret the scope of its own authority. Every exercise of authority is based on an interpretation of that authority. However, when a dispute arises as to the legality of that interpretation, the final decision is in the hands of the judiciary. Indeed, a democracy is based on the nonfinality of decisions by the legislative and executive branches about the scope of their authority and the legality of their actions. The separation of powers does not mean the absolutism of each branch within its zone. The principle of checks that characterizes the modern separation of powers is at work, according to which the judicial branch has the final authority, in cases of dispute, to determine the bounds of authority and the legality of the activity of the other branches. Any other solution would undermine democracy itself. This is because in order for there to be a separation of powers, there must be a system of deciding whether one branch has deviated from its authority or exercised it illegally. If this system were located within the legislative or executive branch, one of those branches would enjoy absolutism. We need a system of adjudication that is external to the branch that has allegedly deviated from its authority or exercised it illegally. Such a system must be independent of the executive and legislative branches and must act objectively, with the sole goal of actualizing the constitution. This system requires that the final authority to decide the legality of any branch's acts be vested in the judicial branch. There is no superior system for fulfilling this task of checking whether the other branches are acting with authorization. The independence of judges, the fact that, unlike members of the legislature, they are not popularly elected, their political nonaccountability, and their professional training as authorized interpreters of the law make them the most qualified to fulfill the function of supervising the separation of powers. Indeed, the national constitution authorizes the judiciary to adjudicate disputes and in doing so, to determine the law that decides the dispute. As Chief Justice Marshall held in 1803, "It is emphatically the province and duty of the judicial department to say what the law is."[66] The same idea was expressed by Lord Bingham two hundred years later: "The function

---

[66] *Marbury v. Madison*, 5 U.S. (1 Cranch) 137, 177 (1803).

of independent judges charged to interpret and apply the law is universally recognised as a central feature of the modern state, a cornerstone of the rule of law itself."[67]

When a court rules that a statute is unconstitutional and invalidates it, it does not undermine the legislature or violate separation of powers. The legislative authority does not include the authority to pass unconstitutional statutes. The authority to decide the boundaries of legislation and its constitutionality belongs to the judiciary, as part of adjudicating the dispute before it.

When the judiciary determines that the executive branch deviated from its authority or exercised it illegally and thus invalidates the action, it does not infringe upon executive authority and it does not violate the principle of separation of powers. On the contrary: the ones who violated the principle of separation of powers are those who deviated from their authority or acted illegally. A court that invalidates these actions preserves this principle and restores the balance that has been upset. "The proper constitutional relationship of the executive with the courts is that the courts will respect all acts of the executive within its lawful province, and that the executive will respect all decisions of the courts as to what its lawful province is."[68]

In response to this principle, the following argument may arise: True, a branch of government should not judge itself. It is therefore appropriate that the final decision about the legality of the activities of the legislative and executive branches should be taken by a mechanism external to those branches, that is, the judiciary. The same logic, however, requires that the mechanism for making a final decision about whether the judiciary deviated from its authority or exercised it illegally be external to the judicial branch itself. If the judiciary indeed guards the boundaries of authority of the other branches, who guards the guards themselves (*sed quis custodiet et ipsos custodies*)? Doesn't it create a conflict of interest for the judiciary to judge itself?

[67] *A(FC) v. Secretary of State for the Home Department* [2004] UKHL 56 (sec. 42).
[68] *M. v. Home Office* [1992] Q.B. 270, 314. (Nolen, J.)

The question is valid, and it has no completely satisfactory answer. The best we can say is that judges, because of their education, profession, and role and because of the procedural and substantive restrictions on their discretion, are trained and accustomed to dealing with conflicts of interest. Despite the fact that most judicial rulings affect the judge as a person, no one suggests that a judge should not have the authority to adjudicate. Indeed, judges are obligated to act objectively in order to actualize the purpose of the constitution and the law. Judges must act devoid of personal interest in the results of the adjudication, because in adjudicating, they are not fighting for their own power. These facts ensure that, more than any other branch, judges can be trusted to adjudicate objectively and appropriately. True, there is no complete trust, but there is also no better solution. All that can be said is that judges are accountable. Their accountability—judicial, not political—does not affect their independence. This judicial accountability provides a partial answer to the dilemma of who will guard the guardian.[69] An additional source of accountability is the checks and balances exercised by the other two branches of government, which we discussed.[70] Of course, we may conceive of creating a fourth branch that would decide whether judges deviated from their authority or exercised it illegally. If this fourth branch acted as judges are supposed to act, it itself would become the judicial branch, and the problem would remain of who would guard it. At a certain stage of the search for the ideal solution, which we do not have, we must decide to make do with an optimal solution, and the current solution is optimal.

IS SEPARATION OF POWERS CONSTITUTIONALIZED?

Most constitutions determine the powers of the three branches of government. Do they also entrench the value of the separation of powers? Most constitutions do not include a specific article

[69] See Mauro Cappelletti, "Who Watches the Watchmen? A Comparative Study of Judicial Responsibility," 31 *Am. J. Comp. L.* 1(1983).
[70] *Supra* p. 40.

enshrining the concept of separation of powers. In such cases, is it a constitutional concept that trumps legislation? Does a branch of government that violates the separation of powers act in violation of the constitution? In my opinion, the answer to these questions is yes. The democratic value of separation of powers, and not just the de facto division of authority among the different branches, is itself a constitutional concept, superior to legislation. True, the constitution may not contain an explicit provision recognizing the principle of separation of powers. Nevertheless, the principle of separation of powers is a constitutional principle. Such recognition is required by the purposive interpretation of the constitution. This principle may not be written in the lines of the constitution, but it is written between the lines. It derives implicitly from the language of the constitution. It is a natural outgrowth of the structure of the constitution—which distinguishes between three branches of government and discusses each of them in a separate chapter—and from the entirety of their provisions.

THE ROLE OF THE JUDGE IN PROTECTING THE SEPARATION OF POWERS

The role of the judge in a legal system whose values are democratic is to preserve and protect the separation of powers. This role is expressed in a variety of ways. In this section I discuss just a few. First, legislation or administrative action that undermines the principle of separation of powers is unconstitutional and may be declared invalid. This would happen, for example, if the legislature enacted a statute providing that the decision over whether a statute is constitutional be assigned to the legislature itself, not to the courts. Such a statute would be unconstitutional. It would take away the authority granted to the judiciary by the constitution to interpret the constitution and give it to the legislature. In doing so, the legislature would violate the principle of separation of powers. This example is not merely hypothetical. It occurred, de facto, in South Africa, where the racist separation at the base of apartheid was grounded in a statute. The Appellate Division of South Africa held that the statute was unconstitutional because it contradicted legislation of a higher normative level.[71] To overcome this decision, the legislature enacted a second statute that provided that an appeal of the constitutionality of the statute establishing apartheid would be adjudicated by parliament, sitting as "the High Court of Parliament." The Appellate Division reviewed this second statute and held it unconstitutional because it infringed upon the authority of the court to exercise judicial review over the constitutionality of statutes.[72] This is an extreme example, and one we hope will not reappear. The State of Israel supplied an additional extreme example. Two coalition parties, the Israeli Labor Party and the Shas Movement, reached a coalition agreement including the following provision (Section 3): "If the status quo on religious issues is violated [by judicial ruling—A.B.], the parties agree to correct the violation through appropriate legislation." The legality of this agreement was raised before the Supreme Court and was met with sharp criticism by each judge in the panel hearing the case. In my dissent, I wrote that, in my opinion, this agreement violated the separation of powers. I added that:

> Section 3 of the coalition agreement destroys the bridge upon which the separation of powers rests. It dismantles the partnership between the branches in the legislative project. It builds a wall between the legislative branch and the judicial branch. It creates a disconnect between the legislative branch and the judicial branch. It calls upon the legislative branch to change the interpretation of the judiciary without weighing it on the merits, without evaluating its advantages and disadvantages, and without studying it at all. Even if the judicial interpretation is rendered necessary by the structure of government, even if it naturally and rationally derives from the range of principles and values, even if it serves the most interests and values deserving of preservation, and even if it is strongly linked to the entirety of regulations in the legal system—the legislature is not even to throw a passing glance at the judicial decision, its holding, or its explanations.

[71] See *Harris v. The Minister of Interior*, 1951 (2) S.A. 428 (A).
[72] *Ministry of Interior v. Harris*, 1952 (4) S.A. 769. The story is told in Forsyth, *In Danger for Their Talents* 58 (1985).

The legislative eye is not to read the decision. The legislative ear does not hear it. The legislative heart does not feel it . . . section 3 of the coalition agreement . . . violates the principle of separation of powers. In my opinion, it is not just an inappropriate decision. It is an invalid decision, because it wreaks serious harm to the fundamental conceptions of our constitutional regime. It violates our constitutional public policy.[73]

These extreme examples do not reflect the full scope of issues arising from the need to preserve the separation of powers. Here is an additional example: The Parliament may not excuse itself from its authority to legislate by transferring that power to the executive branch (the nondelegation doctrine). Even though there is recognition of the executive's broad authority to enact administrative regulations, the general policies and basic criteria constituting the basis of the action must be established in legislation.[74]

THE SEPARATION OF POWERS AND STATUTORY INTERPRETATIONS

Statutory interpretation is a second area in which the judge plays the role of preserving and protecting separation of powers. It is presumed—though the presumption is rebuttable—that legislative provisions are designed to actualize the separation of powers, not violate it. Ordinary legislation seeking to enact a scheme that violates the separation of powers must say so explicitly.

The purpose of every statute is to keep the legislative authority within the parliament. In the absence of explicit authorization, the legislative authority of the other branches is not to be recognized. "Unless granted authority by the primary legislature, the secondary [administrative—A.B.] legislature has nothing. The secondary legislature can only draw its strength from the authority imparted

---

[73] H.C. 5364/94, *Velner v. Chairman of Israeli Labor Party*, 49(1) P.D. 758, 791.
[74] H.C. 3267/97, *Rubinstein v. Minister of Defense*, 52(5) P.D. 481, 502; [1998–9] IsrLR 139, 163. *See also* Kommers, *supra* p. 22, note 9 at 138; Laurence H. Tribe, *American Constitutional Law* (3d ed. 2000); Uwe Kischel, "Delegation of Legislative Power to Agencies: A Comparative Analysis of United States and German Law," 46 *Admin. L. Rev.* 213 (1994).

by the governing statute, which defines the framework of activity permitted it."[75] Furthermore, once the authority to enact secondary legislation is granted, it is presumed that such authority is designed to actualize the primary regulations determined in the primary legislation.

It is presumed that legislation imparts executive authority to the executive branch (the government). The selection of one of multiple legal ways of executing the law is in the hands of the executive branch. This is the "zone of reasonableness," which is directly derived from the separation of powers.

It is presumed that legislation imparts the authority to judge to the judicial branch. The presumption is that the purpose of any legislation is not to deny the court's power to adjudicate (ouster of jurisdiction) or to limit the scope of its discretion in exercising its judicial authority.

If a statute includes an explicit provision negating or restricting the principle of separation of powers, the court will give it full interpretive validity. The statute will be interpreted in such a way as to infringe or violate the principle of separation of powers. In a case like this, a question will of course arise as to whether the legislative provision, as interpreted, is constitutional. This question of constitutionality is distinct from the presumption we discussed. The presumption affects the meaning to be given to the statute. The issue of meaning is different from the issue of validity, though the two are related. The more significant weight we accord the presumption about the meaning of the legislative provision, the lower the risk of having to invalidate the provision.

THE SEPARATION OF POWERS AND PROTECTION OF COURTS' JURISDICTION

A third way in which the courts preserve the separation of powers is through the rule that a court that has jurisdiction must exercise it. When jurisdiction is left to the discretion of the court (discretionary

[75] *See* H.C. 337/81, *Mitrani v. Minister of Transportation*, 37(3) P.D. 337, 357 (Shamgar, J.).

jurisdiction), the presumption is in favor of exercising it. The need to preserve the separation of powers motivates this presumption. Situations in which the courts refrain from exercising their jurisdiction will be rare and exceptional. Indeed, a court that refrains from exercising its jurisdiction violates the separation of powers. The result of refraining to exercise jurisdiction is that an illegal act remains in effect, undermining the principle of checks and balances.

THE SEPARATION OF POWERS AND THE POWER TO INTERPRET

Fourth, the principle of separation of powers leads to the conclusion that the courts have the authority to give the constitution and legislation a binding interpretation. My view is therefore that the final word on constitutional and statutory interpretation belongs to the court. The interpretation given by members of the constitutional assembly or legislature to the constitution or to statutes is not binding on a judge who interprets them. The principle of separation of powers prevents a situation in which the hands of the court are bound to the interpretation given by the constitutional assembly or legislature.

Similarly, the interpretation that the executive branch gives to a statute that it implements does not require a judge to give that same statute a similar interpretation. The court is free to consider the administrative interpretation, but it is not free to shake off its own interpretive authority and transfer such authority to the executive branch.[76]

Different Models of the Separation of Powers

We all speak of separation of powers, but there is substantial variety in the content hidden behind this label. In conversations with judges and law professors in the United States, I have found that

[76] *See infra* p. 246.

despite the common rhetoric of separation of powers, many in the American legal community conceive of this principle very differently than I do. Here, I do not refer to potential differences in the concept of separation of powers that may exist between a presidential democracy like that of the United States and a parliamentary democracy like that of the United Kingdom, Canada, Australia, and Israel. Instead, I refer to differences in the concept of the role of the judiciary within the separation of powers and the relationship of the judiciary to the legislative and executive branches.

For example, it appears that the accepted approach in the United States is that if the courts were to void a presidential pardon because it was given for improper motives, the court would violate the principle of separation of powers; if the court were to void a Senate impeachment proceeding because it had defects,[77] the court would violate the principle of separation of powers;[78] if the court were to order the President to dismiss a Secretary of State who was facing criminal proceedings, the court would violate the principle of separation of powers. In contrast, I would say the court actions described in these examples conform to the principle of separation of powers. Indeed, in my view, separation of powers means that every branch may act independently only as long as it acts lawfully within its jurisdiction. When a branch of state acts unlawfully— whether it exceeds its authority or exercises its authority for unlawful reasons—it is the role of the judiciary, as part of the principle of separation of powers, to ensure that the unlawful action is voided. For this reason, I do not see any difference between a case in which the executive or legislature acts contrary to the constitution[79] and a case in which these branches act contrary to any other legal norm.

---

[77] *But see* Nixon v. United States, 506 U.S. 224, 253–54 (1993) (Souter, J., concurring in the judgment) (suggesting that judicial review may be warranted if the Senate impeached a person "upon a coin toss").

[78] *See* 1 Tribe, *supra* p. 35, note 57, § 2-7, at 152–53 (noting that impeachments are generally considered beyond the reach of American judicial review).

[79] Such was the case in *Powell v. McCormack*, 395 U.S. 486 (1969), in which the Supreme Court held that Congress had unlawfully refused to seat an elected congressman who satisfied the criteria for House membership contained in Article I, Section 2. *Id.* at 489.

Under my approach, the principle of the rule of law always binds the branches, irrespective of the source of the legal norm.

If we wish to avoid invalidating executive or legislative acts that are contrary to law, we should do so not by negating the judiciary's power to invalidate illegal acts but rather by changing legal norms themselves, so that the acts in question are no longer unlawful. If the presidential pardon power allows the President to grant pardons based on considerations such as a family relationship or monetary payment, then there is no basis for judicial disqualification of pardons of this type. The reason is not that judicial review would violate the principle of separation of powers. Rather, the reason is simply that the action is lawful, so the claim should be dismissed on the merits. The same is true of the other examples that I have given above. I have difficulty with the view that, in situations like these, the principle of separation of powers is an obstacle to judicial review. Rather, in my view, it is precisely this principle that is the source of judicial review.

DEMOCRACY AND THE RULE OF LAW

The Nature of the Rule of Law

One of the basic principles of democracy is the rule of law. This is a complex, multilayered, and opaque concept.[80] To understand it, one must differentiate between three aspects of the rule of law. The first is a formal aspect: making the law rule. The second aspect is a jurisprudential (doctrinal) one, concerning the minimal conditions for the existence of law in society. The third aspect is substantive and concerns the rule of law that properly balances between the

---

[80] For a discussion on this topic, see Cass, *supra* p. 16, note 36; Paul Craig, *"Formal and Substantive Conceptions of the Rule of Law: An Analytical Framework"*, 1997 *Pub. L.* 467; Trevor R. S. Allan, *Constitutional Justice, A Liberal Theory of the Rule of Law* (2001); Paul Craig, *"Constitutional Foundations, the Rule of Law and Supremacy,"* 2003 *Pub. L.* 92; Michael Neumann, *The Rule of Law: Politicizing Ethics* (1998).

individual and society. The boundaries among these that aspects are blurred. There is significant overlap between them. However, there is an essential difference among them that must not be ignored. When we say that a fundamental principle of democracy is the rule of law, we refer to all three aspects. One cannot settle for only one of them. From the standpoint of democracy, the most important of the meanings is the substantive rule of law. That is the foundation.

Upon this foundation doctrinal rule of law is built. The formal rule of law is the crossbeams. According to this approach, worthy law, which arises from the substantive and moves up to the doctrinal floor, should be made to rule the members of society and the branches of government. If you pull out the foundation, the crossbeams fall. I am afraid that our overemphasis of the rule of law as "making law rule" blurs the foundational assumptions upon which the law and its rule are constructed. These assumptions are democracy, which places at its center the individual acting within the framework of the state, which in turn acts through representatives; and majority rule.

The rule of law, including its three aspects, is a basic principle in democracy. Each judge must fulfill it; each judge must guard against its infringement. This principle is the source of the trend of opening the courthouse doors to the petitioner wishing to protect the rule of law: without a court of law, there is no law. This principle also explains the need for judicial review of governmental actions. Derived from this is judicial review of the constitutionality of the law, which preserves the rule of law over the rule maker. This principle is also the justification for judicial review of the legality of secondary legislation and of other actions of public administration.

The Rule of Law, not the Rule of Men or Women

It is sometimes emphasized that the rule of law conflicts with the rule of men or women. Can the rule of law be maintained without granting authority to functionaries in public agencies? Can the rule of law be maintained without granting discretion to people? The answer is that the rule of law does not negate the granting of authority to governmental agencies. However, it demands that the functionary's authority not be absolute; that the primary arrangements regarding the contents of that authority be grounded in legislation; that the authority be used according to the norms of administrative law, intended to ensure fairness and equality in its use; and that judicial review of the use of administrative authority be maintained.

The Formal Aspect of the Rule of Law

The concept of the rule of law has numerous meanings.[81] However, everyone agrees that the rule of law means, at a minimum, rule by law. That is its formal aspect, whereby, as I have written,

> [A]ll actors in the State, whether private individuals and corporations or branches of government, must act according to the law, and violations of the law must meet with the organized sanction of society. The rule of law, in this sense, has a double meaning: the legality of government and enforcement of the law. This is a formal principle; we are concerned not with the content of the law but with the need to enforce it, whatever its content. The rule of law in this sense is connected not to the nature of the regime but to the principle of public order.[82]

In this sense it can be said, as Justice Anton in Scalia aptly put it, that the rule of law is a law of rules.[83]

---

[81] See Cass, *supra* p. 16, note 36 at 1 ("[T]he rule of law still means very different things to different people"); Paul Craig, "Formal and Substantive Conceptions of the Rule of Law: An Analytical Framework," 1997 *Pub. L.* 467 (exploring both formal and substantive concepts of the rule of law, as articulated by various scholars); See *The Rule of Law* (Ian Shapiro ed. 1994); *The Rule of Law: Ideal or Ideology* (Allen Hutchinson and Patrick Monahan eds., 1987); Michael Neumann, *The Rule of Law: Politicizing Ethics* (2002).
[82] H.C. 428/86, *Barzilai v. Gov't of Israel*, 40(3) P.D. 505, 621 (Barak, J., dissenting) (English translation available at www.court.gov.il).
[83] Antonin Scalia, "The Rule of Law as a Law of Rules," 56 *U. Chi. L. Rev.* 1175, 1187 (1989). On dissent, *see* Cass Sunstein, *Why Societies Need Dissent* (2003).

But this idea is an impoverished notion of the rule of law. In this weak form, the rule of law exists even in a dictatorship. A friend once told me that during World War II, several Jews were in prison in Germany as a result of sentences received before the war broke out. The Gestapo did not harm those Jews because the law mandated that they not be exterminated in the death camps before finishing their prison sentences, and this rule of law had to be maintained. But when the prisoners finished serving their sentences, the Gestapo was waiting for them at the gate. The prisoners were taken to the death camps and murdered. The formal rule of law was observed.

The Jurisprudential Concept of the Rule of Law

In addition to this formal understanding of the rule of law, the rule of law exists in a jurisprudential sense. According to this concept, the rule of law includes certain minimum requirements without which a legal system cannot exist, and which distinguish a legal system from a gang whose leader imposes his will on everyone else.[84] Professor Lon Fuller calls these requirements collectively the "inner morality of law."[85] Among philosophers, there is disagreement over these minimum requirements. Fuller requires that the law be general; legal rules must be publicized, clear, intelligible, and stable enough to enable citizens to conform to them; the law must not be overly retroactive; statutes should not conflict with one another; the law should not demand the performance of acts beyond one's powers; the rules must be administered as announced.[86] Other philosophers have offered different lists of requirements.[87]

[84] *See* Cass R. Sunstein, *Legal Reasoning and Political Conflict* 101–20 (1996) (discussing the jurisprudential conception of the rule of law).
[85] *See* Lon L. Fuller, *The Morality of Law* 41–94 (rev. ed. 1969).
[86] *See id.* at 39.
[87] *See, e.g.,* John Rawls, *A Theory of Justice* 236–39 (1971); Joseph Raz, "The Rule of Law and Its Virtue," 93 *Law Q. Rev.* 195, 198–202 (1977).

The Substantive Concept of the Rule of Law

Although this jurisprudential concept is important, and I am prepared to regard it as an essential condition for the rule of law, I do not believe that it is enough. It cannot—just as the formal rule of law cannot—release people from the duty of complying with a corrupt statute (*lex corrupta*). Why should we hold inviolable a piece of legislation that gives the government—publicly, prospectively, and in general—the power to deal a mortal blow to human rights? Haim H. Cohen, a judge on the Supreme Court of Israel, rightly said:

> [The rule of law] does not mean only that the ruling authorities in the State act according to law: even totalitarian governments act according to the laws of their countries. Are those not the laws that they themselves enacted for their own purposes and according to their own scheme? Consider the Nazis, who came to power lawfully and committed most of their crimes by virtue of explicit legal authorizations that they made for this purpose: no one would say that "rule of law" reigned in Nazi Germany, and no one would dispute that what reigned there was the rule of crime.[88]

Indeed, it is not proper to identify the rule of law as merely the principle of the legality of government, with jurisprudential requirements added in. Dworkin has rightly said that we must not be satisfied with a "rule-book conception" of the rule of law.[89] It must be extended to the "right conception" of the rule of law. There is certainly no agreement as to the scope of this concept. In my opinion, it means guaranteeing fundamental values of morality, justice, and human rights, with a proper balance between these and the other needs of society.

According to my approach, the rule of law is not merely public order, the rule of law is social justice based on public order. The law exists to ensure proper social life. Social life, however, is

[88] Haim H. Cohen, *Ha-Mishpat* (*The Law*) 143 (1991).
[89] Dworkin, *supra* p. 25, note 18 at 11.

not a goal in itself but a means to allow the individual to live in dignity and develop himself. The human being and human rights underlie this substantive perception of the rule of law, with a proper balance among the different rights and between human rights and the proper needs of society. The substantive rule of law "is the rule of proper law, which balances the needs of society and the individual."[90] This is the rule of law that strikes a balance between society's need for political independence, social equality, economic development, and internal order, on the one hand, and the needs of the individual, his personal liberty, and his human dignity on the other. The judge must protect this rich concept of the rule of law. This perception of the rule of law has practical implications for the methods available to judges in realizing their role and for their relationship to the other branches of government.

The Rule of Law and the Role of the Judge

The role of the judge in a democratic society is to bring about the realization of the rule of law. This task has implications in various areas. Thus, for example, this approach is a justification for the existence of a constitution as a supralegislative norm. Moreover, the enforcement of the rule of law requires judicial review of constitutionality of statutes. The rule of law leads to the conclusion that the final interpreter of the law should be the court, and not the legislature or the executive. Thus the principle of the rule of law affects the formulation of proper interpretive doctrine, based on the rich aspects of the rule of law. This doctrine is purposive interpretation, which takes into consideration the various aspects of the rule of law.[91]

---

[90] H.C. 428/86, *Barzilai v. Gov't of Israel*, 40(3) P.D. 505, 622 (Barak, J., dissenting) (English translation available at www.court.gov.il).
[91] On purposive interpretation, *see infra* p. 125.

FUNDAMENTAL PRINCIPLES

Democracy and Fundamental Principles

Fundamental principles (or values) fill the normative universe of a democracy.[92] They justify legal rules. They are the reason for changing them. They are the spirit (*voluntas*) that encompasses the substance (*verba*). Every norm that is created in a democracy is created against the background of these values. Justice Mishael Cheshin of the Supreme Court of Israel expressed this well when he wrote:

> All of these—principles, values and tenets—are prima facie extralegal, but they serve as an anchor for the law—for every law—and no law can be described without them. A law without that anchor is like a house without foundations; just as the latter will not last, so too a law that has only itself is like a castle in the air.[93]

My position is that every norm, whether expressed in a statute or in case law, lives and breathes within this normative world replete with values and principles. These values create a "normative umbrella" for the operation of the common law and a framework for interpreting all legal texts. The assumption is that every legal norm seeks to give effect to these values.

The common law is replete with fundamental principles. They are the basis for its development. The interpretation of legal texts is dictated by fundamental principles, since they constitute the objective purpose of every legal text.[94] Indeed, a legal norm, whether enacted

[92] For a discussion of how values underlie legal principles, see Robert M. Cover, "The Supreme Court, 1982 Term—Foreword: *Nomos* and Narrative, *Common Values and the* 97 *Harv. L. Rev.* 4 (1983). *See also* Dawn Oliver, *Public-Private Divide* 57 (1999); Dawn Oliver, "The Underlying Values of Public and Private Law," in *The Province of Administrative Law* 217 (Michael Taggert ed., 1997).

[93] C.A. 7325/95, *Yediot Aharonot Ltd. v. Kraus*, 52(3) P.D. 1, 72. (Cheshin, J., dissenting).

[94] *See* William N. Eskridge, Jr., "Public Values in Statutory Interpretation," 137 *U. Pa. L. Rev.* 1007, 1007–09 (1989); Cass R. Sunstein, "Interpreting Statutes in the Regulatory State," 103 *Harv. L. Rev.* 405, 460 (1989), at 426–28.

or in case law, is an organism that lives in its environment. This environment includes the fundamental principles of the system. Indeed, judges are not able to sever themselves from the fundamental values of their societies. They will give expression to them consciously or subconsciously. The use of fundamental principles raises several problems that I wish to consider briefly. I know that this is an area in which different judges are likely to have conflicting opinions. I can only indicate my own view regarding the status and role of fundamental principles in realizing the judicial role.

What Are Fundamental Principles?

Every legal system has its own fundamental principles. Nonetheless, most democratic legal systems share some common ones. As I wrote in one of my opinions:

> These general principles include the principles of equality, justice, and morality. They extend to the social goals of the separation of powers, the rule of law, freedom of speech, freedom of movement, worship, occupation, and human dignity, the integrity of judging, public safety and security, the democratic values of the State and its very existence. These principles include good faith, natural justice, fairness, and reasonableness.[95]

This list is certainly not exhaustive. It is composed of three types of fundamental principles: ethical values (such as justice, morality, and human rights), social purposes (such as the existence of the state and public safety within it, certainty and stability in interpersonal arrangements, and human rights), and proper ways of behavior (such as reasonableness, fairness, and good faith). The distinctions among the three types are not precise, and there is considerable overlap. It is sufficient to point out that we are concerned with general and accepted principles that form a central element of the legal system. They constitute both the principles and the policies of the legal system.[96]

---

[95] Cr.A. 677/83, *Borochov v. Yefet*, 39(3) P.D. 205, 218.
[96] Dworkin distinguishes between principle and policy. *See* Dworkin, *supra* p. xiii, note 20, at 244. I do not insist on this distinction. *See also* N. MacCormick, "On

The Sources of the Fundamental Principles

Since there is usually no central text that articulates the fundamental principles of the legal system, how will the judge derive them? One thing is clear: judges must not impose their own personal, subjective perceptions of the fundamental principles on the society in which they operate. Judges should not reflect their own principles but rather the fundamental principles that are implied by the legal system and the ethos that it characterizes.[97] The nature of the fundamental principles and the balance among them are determined by the fundamental positions and fundamental beliefs of the society, such as those written into its constitution or its declaration of independence. Judges also learn of the fundamental principles from the structure of the democratic regime itself, including principles about the separation of powers, the rule of law, and the independence of the judiciary. From the democratic nature of the state, judges can infer the existence of human rights. Indeed, there is a reciprocal relationship between the democratic nature of the state and its fundamental principles: judges learn of the democratic nature of the state from its fundamental principles. And from this democratic nature, and the different statutes that characterize it, they may derive the state's fundamental principles.

New and Old Fundamental Principles

Fundamental principles do not live forever. New fundamental principles come into the system, while outdated ones leave the system. New fundamental principles find expression in new constitutions and in new statutes consistent with the new constitutions. But even in the absence of new constitutions and new statutes, the introduction of new fundamental principles is made possible by case law. The judge is faced with the difficult and complex tasks of recognizing new fundamental principles and removing outdated ones from the

---

Reasonableness," in *Les notions a contenu variable en droit* chs. 5–8 (Chaim Perelman and Raymond Vander Elst eds., 1984).

[97] *See* Cardozo, *supra* p. xv, note 25 at 88–89, 108.

system. Judges must understand the legal system in which they operate and feel the pace and direction of its development. They must introduce into the system only those fundamental principles that are ripe for recognition.[98] Different values are gradually absorbed and gradually ripen until the moment arrives when judges ought to recognize them as fundamental values of their systems. We are concerned, therefore, with a lengthy social process. This process was discussed by President Agranat of the Supreme Court of Israel:

The conception and birth of these truths are the result of social thought. Their creation and development are the outcome of clarifications and elucidation through social organs (political parties, newspapers, various associations and professional organizations, etc.). Only after they have undergone this process of initial crystallization does the State—i.e., the laws of the legislature, the regulations and rulings of the executive, and the judgments of the courts—come and reshape them, translate them into the language of law, and impress on them the positive and binding stamp of the law. The explanation for this is as follows: the role of the State is—so democracy teaches us—to fulfill the will of the people and to give effect to norms and standards that the people cherish. What follows from this is that a process of "common conviction" must first take place among the enlightened members of society regarding the truth and justice of those norms and standards before we can say that a general will has been reached that these should become binding with the approval and sanction of the positive law. It should be noted that the "common conviction" is not that these norms and standards are yet to be born, but that they exist in the present and contain truth, even though they lack an official statutory stamp of approval. It follows that the social consensus regarding the truth and justice of one norm or another must precede legal recognition from the State, and the process of creating this kind of social consensus does not

[98] See Joseph Raz, "Legal Principles and the Limits of Law," 81 *Yale L.J.* 823, 849 (1972) ("In most countries one of the most general principles restraining judicial discretion enjoins judges to act only on those values and opinions which have the support of some important segment of the population"); Harry H. Wellington, "Common Law Rules and Constitutional Double Standards: Some Notes on Adjudication," 83 *Yale L.J.* 221, 236 (1973).

begin and end in a day; it is a process of gradual development that continues for a long time and is sometimes renewed.[99]

Generally, values that are insufficiently developed and that do not enjoy social recognition and agreement should not be introduced into the legal system judicially. This notion was discussed by Justice Holmes:

> As law embodies beliefs that have triumphed in the battle of ideas and then have translated themselves into action, while there still is doubt, while opposite convictions still keep a battle front against each other, the time for law has not come; the notion destined to prevail is not yet entitled to the field. It is misfortune if a judge reads his conscious or unconscious sympathy with one side or the other prematurely into the law, and forgets that what seem to him to be first principles are believed by half his fellow men to be wrong.[100]

At times judges may find certain values to be fundamental and proper, but this reason alone should not generally be sufficient for judges to recognize them as fundamental values of the system. In principle, judges should recognize only values that appear to be fundamental to the society in which they live and operate. The social consensus around fundamental views is usually what ought to guide judges with regard to both the introduction of new fundamental principles and the removal from the system of fundamental principles that have become discredited.

The Status and Weight of Fundamental Principles

Fundamental principles play various roles in the law. They are the reason for creating new legal norms and for changing existing norms. They influence the legislature in creating legislation and influence the judge in developing the common law. They are sources of rights and duties, and they are criteria for the validity of

[99] H.C. 58/68, *Shalit v. Minister of Interior*, 23(2) P.D. 477, 602.
[100] Oliver Wendell Holmes, "Law and the Court," in *Collected Legal Papers* 210, 239 (1952), at 291, 294–95.

legal norms. As we shall see when we discuss purposive interpretation and objective purpose,[101] fundamental principles are an interpretive tool for all legal texts.

The legal status of fundamental principles is determined by their normative sources. Fundamental principles derived from the constitution have constitutional status; fundamental principles derived from statutes have statutory status; fundamental principles derived from the common law have common law status. This framework leads to an important question: Are there principles so fundamental that they have, in a legal system with a formal constitution (such as the United States), supraconstitutional weight,[102] or in a legal system with no formal constitution (such as England and New Zealand), supralegislative status?[103]

Fundamental principles reflect ideals. What makes them unique is that they can be realized at different levels of intensity. When fundamental principles conflict, they do not cancel each other out. Instead, the result of the conflict is a redefinition of the scope of each principle's boundary. The two conflicting principles continue to apply in the legal system, and a proper balance is maintained between them.

As discussed by Dworkin,[104] an important quality that characterizes principles is that they have "weight." It is possible to resolve a conflict between principles by means of "balancing" their respective

---

[101] *Infra* p. 125.

[102] The question arises whether every constitutional amendment that complies with the formal provisions relating to amendments is constitutional. Alternatively, is it perhaps possible to recognize constitutional amendments as unconstitutional? *See* Laurence H. Tribe and Michael C. Dorf, *On Reading the Constitution* 102–103, 110 (1991), 110; John Vile, "The Case Against Implicit Limits on the Constitutional Amending Process," in *Responding to Imperfection: The Theory and Practice of Constitutional Amendment* 191 (Sanford Levinson ed., 1995). The most interesting judicial treatment of this issue comes from the Indian Supreme Court. In a series of decisions, the court established that a constitutional amendment is unconstitutional if it changes the constitution's basic structure and framework. *See* Matthew Abraham, "Judicial Role in Constitutional Amendment in India: The Basic Structure Doctrine," in *The Creation and Amendment of Constitutional Norms* 195, 201–04 (Mads Andenas ed., 2000).

[103] *See* Robin Cooke, "Fundamentals," 1988 *N.Z. L.J.* 158, 164; Harry Woolf, "Droit Public—English Style, 1995 *Pub. L.* 57, 67.

[104] See Dworkin, *supra* p. xiii, note 18 at 26–27.

weights. The weight of a fundamental principle reflects its relative social importance, its place in the legal system, and its value within the entire array of social values. Similarly, it is possible to speak of a "gravitational force" of fundamental values. This gravitational force varies according to the nature of the principles, their sources, and their importance. William Eskridge rightly points out that "[p]ublic values have a gravitational force that varies according to their source (the Constitution, statutes, the common law) and the degree of our historical and contemporary commitment to these values."[105]

How does the judge determine the weights of the various fundamental principles? The answer to this question is difficult. Legal science has not yet developed a satisfactory theory of values, and it is questionable whether such a theory could ever be developed. But it is certainly possible to say that a fundamental principle enshrined in a superior norm, such as a constitution, is of greater weight than a fundamental principle enshrined in an inferior norm, such as a statute or common law. A judge can also take into account the weight given to competing fundamental principles in the past. The judge must harmonize the relative weight given to a fundamental principle in one case (freedom of speech versus public safety) with the weight that should be given to that fundamental principle in another case (freedom of expression versus reputation). In doing so, the judge must aspire to uniformity and harmony. But we must admit that in certain cases the matter is subject to judicial discretion. There are many values and principles of substantive democracy. I wish to mention five of them: tolerance, good faith, justice, reasonableness, and public order.

Tolerance

Democracy is based on tolerance. This means tolerance for the acts and beliefs of others. It also means tolerance for intolerance. In a pluralistic society, tolerance is the unifying force that allows people to live together. Indeed, tolerance constitutes both an end

---

[105] Eskridge, *supra* p. 57, note 94 at 1018.

and a means. It constitutes a social goal in itself, which every democratic society should aspire to realize. It serves as a means and a tool for balancing between other social goals and reconciling them, in cases where they conflict with one another. As I have stated in one case:

> Tolerance is a central value on the public agenda. If every individual in a democratic society seeks to realize all of his desires, in the end society will not be able to realize even a small number of its desires. Proper social life is naturally based on reciprocal concessions and mutual tolerance.[106]

Of course, tolerance has its limits.[107] But although it is not an absolute value, it is a central value to be considered and balanced against others.

Tolerance means respect for the personal opinions and feelings of every individual. Tolerance also means attempting to understand others, even if they behave in a way that is unusual, and tolerance means protecting opinions, ideas, and beliefs. Tolerance in religious-secular relations, for example, means recognizing the existence of two important human rights—freedom of religion and freedom from religion—that require accommodation and compromise. Indeed, tolerance means the willingness to compromise: compromise between the individual and society and compromise between individuals. This willingness to compromise does not mean waiving principles, but it does mean waiving the use of all means to realize goals: "Tolerance is not a slogan for accumulating rights, but a criterion for granting rights to others."[108]

---

[106] C.A. 105/92, *Re'em Eng'g Contractors Ltd. v. Municipality of Upper Nazareth*, 47(5) P.D. 189, 211.

[107] *See* Raphael Cohen-Almagor, *The Boundaries of Liberty and Tolerance* 122–31 (1994); Raphael Cohen-Almagor, "Boundaries of Freedom of Expression Before and After Prime Minister Rabin's Assassination," in *Liberal Democracy and the Limits of Tolerance* 79, 81 (Raphael Cohen-Almagor ed., 2000); Mary Warnock, "The Limits of Toleration," in *On Toleration* 123, 139 (Susan Mendus and David Edwards eds., 1987). *See generally* Lee Bollinger, *The Tolerant Society* (1988); Susan Mendus, *Justifying Toleration* (1988); David A.J. Richards, *Toleration and the Constitution* (1986); Michael Walzer, *On Toleration* (1997).

[108] H.C. 257/89, *Hoffman v. Dir. of the W. Wall*, 48(2) P.D. 265, 354.

Good Faith

The second principle of substantive democracy is good faith. I am not referring to the subjective meaning of good faith, which is a lack of evil intent. I am referring to its objective meaning,[109] which determines the standard of behavior for relationships among members of society.[110] In explaining this objective principle, I wrote in one opinion:

> The principle of good faith establishes a standard of behavior for people brought together by life's circumstances. It establishes that this behavior must be honest and fair as required by . . . society's sense of justice. By its very nature, the principle of good faith constitutes an "open" criterion that reflects . . . society's fundamental conceptions about the proper behavior between people. The categories of good faith are never closed; they are never rigid and they do not rest on their laurels. Good faith introduces into our system a foundation of flexibility that allows the system to adapt itself to the needs of changing life. It allows the law to bridge the gap between the needs of the individual and the needs of society; between individualism and community. It is a conduit through which the law absorbs new ideas. Good faith does not assume benevolence. Good faith does not require a person not to take account of his own personal interest. In this way, the principle of good faith is different from the principle of fiduciary duty (which applies to

[109] *See* Robert S. Summers, "The General Duty of Good Faith—Its Recognition and Conceptualization," 67 *Cornell L. Rev.* 810, 829–30 (1982).

[110] This concept has been developed mainly in Continental law, and especially in German law. The German Civil Law Code provides (in English translation) that "[t]he debtor is bound to effect performance according to the requirements of good faith, giving consideration to common usage" (§ 242 BGB). Israel has a similar provision, according to which every legal action, such as a contract, must be executed in good faith. *See* The Contracts (General Part) Law, 1973, 27 L.S.I. 123, § 39 (1972–73). Before legislation was enacted to this effect, Israeli common law recognized this principle. On good faith in contract law, see Steven J. Burton and Eric G. Anderson, *Contractual Good Faith: Formation, Performance, Breach, Enforcement* (1995); "Good Faith," in *Contract: Concept and Context* (Roger Brownsword, Norma J. Hird, and Geraint Howells eds., 1999); *Good Faith and Fault in Contract Law* (Jack Beatson and Daniel Friedmann eds., 1995).

a director, agent, guardian, or civil servant). The principle of good faith determines the standard of behavior for people concerned with their own interest. The principle of good faith determines that protection of one's own interest must be done fairly and with consideration for the justified expectations and proper reliance of the other party. Person-to-person, one cannot behave like a wolf, but one is not required to be an angel. Person-to-person, one must act like a person.[111]

The main application of the principle of good faith is in private law, for in public law the public authority has a heavier duty than the one derived from the principle of good faith. The judge develops private law using the principle of good faith, and uses good faith to interpret, for example, contracts[112] and wills. Courts have held that every power given to an individual in private law should be exercised in good faith, including procedural rights, property rights, contract negotiations,[113] and performance of contracts.[114]

Justice

Democracy is based on justice.[115] A regime based entirely on injustice, in which justice is not one of the foundational principles, loses its democratic character, and it appears that it loses its character as law. Indeed, justice is the goal of law. Justice is a standard for evaluating the law. I am convinced that many judges, once they have exhausted

[111] C.A. 6339/97, *Roker v. Salomon*, 55(1) P.D. 199, 279 (citations omitted).
[112] *See* Steven J. Burton and Eric G. Anderson, "The World of a Contract," 72 Iowa L. Rev. 861, 873 (1990); Martijn Willem Hesselink, "Good Faith", in *Towards a European Civil Code* 285, 294 (Arthur Hartkamp et al. eds., 1998).
[113] This concept has not yet been recognized as a general legal principle in the United States. *See* E. Allan Farnsworth, *Contracts* § 4.26, at 312 (1998); E. Allan Farnsworth, "Precontractual Liability and Preliminary Agreements: Fair Dealing and Failed Negotiations," 87 *Colum. L. Rev.* 217, 221 (1987).
[114] This principle is accepted in United States law. Farnsworth, *supra* p. 66, note 113, § 7.17, at 550–53.
[115] Much has been written about justice. See John Rawls, *A Theory of Justice* (1971); Michael Walzer, *Spheres of Justice* (1983); Alasdair MacIntyre, *After Virtue* (2d ed. 1986). On the relationship between democracy and justice, see Ian Shapiro, *Democratic Justice* (1999).

the different values they must balance yet still have not reached a single exclusive solution, aspire to reach the solution they find to be just. Indeed, justice is one of the central values of a legal system. The assumption is that the general purpose of every statute is the realization of justice. Moreover, in my opinion, justice has additional normative force. This additional force, which can be called "residual" force, is as follows: Assuming that in the initial balancing between values (including justice) the scales are even, and that the other considerations, including considerations of justice, balance each other out, the judge has at his disposal the value of justice as a residual value. At the end of judicial activity, toward the conclusion of judicial decision making—in situations of judicial discretion—justice is the appropriate value with which the judge should decide. As judges, we must aspire to reach just solutions: justice for the parties, justice for society, justice in law. When the other values do not lead to decision, it is appropriate for the judge to turn to his sense of justice. This is justice's elation: it is not merely another one of the system's values; it is a residual value, capable of decisiveness in hard cases. Indeed, if in the end the judge arrives at a result that contradicts his sense of justice, the judge must retrace his footsteps. The judge must examine whether he has strayed from the path, for law's aspiration is to be just, and the judge's aspiration is to do justice: "justice, justice shall you pursue."[116]

Reasonableness

WHAT IS REASONABLENESS?

The reasonable person plays a central role in common law. The principle of reasonableness crisscrosses the law of the common law countries. What is reasonableness? There is a tendency to answer this question with the statement that reasonableness is determined according to the circumstances of the case, but what are the relevant circumstances, and what makes an act reasonable? The statement

---

[116] Deuteronomy 16:20.

that the reasonable person is the court does not advance us much, either. How shall I know, as a judge, what a reasonable act is? More than forty years ago Professor Julius Stone pointed out that reasonableness belongs to "categories of illusory reference."[117] We use it in a circular fashion. I made that point in one case, stating that "the reference to the 'reasonable person' is merely metaphoric language . . . when we ask how the reasonable person acts, we are usually answered that the court is the reasonable person, and that it determines the standard of behavior . . . but what really is the level that the court should determine? To this we are usually answered that all depends upon the circumstances of the case. And when we ask what the circumstances of the case are, we are once again answered that they are determined by the standards of the reasonable person. Thus the circle is closed. Indeed, we have before us a sort of vicious circle."[118]

It seems to me that in order to advance the discussion on the issue of reasonableness, we must recognize the fact that reasonableness is not a physical or metaphysical concept but a normative one. The meaning of reasonableness is the discovery of the relevant considerations and the balance between them according to their weight. Reasonableness is a process of assessment. It is not a process of description. It is not a concept defined only by deductive logic. It is not purely rational. MacCormick made this point:

> . . . what justifies resort to the requirement of reasonableness is the existence of a *plurality* of factors requiring to be *evaluated* in respect of their *relevance* to a common *focus of concern* (in this case a decision). Unreasonableness consists in ignoring some relevant factor or factors, in treating as relevant what ought to be ignored. Alternatively, it may involve some *gross* distortion of the relative values of different factors, even though different people can come to different evaluations each of which falls within the range of reasonable opinions in the matter in hand.[119]

---

[117] *See* Julius Stone, *Legal System and Lawyer's Reasoning* 263 (1968).
[118] C.A. 252/86, *Goldfarb v. Klal Insurance Co. Ltd.*, 45(4) P.D. 45, 51.
[119] Neil MacCormick, "On Reasonableness," in *Les notions a contenu variable en droit* (Chaim Perelman and Raymond Vander Elst eds.), 131, 136 (1984).

Thus, reasonableness, more than being a value in and of itself, it is a value function. A decision is reasonable if it has been made by giving appropriate weight to the various facts that must be taken in consideration. I made that point in one case, emphasizing that:

[R]easonableness means weighing all of the relevant considerations, and the granting of appropriate weight to these considerations . . . reasonableness is not a personal issue. It is a substantive issue. The reasonableness of the decision maker is not what makes his or her decision reasonable; rather, the reasonableness of the decision makes the person who made it a reasonable person. The reasonableness of a decision is determined according to the appropriate internal weight given to the major factors that formulate it . . . there is no such thing as reasonableness "in and of itself" . . . reasonableness is always a product of the relevant factors and of the appropriate weight that should be given them in their internal relations. The concept of reasonableness assumes a pluralistic outlook, which recognizes the existence of a number of appropriate considerations and wishes to balance them by giving the "appropriate" weight to the internal relations between them . . . the "appropriate" weight of the relevant considerations is determined according to their power to advance the objectives which lie at the foundation of the act (or decision) whose reasonableness is being tested. Indeed, "appropriate" weight is not a natural phenomenon inherent in the relevant factors. "Appropriate" weight is not determined by logical deduction . . . appropriate weight is an assessment of the extent to which the various factors advance the objectives which the action (or decision) is intended to achieve.[120]

The question is, of course, what weight should be given to the various considerations, and how is that weight determined. Have we not returned to the vicious circle from which we tried to escape?

---

[120] H.C. 935/89, *Ganor v. Attorney General*, 44(2) P.D. 485, 513–514, translated in Itzhak Zamir and Allen Zysblat, *Public Law in Israel* (1996) 365, 348–49.

Various scholars have attempted to answer the question of weight, using techniques of argument and debate. Thus, for example, Perelman developed the concept of legal rhetoric.[121] He researched ways of debate through which one can convince an audience of listeners to agree to an argument. According to his approach, one must grant values the weight to which listeners will agree after hearing the values debate through the use of legal rhetoric. This approach does not advance us very far, since the question is what those arguments are, and what is the weight which a listener in the audience should give them? In the German legal literature, the doctrine of *Topoi* has been developed.[122] According to this doctrine, the various options are listed, the advantages and disadvantages of each option are weighed, and through discussion and the exchange of opinions, the optimal solution is reached. The principle of proportionality and lack of exaggeration are often referred to as key principles that are likely to assist in the determination of a proper balance between competing principled considerations. This outlook cannot avail either, since the question is, when is an action proportionate, and when does it lack exaggeration? MacCormick returns to the reasonable person, who represents Aristotelian wisdom. According to MacCormick, the reasonable person represents the ongoing attempt to get a grip on an objective assessment that will allow detachment from the various subjective points of departure. The reasonable person represents, in his opinion, "our common desire to find common criteria of moral and practical judgment which have at least intersubjective, if not absolutely objective, validity within a given social milieu."[123]

This attempt to find the common standard is a value-oriented one. We are not dealing with the "discovery" of something "found" somewhere, rather with the "construction" of something "new."[124]

---

[121] *See* Chaim Perelman, *The Legal Logic* 90 (1987).
[122] *See* Karl Larenz, *Methodenlehre Der Rechtwissenschaft* 14 (5th ed. 1983).
[123] MacCormick, *supra* p. 68, note 119 at 153.
[124] *Ibid*, at 153–54.

From this MacCormick infers that the weight that should be given to the various values is that which flows from the consent of the universal audience. But what weight is that, and how shall we know what the universal audience is?

What then is a reasonable action (or decision)? According to my view, it is the action (or decision) that locates the relevant values and balances them. The balance is determined by the weight of the values. This weight is determined by the attitude of society (or of the legal community) regarding the relative importance of the values. This attitude is always in flux. The attitudes of society are expressed by the judge using his (limited) discretion.

This grasp of the concept of reasonableness advances our understanding. True, the concept of reasonableness does not give, from within itself, a single and exclusive answer to the question of whether an action is reasonable. That is not its objective. The role of the principle of reasonableness is to ensure flexibility. He who looks for a single and exclusive answer should not use the concept of reasonableness. He should think up all the various possibilities and determine rules about them, assuming this is possible. The decision to resort to a vague concept like reasonableness means taking the risk, *ex ante*, that uncertainty will result from the need to assign weight to clashing values. Moreover, he who desires to refrain from granting discretion to judges should not resort to vague concepts (*Ventilbegriffe; concetti volvola*) and should not use reasonableness. The concept of reasonableness assumes the existence of judicial discretion in a wide variety of situations.

In using judicial discretion regarding reasonableness, just as in using any judicial discretion, the judge is not free to do as he wishes. The judge must locate the relevant values for the resolution of the issue before him. The judge must grant them the very weight that reflects their relative importance in society at the time the decision is made. The judge must balance the values on the basis of that weight. The judge must refrain from resorting to his personal views.

Have we advanced the understanding of the concept of reasonableness? Have we exited the vicious circle? Have we not returned
to the concept that reasonableness is determined by the court as it
considers all of the circumstances? In my opinion, we have
advanced beyond the idea of personification, by which the court is
the reasonable person. The advancement is twofold: first, we have
pointed out that one cannot expect an answer from within the concept of reasonableness, unconnected to the values external to it,
which are in a state of constant clash. Indeed, if the concept of reasonableness could give an answer, from within itself, regarding the
reasonableness of an action, it would lose its character. Second, we
have pointed out a process upon which the concept of reasonableness is based. We have shown that we are dealing with locating conflicting values and balancing them on the basis of their weight. We
have determined that this weight reflects the relative importance of
values in society at the time the balancing is performed. One
should ask no more.

THE ZONE OF REASONABLENESS

An action (or decision) is reasonable if it grants appropriate weight
to the clashing values and principles. The weight of a value is
appropriate if it reflects the attitudes of society regarding what is
appropriate in the relationship between that value and the other
relevant values. Sometimes there is only one appropriate weight for
the competing relevant values, but sometimes the competing values can be given various appropriate weights. The standard of societal attitudes is not sensitive or fine enough always to grant the
competing values a single and exclusive weight. A "zone of reasonableness" that contains all the reasonable possibilities is created.
The boundaries of the zone of reasonableness are determined by
the appropriate balance between the various interests and values
wrestling for superiority. The relevant interests and values are
determined by the relevant field in which the action is examined
and against the background of the foundational principles of the

system and its ethos. The zone itself is determined according to the weight and balance between these interests.

What should a judge do when confronted with a zone of reasonableness? The answer depends on the role in which the judge is performing at that moment. If the judge is developing the common law and the zone of reasonableness relates to various reasonable common law solutions between which he can choose, the judge must choose the solution that seems best to him. The same applies if the zone of reasonableness relates to reasonable interpretations of a statute. The judge must choose from among the reasonable interpretations the interpretation which seems best to him. However, if the judge is performing judicial review of an administrative decision, and the administrative decision falls within the zone of reasonableness, the judge must refrain from invalidating it simply because he prefers a different reasonable decision that lies within the zone.

This answer is deduced from considerations of the separation of powers. The role of the judge is to bridge the gap between the law and the ever-changing reality of life, and to protect the constitution and its values. The judge does so, *inter alia*, through the development of the common law and the interpretation of statutes. Whether in the development of the common law or in the interpretation of statutes, the obligation imposed on the judge is to use his discretion in such a way that the solution that he thinks should be chosen is drawn from the zone of reasonable solutions. Therefore, a Supreme Court justice or appellate court judge cannot make do with the fact that the interpretation given by the lower court judge is one of two reasonable solutions from which the former chooses. The responsibility is that of the judge hearing the appeal. The same applies to the reasonable interpretation which the administration gives to a statute. According to the principle of separation of powers, the interpretation of the provisions of the statute is the responsibility of the judge.[125] The judge must give the statute the interpretation that seems to him to be right. The judge must

---

[125] *See* infra p. 246.

not make do with the fact that the interpretation falls within the zone of reasonableness and that a public official was permitted to have reached it.

The situation is different when the judge engages in judicial review of administrative actions. According to the principle of separation of powers, the judge must ask himself if the action of the administration is legal. Since the action of the administration falls within the zone of reasonableness, it balances legally between the relevant values, and is therefore legal. The judge must refrain from invalidating a decision simply because he would have reached a different reasonable solution if he were a public official. The judge is not an administrative official, and the principle of separation of powers obligates the judge only to determine whether the decision was reasonable; it does not allow the judge to substitute the administrative discretion with his own discretion. In this respect, the action of the public administration is different from its activity in interpreting statutes. The former is, according to the separation of powers, the responsibility of public administration. Therefore, it suffices that such action falls within the zone of reasonableness. The latter is, according to the separation of powers, the responsibility of the judge. It does not suffice that such interpretation is within the zone of reasonableness. It must be the (reasonable) choice of the judge himself.

Reasonableness performs an important role in the activity of a judge. It is an important tool by which the judge fulfills his role. In the development of the common law, reasonableness is one of the main concepts. "The reasonable person" is one of the key figures in the common law, and reasonableness is placed at the foundations of a tangled system of judicial precedents. Thus, for example, in tort law the central tort is negligence, one of whose major components is negligent behavior, that is to say the lack of reasonableness. In administrative law, reasonableness determines the proper ways to use administrative discretion. Judicial discretion must also be used reasonably.

Reasonableness is the bridge with which the law is likely to provide modern and appropriate solutions to new social problems.

Being a vague concept, it is fit to perform this role; being a reflection of values wrestling for priority, it assists in designing the modern legal order, which gives solutions to current problems. Through reasonableness it is possible to ensure that the values of the constitution will be applied, not just theoretically but de facto.

Public Order

Law has a calling. It is meant to serve the individual and society. The good of society is a value which the law of a democratic state should aspire to realize. Indeed, besides the individual's rights in relation society, the individual has duties toward society.[126] Law is not just human rights. It is also human duties, and the duty of each individual is to advance the public order. This order is of comprehensive application. It covers both the assurance of state security and public peace and the assurance of the rights and good of the individual. Public order is a flexible value that changes from time to time. It is an "open" value that is filled with content according to the development of societal life.

Public order is an important value in democratic society. Without the realization of public order (exemplified by public peace and security), it is impossible to assure the realization of other democratic values, including human rights. Of course, a regime ensuring only public order is not a democratic regime. A democratic regime is a regime that ensures an appropriate level of public order alongside a recognition of human rights. Therefore, public order should be included as one of the fundamental values of any democratic society. Every statute should be interpreted as having the purpose of realizing the public order.

Protecting the public order is among the fundamental principles of our regime. The existence of the state, its eternality, and its demo-

---

[126] *See* Douglas Hodgson, *Individual Duty Within a Human Right Discourse* (2003).

cratic character are part and parcel of the fundamental principles of the state. Neither the individual nor society will be able to express their ethos if the public order is not protected. Without order there is no liberty . . . the ensuring of reciprocal tolerance, human dignity, and the existence of an independent system of courts, which adjudicates without external influences, is among the fundamental values of the state. Every state has its collective identity, its national history, and its social aspirations. Protection of all of these is among the fundamental values of the state. Democracy is not anarchy. "Democracy need not commit suicide in order to prove its vitality."[127]

INDEPENDENCE OF THE JUDICIARY

Democracy and Judicial Independence

Judicial independence is a central component of any democracy[128] and is crucial to separation of powers, the rule of law, and human rights. It is also, however, a component that stands on its own. It is part of any democratic constitution, whether mentioned expressly or merely implied.[129] It is an inseparable part of any constitutional scheme. Lord Steyn of the House of Lords addressed

---

[127] H.C. 14/86, *Laor v. Film & Play Review Bd.*, 41(1) P.D. 421, 433 (Barak, J.).
[128] *See Judicial Independence: The Contemporary Debate* (Shimon Shetreet and Jules Deschênes eds. 1985); G. Eckhoff, "Impartiality, Separation of Powers and Judicial Independence," 9 Scandinavian Studies in Law 11(1965); Stephen Breyer, "Judicial Independence in the United States", 40 St. Louis U. L.J. 989 (1996); Martin L. Friedland, *A Place Apart: Judicial Independence and Accountability in Canada* (1995); Robert Stevens, *The English Judges: Their Role in the Changing Constitution* 76 (2002); *Judicial Independence at the Crossroads: An Interdisciplinary Approach* (Stephen B. Burbank and Barry Friedman eds., 2002); Eli Salzberger, "A Positivist Analysis of the Doctrine of Separation of Powers, or: Why Do We Have an Independent Judiciary?" 13 Int'l Rev. Law Econ. 349 (1993); Antonio Lamer, "The Rule of Law and Judicial Independence: Protecting Core Values in Times of Change," 45 U.N.B. L.J. 3(1996). Bingham, supra p. xiii, note 15 at 55. For a comparative review of judicial independence, see *Traite d'organisation judiciaire compare* (tom II 2004).
[129] *See Manitoba Provincial Judges Assn v. Manitoba* [1997] 3 S.C.R..

this point: "the judiciary can effectively fulfill its role only if the public has confidence that the courts, even if sometimes wrong, act wholly independently."[130]

Constitutions of nondemocratic countries also include provisions concerning human rights. These provisions, however, are a dead letter, because there is no independent judiciary to breathe life into them.[131] Judicial independence has a dual goal: to guarantee procedural fairness in the individual judicial process and to guarantee protection of democracy and its values. In the words of Chief Justice Lamer of the Supreme Court of Canada, "Judicial independence is essential for fair and just dispute-resolution in individual cases. It is also the life blood of constitutionalism in democratic societies."[132] Without judicial independence, there is no preservation of democracy and its values. The existence of judicial independence depends on the existence of legal arrangements that guarantee it, arrangements that are actualized in practice and are themselves guaranteed by public confidence in the judiciary.

The accepted view is that judicial independence is composed of two foundations. Only together do the two guarantee the independence of the judiciary. These two foundations are the independence of the individual judge and the independence of the judicial branch. Siracuse's Draft Principles on the independence of the judiciary addressed these two foundations of judicial independence:

Independence of the judiciary means:

(1) that every judge is free to decide matters before him in accordance with his assessment of the facts and his understanding of the law, without any improper influences, inducements, or pressures, direct or indirect, from any quarter or for any reason, and

---

[130] *Johan Steyn*, "The Case for a Supreme Court," 118 Law. Q. Rev. 382, 388 (2002); Owen Fiss, *The Law as It Could Be* 59 (2003).
[131] See McLachlin, "The Role of the Court," *supra* p. ix, note 1 at 57.
[132] *Beanregand v. Canada* [1986] 2 S.C.R. 56, 70.

(2) that the judiciary is independent of the executive and legislature, and has jurisdiction, directly, or by way of review, over all issues of a judicial nature.[133]

These two foundations are cumulative. Neither is sufficient by itself.

Personal Independence

A crucial condition for judicial independence is the personal independence of the judge. This is a constitutional principle. In some countries it is explicitly established in the constitution. Other countries derive it as an implied provision of the constitution. Judicial independence means that in judicial adjudication, the judge is free of all pressures. I do not mean freedom from internal pressure, which is sometimes expressed in a judge's deliberations concerning the judicial decision. Such deliberation is often related to the social reality of which the judge is a part and to societal trends which the judge must balance. A judge's freedom from pressure refers to freedom from external pressure, regardless of the source. Personal independence is independence from relatives and friends, independence from the litigating parties and the public, independence from fellow judges and judges responsible for managing the system (including the president or chief judge of the court), independence from officeholders in the other branches of government. The judge's master is the law. The judge has no other master. From the moment a person is appointed as judge, he must act without any dependence on another.

The independence of the individual judge means that the judge is subject to no authority other than the law. This authority includes, of course, the authority of case law determined by the courts whose opinions bind the judge. Judicial independence does not mean release from the chains of binding precedent or other

---

[133] Cited in Shetreet and Deschênes, *supra* p. 76, note 128 at 414 (article 2).

judicial instructions that bind the judge. These are part of the law to whose authority the judge is subject.

Judicial independence means building a protective wall around the individual judge that will guard against the possibility of influencing decisions by influencing the conditions of his employment. For example, a judge should not be removed from office except as the result of a judicial proceeding, based on reasons related to improper behavior in the fulfillment of his office. In my opinion, such a process should be run by a body composed entirely or partly of other judges. In the United States, the Senate has the authority to cause a (federal) judge to be removed from office by holding an impeachment process.[134] In my opinion, this is not an appropriate arrangement. The threat of impeachment proceedings is subject to exploitation by politicians seeking to influence judges. Removing a judge from office must be done exclusively through a proceeding that guarantees the independence of the judge in his tenure. Such a proceeding should be run by judges, not politicians. It should be run as a trial in every way.

Judges should be protected against reductions or erosions in their salaries.[135] Further, a judge's salary and conditions of service should not be set by the executive branch. In my opinion, the salaries of judges should be set by an independent body chosen by the parliament, and not by the parliament itself.[136]

Personal independence requires administrative independence of the individual judge. Obviously, the judge is part of an administrative framework and must act according to its rules. Judicial independence is not a license for administrative lawlessness. Those rules, however, must guarantee that judges are not subject to pressure that infringes on their independence. For example, the permanent location of a judge's seat should not be changed except to fulfill clear administrative needs. The president (or chief judge)

---

[134] See Article II, § 4 of the Constitution.
[135] See Article III, § 1 of the Constitution.
[136] *See Manitoba Provincial Judges Assn v. Manitoba* [1997] 3 S.C.R. 3; *Valente v. The Queen* [1985] 2 S.C.R. 673, 704 (Cam.).

of each court establishes the organizational frameworks to which judges are subject. The court president, including the Supreme Court president, cannot tell judges how to exercise their judicial discretion unless those instructions are part of a judgment binding the judges. Indeed, judges' personal independence is independence from those who surround them. On matters of adjudication, the judge is alone. He is subject to no authority other than his understanding of the law.

Institutional Independence

Personal independence is a necessary condition for judicial independence. It is not a sufficient condition. A crucial condition is institutional independence. A judge's personal independence is incomplete unless it is accompanied by the institutional independence of the judicial branch, designed to ensure that the judicial branch can fulfill its role in protecting the constitution and its values.[137]

Institutional independence is designed to build a protective wall around the judicial branch that prevents the legislative and executive branches from influencing the way judges realize their roles as protectors of the constitution and its values. The judicial branch must therefore be run, on the organizational level, in an independent manner. It should not be part of the executive branch and should not be subject to the administrative decisions of the executive branch.

The independence of the judicial branch must, of course, be part of the checks and balances mandated by the separation of powers. Therefore, the judicial branch should not determine its own budget: the judicial branch's budget should be set by the legislative branch, and the judicial branch should give the legislative branch an accounting of the way it is run.

[137] See Patricia Hughes, "Judicial Independence: Contemporary Pressures and Appropriate Responses," 80 *Can. Bar. Rev.* 181, 186 (2000); Aharon Barak, "Independence of the Judicial Branch," in *Judicial Independence Today: Liber Amicorum in Onore di Giovanni Longo* 49 (1999).

HUMAN RIGHTS

Human Rights and Democracy

We live in an age of human rights.[138] As Justice Pikis, president of the Supreme Court of Cyprus, rightly observed:

> The essence of human rights lies in the existence within the fabric of the law of a code of unalterable rules affecting the rights of the individual. Human rights have a universal dimension, they are perceived as inherent in man, constituting the inborn attribute of human existence to be enjoyed at all times in all circumstances and at every place.[139]

We are experiencing a human rights revolution as a result of World War II and the Holocaust.[140] Indeed, a central element of modern democracy is the protection of constitutional, statutory, and common law human rights. Without these rights, we cannot have democracy. Take human rights out of democracy and democracy loses its soul; it becomes an empty shell. It is the task of the judge to protect and uphold human rights. Justice McLachlin of the Supreme Court of Canada rightly said that "[t]he courts are the ultimate guardians of the rights of society, in our system of government."[141] These rights are the rights of man as an individual, as

---

[138] *See* Norberto Bobbio, *The Age of Rights* 32 (Allan Cameron trans., 1996) (1990) (discussing "the increasing importance given to the recognition of human rights in international debates, among cultured people and politicians, in working groups and government conferences"); Louis Henkin, *The Age of Rights IX* (1990) ("Ours is the age of rights. Human rights is the idea of our time, the only political-moral idea that has received universal acceptance").

[139] Pikis, *supra* p. ix, note 1 at 9.

[140] *See* Charles R. Epp, *The Rights Revolution: Lawyers, Activists, and Supreme Courts in Comparative Perspective* (1998); Lorraine E. Weinrib, "The Supreme Court of Canada in the Age of Rights: Constitutional Democracy, The Rule of Law and Fundamental Rights Under Canada's Constitution", 80 *Can. B. Rev.* 699, 701 (2002) ("We live in the age of rights. In the aftermath of the Second World War, commitment to the principles embodied in the modern idea of human rights has intensified in the West, although the record of achievement is undeniably blemished").

[141] McLachlin, "The Role of the Court," *supra* p. ix, note 1 at 57.

well as his rights as a member of a minority group.[142] Judges must protect these rights. Judges must resolve cases of conflict between individual and group rights.

The Scope of Rights and Their Limitations

Human rights are not absolute; the scope of the right of one individual is limited by the right of another. The right of the individual is also limited by the needs of society.[143] Every legal system has its own express or implied limitation clauses for balancing the right of the individual against society's demands.[144] In Canada, the limitation clause operates so that the human rights set out in the Canadian Charter of Rights and Freedoms are subject "only to such reasonable limits prescribed by law as can be demonstrably justified in a free and democratic society."[145] In Israel, the limitation clause provides that "[t]he rights under this basic law may only be infringed by a law that befits the values of the State of Israel, is intended for a proper purpose, and to an extent that is not excessive."[146] The most detailed general limitation clause is found in the constitution of South Africa:

> The rights in the Bill of Rights may be limited only in terms of law
> of general application to the extent that the limitation is reasonable

---

[142] See Beverley M. McLachlin, *Democracy and Rights: A Canadian Perspective* 3 (2000) (unpublished manuscript, on file with the Harvard Law School Library).
[143] *See* Robert Alexy, *A Theory of Constitutional Right* (trans. Julian Rivers, 2002).
[144] *See* The Limitation of Human Rights in Comparative Constitutional Law 1–112 (Armand de Mestral et al. eds., 1986) (a series of essays considering limitations on human rights in Canada, Europe, and the United States); Alexandre Charles Kiss, "Permissible Limitations on Rights," in *The International Bill of Rights: The Covenant on Civil and Political Rights* 290 (Louis Henkin ed., 1981) (examining public interest limitations embedded in various human rights provisions of the International Covenant on Civil and Political Rights).
[145] On the Canadian limitation clause (Article 1), see Peter W. Hogg, *Constitutional Law of Canada* 864 (4th ed. 1997); Janet L. Hiebert, *Limiting Rights: The Dilemma of Judicial Review* (1996).
[146] Basic Law: Human Dignity and Liberty § 8 (1992).

and justifiable in an open and democratic society based on human dignity, equality and freedom, taking into account all relevant factors, including—a. the nature of the right; b. the importance of the purpose of the limitation; c. the nature and extent of the limitation; d. the relation between the limitation and its purpose; and e. less restrictive means to achieve the purpose.[147]

In Canada, Israel, and South Africa, the limitation clause applies across all the rights established by the constitution. In other constitutions and international instruments,[148] particular rights have their own unique limitation formulas. In the absence of express limitation clauses prescribed by the constitution—which is the case in the United States with reference to several human rights—the courts develop the limitation formulas through case law. The "levels of scrutiny" developed by United States law can fit into this category. Such limitations, whether in the written constitution or outside it, reflect the idea that human rights are not the rights of a person on a desert island. Robinson Crusoe (sans Friday) does not need human rights. Human rights are the rights of a human being as part of society. The rights of the individual must conform to the existence of society, the existence of a government, and the existence of national goals. The power of the state is essential to the existence of the state and the existence of human rights themselves. Therefore, limitations on human rights reflect a national compromise between the needs of the state and the rights of the individual. This balance is intended to prevent the sacrifice of the state on the altar of human rights. As I once stated:

A constitution is not a prescription for suicide, and civil rights are not an altar for national destruction (compare Jackson J. in *Terminiello v.*

---

[147] S. Afr. Const. § 36(1).

[148] *See, e.g.*, art. 10 (freedom of expression) of the Convention for the Protection of Human Rights and Fundamental Freedoms. Article 10(1) provides the scope of freedom of expression. Article 10(2) provides the limitation.

Chicago). The laws of a people should be interpreted on the basis of the assumption that it wants to continue to exist. Civil rights derive from the existence of the State, and they should not be made into a spade with which to bury it.[149]

Similarly, human rights should not be sacrificed on the altar of the state. After all, human rights are natural rights that precede the state. Indeed, human rights protections require preservation of the sociopolitical framework, which in turn is based on recognition of the need to protect human rights. Both the needs of the state and human rights are part of one constitutional structure that simultaneously provides for human rights and allows them to be limited. A unique feature of democracy is that the scope and limits of human rights derive from a common source. Justice Dickson of the Canadian Supreme Court nicely noted this peculiar underpinning of democracy with the following comment about Canada's limitation formula: "The underlying values and principles of a free and democratic society are the genesis of the rights and freedoms guaranteed by the *Charter* and the ultimate standard against which a limit on a right or freedom must be shown, despite its effect, to be reasonable and demonstrably justified."[150]

This is the constitutional dialectic. Human rights and the limitations on them derive from the same source, and they reflect the same values.[151] Human rights can be limited, but there are limits to the limitations. The role of the judge in a democracy is to preserve both of these limitations. Judges must ensure the security and existence of the state as well as the realization of human rights; judges must determine and protect the integrity of the proper balance.

---

[149] E.A. 2/84, *Neiman v. Chairman of Cent. Elections Comm. for Eleventh Knesset*, 39(2) P.D. 225, 310 (citation omitted) (English translation available at www.court.gov.il).

[150] *The Queen v. Oakes*, [1986] S.C.R. 103, 136.

[151] *See* Weinrib, *supra* p. xix, note 34 at 127–28.

Human Dignity

Most central of all human rights is the right to dignity.[152] It is the source from which all other human rights are derived. Dignity unites the other human rights into a whole.[153] It also constitutes a right in itself and is recognized as such in several constitutions.[154] The right of dignity reflects the "recognition that a human being is a free agent, who develops his body and mind as

[152] *See* Edward J. Eberle, *Dignity and Liberty: Constitutional Visions in Germany and the United States* 1 (2002); *The Concept of Human Dignity in Human Rights Discourse* (David Kretzmer and Eckart Klein eds., 2002); *Human Dignity: This Century and the Next* 3–97 (Rubin Gotesky and Ervin Laszlo eds., 1970); Izhak Englard, "Human Dignity: From Antiquity to Modern Israel's Constitutional Framework," 21 *Cardozo L. Rev.* 1903 (2000); G.P. Fletcher, "Human Dignity as a Constitutional Value," 22 *U.W. Ont. L. Rev.* 171, 171 (1984) ("No one would question whether the protection of human dignity was a primary task of the contemporary legal culture"); A.I. Melden, "Dignity, Worth, and Rights," in *The Constitution of Rights: Human Dignity and American Values* 29, 46 (Michael J. Meyer and William A. Parent eds., 1992) ("[A]ttention to human rights is of the first importance for the promotion of the dignity and the worth of human beings"); Jordan J. Paust, "Human Dignity as a Constitutional Right: A Jurisprudentially Based Inquiry into Criteria and Content," 27 *How. L.J.* 145, 223 (1984) ("[H]uman rights law provides a rich set of general criteria and content for supplementation of past trends in Supreme Court decision[s] about human dignity"). *See also* Paulo Cesar Carbonari, "Human Dignity as a Basic Concept of Ethics and Human Rights," in *Dignity and Human Rights: The Implementation of Economic, Social and Cultural Rights* (Berman Klein Goldewijk et al. eds., 2002).
[153] *See* William J. Brennan, Jr., "The Constitution of the United States: Contemporary Ratification," 27 *S. Tex. L. Rev.* 433, 438 (1986) ("[T]he Constitution is a sublime oration on the dignity of man, a bold commitment by a people to the ideal of libertarian dignity protected through law"); Walter F. Murphy, "An Ordering of Constitutional Values," 53 *S. Cal. L. Rev.* 703, 745 (1980) ("The basic value in the United States Constitution, broadly conceived, has become a concern for human dignity").
[154] The German Constitution, for example, provides that "[t]he dignity of man shall be inviolable. To respect and protect it shall be the duty of all state authority." F.R.G. Const. art. 1, translated in *Basic Law for the Federal Republic of Germany* (1991). On dignity in the German Constitution, see Currie, *supra* p. 22, note 9 at 314–16; Eberle, *supra* p. 85, note 152 at 41; Kommers, *supra* p. 22, note 9 at 298. In Israel, Basic Law: Human Dignity and Freedom provides: "2. The life, body or dignity of any person shall not be violated . . . 4. Every person is entitled to protection of his life, body and dignity."

he wishes, and the social framework to which he is connected and on which he depends."[155] Human dignity is therefore the freedom of the individual to shape an individual identity. It is the autonomy of the individual will. It is the freedom of choice. Human dignity regards a human being as an end, not as a means to achieve the ends of others.

When human dignity is expressly mentioned in a constitution, the scope of its application as a right is determined by its relationship with other rights, in accordance with the structure of rights protection in that particular constitution. Therefore, the same right of dignity may have a different scope in different constitutions.

In Israel's constitution, the right to dignity includes four elements. First, human dignity is the dignity of each human being "as a human being." This is the source of the viewpoint that human dignity includes the equality of human beings.[156] Discrimination infringes on a person's dignity. Human dignity assumes equality of the (other) rights that people have and equality of opportunity and benefits.

Second, human dignity is a person's freedom of will. This is the freedom of choice given to people to develop their personalities and determine their own fate. People are spiritual entities who enjoy the freedom to develop themselves. This is the source of my view that at the core of human dignity is the autonomy of the individual will.

Third, human dignity is infringed if a person's life or physical or mental welfare is harmed. The death penalty contradicts human dignity.[157] Life imprisonment with no chance of early release contradicts human dignity. Torture contradicts human dignity. Humiliation, blows, confiscation, forced labor—all infringe on human dignity. Human dignity is infringed when a person lives in humiliating conditions that negate his humanity. Human dignity

---

[155] H.C. 5688/92, *Wechselbaum v. Minister of Def.*, 47(2) P.D. 812, 827 (Isr.).
[156] Louis Henkin, "Human Dignity and Constitutional Rights," in *The Constitution of Rights: Human Dignity and American Values* 212 (1992).
[157] *See S. v. Makwanyane* (1995) 3 SA 391, 437 (c.c.) (S.Afr.).

assumes the guarantee of the minimum conditions of (physical and mental) existence.

> A person living in the street, with no home, is a person whose human dignity is infringed; a person who goes hungry is a person whose human dignity is infringed; a person who has no access to basic medical care is a person whose human dignity is infringed; a person forced to live under humiliating physical conditions is a person whose human dignity is infringed.[158]

Fourth, human dignity assumes that the individual is not a means for satisfying the needs of another individual. Every person is a world unto himself, and an objective unto himself. It assumes a society predicated on the desire to protect the human dignity of each of its members. Therefore, the right to human dignity cannot be infringed without an appropriate procedure. Harming a person without first granting a hearing infringes upon human dignity. Many rights of the accused derive from his dignity as a human being. For example, the presumption that every person is innocent until proven guilty by law is part of human dignity; the right of the accused to a fair trial is part of human dignity; the right of the accused to a speedy trial is part of human dignity. The right of a person to know the charges against him or why he has been arrested, and his ability to defend effectively against those charges, are part of human dignity. Thus, imposing criminal liability and criminal imprisonment for behavior that lacks a criminal *mens rea* ("strict liability crimes") infringes on human dignity; imposing criminal responsibility on behavior that did not constitute a crime at the time it occurred infringes on human dignity.

Human dignity is not an absolute right. Unless otherwise provided,[159] it may be infringed upon according to the limitation clause existing in the legal system. Thus, many provisions of the criminal law affect dignity, but they are constitutional, since they comply with the limitation clause.

[158] L.C.A. 4905/98, *Gamzu v. Yeshayahu*, 55(3) P.D. 360, 375. (Barak, P.).
[159] Such a provision is found in Article 1 of the German Constitution.

When human dignity is not mentioned expressly in a constitution, as is the case in the United States, Canada, and many other countries, the question arises as to whether human dignity can be recognized as a human right in these legal systems. A way of recognizing a constitutional right to dignity in those systems is through interpretation of specific rights, mainly the right to equality.[160] It can also be recognized through interpretation of the whole bill of rights, whereby human dignity either is implied by the overall structure of the rights or is derived from their "penumbras."[161]

CRITICISM AND RESPONSE

The Criticism

I am aware that my theory of the role of a judge in a democracy is not universally accepted. It may be said that legislation and adjudication serve wholly different functions and that a judge is neither a senior nor a junior partner of the legislature. It may also be said that my approach to the judicial role departs from the proper outlook on separation of powers and democracy, for democracy, both formal and substantive, is too important to be left to the protection of judges who are not elected or otherwise accountable to the people. Who will guard the guardians? It may even be argued that my approach is based on judicial "imperialism,"[162] conferring on judges an inappropriately prominent status. These criticisms are important, and I take them seriously. They accompany me always and restrain me always. However, there are proper answers to these criticisms. I do not claim that the court can cure every ill of society, nor do I claim that it can be the primary agent for social

---

[160] See Law v. Canada [1999] 1 S.C.R. 497, 507 (Can.).

[161] See Griswold v. Connecticut, 381 U.S. 479, 484 (1965) ("[S]pecific guarantees in the Bill of Rights have penumbras, formed by emanations from those guarantees that help give them life and substance").

[162] See Nathan Glazer, "Toward an Imperial Judiciary?" Pub. Int., Fall 1975, at 104, 122.

change.[163] I do not claim that the court is always the most effective branch for the resolution of disputes. My claim is much more limited: I claim that the court has an important role in bridging the gap between law and society and in protecting the fundamental values of democracy, with human rights at the center.

The Role of the Judge as Creator of the Common Law

Within the field of common law, almost a thousand years of history validate my approach. If the common law does not merely declare what has existed since time immemorial—and I do not think that anyone still believes this myth—then it is hard to deny the creative role of the judge in the common law. Judges created and developed the common law.[164] Judges bridged the gap between law and society by giving expression to the fundamental principles of society. And judges are responsible for using the common law to fit solutions to life's changing needs. Naturally, over the years, judges made mistakes. But there were many achievements, too. It is difficult to forget Lord Mansfield's statement, "the black must be discharged,"[165] releasing in 1772 a black slave who fled to England from his American master. Lord Mansfield issued this statement after the court heard from counsel for the slave that "the air of England was too pure for slavery."[166] It was the judge who declared and gave effect to the fundamental values on which the common law is founded. The judge must protect and promote these fundamental values. In these activities, the main responsibility rests with the judge, the senior partner.

---

[163] See generally Gerald N. Rosenberg, The Hollow Hope: Can Courts Bring about Social Change? 343 (1991) (examining the ability of courts to enact social change and concluding that "[t]o ask [courts] to produce significant social reform is to forget their history and ignore their constraints").

[164] See M.A. Eisenberg, The Nature of the Common Law, (1988); Michael McHugh, "The Law-Making Function of the Judicial Process," 62 Austl. L.J. 15, 16 (1988).

[165] "The Case of James Sommersett," 20 How. St. Tr. 1, 82 (K.B. 1772).

[166] Id. at 79.

The Role of the Judge as Interpreter
of the Constitution and Statutes

The role of the judge is to interpret the constitution and statutes, and the system of interpretation is usually determined by judges. This implies that each branch of the state cannot devise its own interpretive system. The rule of law would be undermined if the system of interpretation accepted by judges were not binding on the legislature and the executive.[167] The difficulty, of course, is that there is no single interpretive system.[168] Changes in the law that aim to bridge the gap between law and society alter the systems of interpretation. We do not interpret statutes today in the same way that they were interpreted 200 or 100 or even 50 years ago. In any event, I accept the system of interpretation that allows me, in interpreting both the constitution and statutes, to take into account my status as a junior partner in the legislative enterprise and to realize my role as a judge.

Thus far, my response to criticism regarding the interpretation of the constitution and statutes has been to demonstrate that my view is legitimate. But is it the right approach? In my opinion, the

---

[167] This issue is not free of uncertainty in United States law. *See* Larry Alexander and Frederick Schauer, "On Extrajudicial Constitutional Interpretation," 110 *Harv. L. Rev.* 1359, 1362 (1997) (defending the "assertion of judicial supremacy without qualification 'against' accepted wisdom"); Scott E. Gant, "Judicial Supremacy and Nonjudicial Interpretation of the Constitution," 24 *Hastings Const. L.Q.* 359, 364 (1997) ("[V]iews about the descriptive or normative appropriateness of judicial supremacy are by no means uniform"); Allan Ides, "Judicial Supremacy and the Law of the Constitution," 47 *UCLA L. Rev.* 491, 519 (1999) ("I am reluctant to subscribe to any theory of constitutional law that downplays the significance of the Court's power over the law of the Constitution"); Neal Kumar Katyal, "Legislative Constitutional Interpretation," 50 *Duke L.J.* 1335, 1336 (2001) ("The structural variances between the courts and Congress can be analyzed profitably to develop a theory of interbranch interpretation"); William D. Popkin, "Foreword: Nonjudicial Statutory Interpretation," 66 *Chi.-Kent L. Rev.* 301 (1990) (introducing a symposium focusing on statutory interpretation by bodies other than courts, including agencies and Congress).

[168] *See infra* pp. 122–25.

answer is yes. If one can rely on the objectivity, integrity, and balance that judges employ as creators of common law, why can one not rely on them to fulfill that same role as interpreters of the constitution and statutes? If we are trusted as senior partners, why are we not trusted as junior partners? Naturally, in our interpretive approach, we will not depart from the language of the constitution and statutes by giving them a meaning that their language cannot sustain. But within the range of possible linguistic meanings, and taking into account—to different degrees—the intentions of the authors of the constitution and statutes, why do we not recognize that when judges interpret the constitution and statutes, just as when they create the common law, they have a role to play in protecting democracy and in bridging the gap between society and law?

The Role of the Judge and Judicial Review of the Constitutionality of Statutes

Critics argue that the nonaccountability of judges should deprive them of the power to void statutes. Such power must only be given to the representatives of the people, who are accountable to them. This is the countermajoritarian argument made again and again. In my opinion, this argument is extremely problematic.[169] First, some constitutions contain express provisions for judicial

---

[169] *See* Daniel A. Farber and Suzanna Sherry, *Desperately Seeking Certainty: The Misguided Quest for Constitutional Foundations* 140, 145 (2002) (noting that "[a]lthough the countermajoritarian difficulty has a core of truth, it has been blown out of proportion") and *id*. at 199. *See also* Steven P. Croley, "The Majoritarian Difficulty: Elective Judiciaries and the Rule of Law," 62 *U. Chi. L. Rev.* 689 (1995); Barry Friedman, "Dialogue and Judicial Review," 91 *Mich. L. Rev.* 577 (1993); Barry Friedman, "The History of the Countermajoritarian Difficulty, Part One: The Road to Judicial Supremacy," 73 *N.Y.U. L. Rev.* 333 (1998); Mark A. Graber, "The Nonmajoritarian Difficulty: Legislative Deference to the Judiciary," 7 *Stud. in Am. Pol. Dev.* 35 (1993); Steven L. Winter, "An

review of the constitutionality of statutes. In such circumstances, the legitimacy of judicial review should not be in doubt. The only remaining question in these situations is whether the constitutional arrangement is proper and consistent with the society's perception of democracy.[170] Second, if the countermajoritarian argument is correct, then states ought to refrain from making a constitution. After all, a constitution is not a democratic document since it negates, in certain circumstances, the power of the current majority.[171] Therefore, if a constitution is desirable, we cannot attribute much weight to countermajoritarian considerations.[172] Justice Dieter Grimm of the German Constitutional Court rightly observed that "Constitutional adjudication is just as little irreconcilable with democracy as constitutionalism itself is."[173] But if a constitution is democratic, then its implementation by courts is democratic; if demo-cracy is not merely the rule of the majority but also the protection of human rights, then judicial review to ensure that acts and legislation are constitutional and consistent with substantive democracy—thereby giving

---

Upside/Down View of the Countermajoritarian Difficulty," 69 *Tex. L. Rev.* 1881, 1924 (1991). Farber and Sherry observe that "[o]ne might call these scholars the anticounter majoritarianists." Farber and Sherry, *id. supra* p. 91, note 169 at 199; Koopmans, *supra* p. xii, note 10 at 104.

[170] *See* in *Re B.C. Motor Vehicle Act*, [1985] 2 S.C.R. 486, 497 ("It ought not to be forgotten that the historic decision to entrench the *Charter* in our Constitution was taken not by the courts but by the elected representatives of the people of Canada. It was those representatives who extended the scope of constitutional adjudication and entrusted the courts with this new and onerous responsibility. Adjudication under the *Charter* must be approached free of any lingering doubts as to its legitimacy").

[171] *See generally* Robert Dahl, *How Democratic Is the American Constitution?* (2001) (exploring the vital tension between the belief of Americans in the legitimacy of their Constitution and their belief in the principles of democracy).

[172] *Cf.* John Rawls, *Political Liberalism* 233 (1993) (observing that "constitutional democracy is dualist," constraining the current majority to protect original democratic guarantees).

[173] Dieter Grimm, "Constitutional Adjudication and Democracy," 33 *Isr. L. Rev.* 193, 196 (1999).

expression to the role of the judge—is not antidemocratic.[174] I discussed this in one case, where I said:

> Democracy is a delicate balance between majority rule and the fundamental values of society that rule the majority. . . . [W]hen the majority deprives the minority of human rights, this harms democracy. . . . [W]hen judges interpret provisions of the Constitution and void harmful laws, they give expression to the fundamental values of society, as they have evolved throughout the history of that society. Thus they protect constitutional democracy and uphold the delicate balance on which it is based. Take majority rule out of constitutional democracy, and you have harmed its essence. Take the rule of fundamental values out of constitutional democracy, and you have harmed its very existence. Judicial review of the constitutionality of statutes allows society to be honest with itself and to respect its fundamental tenets. This is the basis for the substantive legitimacy of judicial review. . . . [T]hrough judicial review we are faithful to the fundamental values that we imposed on ourselves in the past, that reflect our essence in the present, and that will guide us in our national development as a society in the future.[175]

---

[174] See Dworkin, *supra* p. 33, note 49 at 35 ("Would it offend democracy if a British court had the power to strike down the blasphemy law as inconsistent with the [European Convention of Human Rights]? No, because the true democracy is not just *statistical* democracy, in which anything a majority or plurality wants is legitimate for that reason, but *communal* democracy, in which majority decision is legitimate only if it is a majority within a community of equals"); Pikis, *supra* p. ix, note 1 at 9 ("[H]uman rights require constitutional entrenchment with corresponding power on the part of the judiciary to void or derogate from legislation offensive to or incompatible with human rights."). *See also* Erwin Chemerinsky, "The Price of Asking the Wrong Question: An Essay on Constitutional Scholarship and Judicial Review," 62 *Tex. L. Rev.* 1207, 1211–26 (1984) (arguing that the countermajoritarian difficulty is based on a misdefinition of democracy as majority); Erwin Chemerinsky, "The Supreme Court, 1988 Term—Foreword: The Vanishing Constitution," 103 *Harv. L. Rev.* 43, 74–77 (1989).

[175] C.A. 6821/93, *United Mizrahi Bank Ltd. v. Migdal Coop. Vill.*, 49(4) P.D. 221, 423–24. *See also* Rosalie Silberman Arbella, "The Judicial Role in a Democratic State," 26 *Queen's L.J.* 573, 577 (2001) ("The most basic of the central concepts we need back in the conversation is that democracy is not—and never was—just about the wishes of the majority. What pumps oxygen no less

Indeed, in a constitutional democracy neither the legislature nor the judiciary is supreme. Only the constitution is supreme. When a constitution is adopted, the legislature is obliged to uphold its provisions. The task of the court is to protect the provisions of the constitution and ensure that the legislature fulfills its obligation.[176] This was aptly expressed by Justice McLachlin when she said:

> The elected legislators are subject to the Constitution and must stay within its bounds, as must the courts. The courts have the duty to rule on whether the elected legislators have done so. Democracy is more than mere populism; it is the lawful exercise of powers conferred by the constitution. . . . When the courts hold a law to be invalid, they are not limiting parliamentary supremacy. They are merely expounding the limits that the Constitution imposes on Parliament. The claim that the Charter has replaced parliamentary supremacy by judicial supremacy is not true; rather, it is a myth.[177]

Third, the countermajoritarian argument does not give sufficient weight to the possibility of changing the constitution. Many constitutions are more easily amended than the United States Constitution is. Frequently the legislature itself may amend the constitution by a special supermajority of its members.

We are still left with the nonaccountability argument, which claims that it is inappropriate for the judge, who is not accountable to the public, to exploit constitutional vagueness and "majestic generalities"[178] by giving expression to his subjective beliefs. In such circumstances, the opinion of the legislature, which reflects the will of the majority, should receive preference. My answer to the nonaccountability argument is twofold. First, it is a mistake to assume that to be a true democracy, every organ of the state must

---

forcefully through vibrant democratic veins is the protection of rights, through courts, *notwithstanding* the wishes of the majority").

[176] *See* Brian Dickson, "The *Canadian Charter of Rights and Freedoms:* Dawn of a New Era?" 2 *Rev. Const. Stud.* 1, 12 (1994).

[177] Beverley McLachlin, "Charter Myths," 33 *U.B.C. L. Rev.* 23, 31 (1999) (emphasis omitted).

[178] *Fay v. New York*, 332 U.S. 261, 282 (1947).

be accountable to the public as the legislature is. Accountability to the people is necessary for the legislature. But such accountability is not required from the judiciary, which has another type of accountability. The question is not whether every organ of the state is accountable as the legislature is. The question is, as Daniel A. Farber and Suzanna Sherry put it, "whether the system as a whole fits our concept of democracy."[179]

Second, it is a myth that judges always give expression to their subjective beliefs. According to my view—both normatively and descriptively—the judge gives expression not to his own beliefs but to the deep, underlying beliefs of society. The key concept is judicial objectivity[180] "Judicial objectivity underlies judicial review of the constitutionality of statutes. In giving weight to the various considerations, the judge aspires, to the best of his ability, to judicial objectivity. He does not reflect his subjective values and his personal considerations."[181] The judge must reflect the beliefs of society, even if these are not the judge's own beliefs. The judge gives expression to the values of the constitution as they are understood by the culture and tradition of the populace in its progress through history. The judge reflects the fundamental tenets of the people and the national credo rather than his personal beliefs. In this way, the judge gives effect to the constitution and to democracy. Thus, the choice is not between the wishes of the people and the wishes of the judge. The choice is between two levels of the wishes of the people. The first, basic level reflects the most profound values of society in its progress through history; the second, ad hoc level reflects passing vogues. As Justice Iacobucci of the Supreme Court of Canada has observed:

> Democratic values and principles under the *Charter* demand that legislators and the executive take these into account; and if they fail to do so, courts should stand ready to intervene to protect these democratic

---

[179] Farber and Sherry, *supra* p. 91, note 169 at 141.
[180] *See infra* p. 101.
[181] C.A. 6821/93, *United Mizrahi Bank Ltd. v. Migdal Coop. Vill.* 49(4) P.D. 221, 426 (Isr.).

values as appropriate. . . . [J]udges are not acting undemocratically by intervening when there are indications that a legislative or executive decision was not reached in accordance with the democratic principles mandated by the *Charter*.[182]

It is the judge—who enjoys independence and does not need to stand for reelection every few years[183]—who is best equipped for succeeding in the difficult task of choosing between these two levels. It is the legislator—who must stand for reelection, and who needs the approval of the voters—who is ill-suited to make this choice.[184] According to this line of thinking, only the judge, who has nothing to hamper his independence, is capable of, and suited for, reflecting the fundamental values of society. It is only the judge who can give effect to substantive democracy. Indeed, I contend that the most important asset judges have in fulfilling their role is the lack of direct accountability to the public.[185] Note that when I say the judge is not accountable I am saying only that he is not accountable in the same way that the legislature is accountable. A judge is not a politician,[186] and his accountability differs from that of the politician. A judge's accountability is not expressed in regular elections by the people. It is expressed in accountability to the legislature, which can respond to a court's ruling with legislation.[187] It is expressed in accountability to the legal community, by the need to give reasons for every judgment—reasons that are accountable on appeal and stand open to public scrutiny. It is expressed in accountability for judicial misconduct.

---

[182] *Vriend v. Alberta*, [1998] 1 S.C.R. 493, 566–67.

[183] Of course, in a number of states in the United States, judges are elected by the people. This phenomenon is regrettable. *See Republican Party of Minn. v. White*, 122 S. Ct. 2528, 2542–44 (2002) (O'Connor, J., concurring).

[184] *See* Alexander M. Bickel, *The Least Dangerous Branch* 24–25 (1962); Rosalie Silberman Abella, "Public Policy and the Judicial Role," 34 *McGill L.J.* 1021, 1033 (1989).

[185] *See* P.S. Atiyah, "Judges and Policy," 15 *Isr. L. Rev.* 346, 369 (1988).

[186] *See Republican Party*, 122 S. Ct. at 2551 (Ginsburg, J., dissenting).

[187] *See Vriend*, [1998] 1 S.C.R. at 566.

Naturally, not everyone believes that judges act objectively, without imposing their subjective views on their societies. But if one assumes judicial objectivity within the framework of the common law, why should one not assume it within the framework of interpreting the constitution and statutes? Admittedly, the activity of a judge in the field of common law differs from the activity of a judge in interpreting a legal text. Nonetheless, both activities are replete with values and principles. If we trust judges to be objective when balancing among various values and principles in the common law, why should we not trust them to be objective when balancing among values and principles in interpreting the constitution and statutes? They are the very same judges. I am aware of the claim that, while the legislature may pass a statute overriding judicial development of the common law, it has no such power over judicial interpretation of a constitution. That does not, however, explain the lack of faith in judicial objectivity in statutory interpretation. After all, the legislature can change the effects of judicial interpretation of a statute by amending the statute, just as it can pass a statute overriding a common law rule. It is also not clear to me why the mere fact that the constitution is difficult to amend should undermine the faith in judicial objectivity apparently present in the common law context. Of course, mistakes have been made in the past. Some were very serious. But judges do not have a monopoly on mistakes. Judges come and go, and most mistakes are corrected by the judges themselves. Those that are not may be corrected by constitutional changes, and in most modern democracies, except for the United States, a special majority of the legislature may make those constitutional changes.[188] Personally, I would encourage this option.

It is possible that, in the final analysis, the question is about finding ways to prevent mistakes in the future. The twentieth century has taught me that the best way is to form a partnership between

---

[188] This type of change may include, at some point, the use of popular referenda. *See* Bruce Ackerman, "The New Separation of Powers," 113 *Harv. L. Rev.* 633, 666 (2000).

the constitution and judges. That is, of course, my subjective approach. But is the approach of my critics not their subjective approach? And if the life of the law is, as Holmes said, not logic but experience, should we not make use of the experience that we accumulated during the twentieth century?[189] Did all the democracies established after World War II and after the fall of the Soviet bloc err in explicitly writing into their constitutions provisions for judicial review of the constitutionality of statutes? Why should we not be allowed to continue this multinational experiment?

---

[189] Oliver Wendell Holmes, *The Common Law* 1 (1881) ("The life of the law has not been logic: it has been experience").

Part Two

THE MEANS OF REALIZING

THE JUDICIAL ROLE

CHAPTER THREE

Preconditions for Realizing the Judicial Role

In this part, I consider several devices through which judges in a democracy may realize their role. Indeed, it is not enough that we know where we need to go. We must develop means (or tools) to help us reach that goal, and the preconditions necessary to allow judges to realize their role must be met. These preconditions vary among democracies, but three are common to all democratic systems of law: (1) judicial impartiality and objectivity, (2) decisions within the social consensus, and (3) public confidence in the judiciary. These are not the only general preconditions, but they seem to me the most important and the most problematic. For all three, we must ensure not only that they are upheld, which is the main point, but also that the public recognizes that they are upheld.

JUDICIAL IMPARTIALITY AND OBJECTIVITY

The Essence of Impartiality and Objectivity

The judge must realize his role in a democracy impartially and objectively. Impartiality means that the judge treats the parties before him equally, providing them with an equal opportunity to make their respective cases, and is seen to treat the parties so. Impartiality means the judge has no personal stake in the outcome.[1] Absence of bias is essential to the judicial process;[2] hence the image

---

[1] Barak, *supra* p. xiii, note 14, at 189.
[2] See *Equality and Judicial Neutrality* (Sheilah L. Martin and Kathleen E. Mahoney eds., 1987).

of justice as blindfolded. With impartiality comes objectivity.[3] It means making judicial decisions on the basis of considerations that are external to the judge and that may even conflict with his personal view.[4] Judges must look for the accepted values of society, even if they are not their values. They must express what is regarded as moral and just by the society in which they operate, even if it is not moral and just in their subjective view.[5] As I wrote in one case:

> It is not his own subjective values that the judge imposes on the society in which he operates. He must balance among various interests according to what appear to him to be the needs of the society in which he lives. He must exercise his discretion according to what seems to him, to the best of his objective understanding, to reflect the needs of society The question is not what the judge wants but what society needs.[6]

Judges with religious or secular outlooks on life ought not impose those outlooks on the society in which they live. When

---

[3] On objectivity generally, see Karl Popper, *Objective Knowledge: An Evolutionary Approach* (1972); Nager, *The View From Nowhere* (1986); Tibor R. Machan, *Objectivity: Recovering Determinate Reality in Philosophy, Science, and Everyday Life* (2004); Richard J. Bernstein, *Beyond Objectivism and Relativism: Science, Hermeneutics and Praxis* (1985). On objectivity in law, see Kent Greenawalt, *Law and Objectivity* (1992); Nicos Stavropoulos, *Objectivity in Law* (1996); Jules L. Coleman, "Truth and Objectivity in Law," 1 *Legal Theory* 33 (1995); Brian Leiter, "Objectivity and the Problem of Jurisprudence," 72 *Tex. L. Rev.* 187 (1993); *Objectivity, Morality, and Adjudication* (Brian Lieter ed., 2001); Brian Lieter, "Law and Objectivity," in *The Oxford Handbook of Jurisprudence and Philosophy of Law* 1969 (Jules Coleman and Scott Shapiro eds., 2002).
[4] *See* Barak, *supra* p. xiii, note 14 at 125; Aharon Barak, "Justice Matthew O. Tobriner Memorial Lecture: The Role of a Supreme Court in a Democracy," 53 *Hastings L.J.* 1205, 1210–11 (2002).
[5] I noted in one case: "The judge must reflect . . . all the fundamental values of the enlightened public, even if he personally does not accept one or another value. . . . [T]he judge must reflect the long-term beliefs of society. He must refrain from imposing his personal beliefs on society. . . ." H.C. 693/91, *Efrat v. Dir. of Population Register*, 47(1) P.D. 781, 781–82.
[6] C.A. 243/83, *Municipality of Jerusalem v. Gordon*, 39(1) P.D. 113, 131 (internal quotation marks omitted).

judges consider the weight of different values, they must do so according to the fundamental views of the society in which they live, not according to their own personal fundamental views.[7]

The Problem of Objectivity and Ways to Solve It

This objectivity makes strenuous demands, requiring the judge to take moral stock of himself. The judge must be aware that he may have values that lack general acceptance and that his personal opinions may be exceptional and unusual. I drew this distinction in one opinion:

> This requirement for objectivity imposes a heavy burden on the judge. He must be able to distinguish between his personal desire and what is generally accepted in society. He must erect a clear partition between his beliefs as an individual and his outlooks as a judge. He must be able to recognize that his personal views may not be generally accepted by the public. He must carefully distinguish his own credo from that of the nation. He must be critical of himself and restrained with regard to his beliefs. He must respect the chains that bind him as a judge.[8]

The judge must be capable of looking at himself from the outside and of analyzing, criticizing, and controlling himself. A judge who thinks that he knows all, and that his opinions are right and proper to the exclusion of all else, cannot properly fulfill his role.

The judge is a product of his times, living in and shaped by a given society in a given era. The purpose of objectivity is not to

---

[7] See *Rochin v. California*, 342 U.S. 165, 170–72 (1952) (arguing that judges, when interpreting the due process clause, should not rely merely on personal and private notions of due process); *W. Va. State Bd. of Educ. v. Barnette*, 319 U.S. 624, 647 (1943) (Frankfurter, J., dissenting) ("As a member of this Court I am not justified in writing my private notions of policy into the Constitution, no matter how deeply I may cherish them. . . ."); Cardozo, *supra* p. xv, note 25 at 88–89, 108 (1921) (arguing that a judge's personal beliefs and idiosyncrasies should not be imposed on the community); McLachlin, "*The Charter*," *supra* p. ix, note 1 at 546 (arguing that judges have a "duty to set aside their personal prejudices and views").

[8] *Efrat*, 47(1) P.D. at 782.

sever the judge from his environment. Rather, its purpose is to allow him to ascertain properly the fundamental principles of his time. The purpose of objectivity is not to rid a judge of his past, his education, his experience, his belief, or his values.[9] Its purpose is to encourage the judge to make use of all of these personal characteristics to reflect the fundamental values of the society as faithfully as possible. A person who is appointed as a judge is neither required nor able to change his skin. The judge must develop sensitivity to the dignity of his office and to the restraints that it imposes. As the ancient Jewish text reminds judges, "Do you imagine that I offer you rulership? It is servitude that I give you."[10] The judge must display the self-criticism and humility that will prevent him from identifying himself with everything good and praiseworthy. A judge must display the self-control that will allow him to distinguish between personal feelings and national aspirations. A judge must display intellectual modesty.

The objectivity required of a judge is difficult to attain. Even when we look at ourselves from the outside, we do so with our own eyes.[11] Nonetheless, my judicial experience tells me that objectivity is possible. A judge does not operate in a vacuum. A judge is part of society, and society influences the judge. The judge is influenced by the intellectual movements and the legal thinking that prevail. A judge is always part of the people.[12] It may be true that the judge sometimes sits in an ivory tower, though my ivory tower is located in the hills of Jerusalem and not on Mount Olympus in Greece. But the judge is nonetheless a contemporary creature. He progresses with the history of the people. All of these elements contribute to the judge's objective perspective.

[9] *See* Abella, *supra* p. 96, note 184 at 1027.
[10] Babylonian Talmud, *Horayot* 10a–b.
[11] *See* Cardozo, *supra* p. xv, note 25 at 13.
[12] *See* William H. Rehnquist, "Constitutional Law and Public Opinion," 20 *Suffolk U. L. Rev.* 751, 768–69 (1986) (explaining that some "currents of public opinion" inevitably influence a judge's decisions, though perhaps in an unconscious way). *See also* Thomas R. Marshall, *Public Opinion and the Supreme Court* (1989).

Moreover, the judge acts within the limits of a court. He lives within a judicial tradition. The same spark of wisdom passes from one generation of judges to the next. This wisdom is mostly unwritten, but it penetrates little by little into the judge's consciousness and makes his thinking more objective. The judge is part of a legal system that establishes a framework for the factors that a judge may and may not consider. The heavier the weight of the system, the greater the objectification of the judicial process.

The Place of Judicial Subjectivity

When judges give expression to the fundamental values of the system, they give expression to the values that, in their eyes, seem proper and basic. Some subjectification of this process is inevitable. Complete objectivity is unattainable. The personal aspect of a judge is always present, and his life experience neither disappears nor can disappear. We would not want it to, because in these situations, it is the judge's personality that finds expression—the same personality that underwent, and passed, the judicial nomination process. We need not, however, go from extreme to extreme. Rejecting complete objectivity does not require us to embrace complete subjectivity. There is a third way, reflected in acknowledging the importance and centrality of judicial objectivity while recognizing unreservedly that it can never fully be achieved. It is enough for a judge to make an honest attempt to objectify his exercise of discretion, recognizing that it cannot be done in every circumstance.

Furthermore, for some issues, the structure of the system grants the judge discretion that is ultimately based on a subjective decision, bounded by the range of considerations from which he chooses. Indeed, objectivity is sometimes unattainable. There are numerous methods of developing the common law. The interpretation of a legal text does not always lead to a unique solution. The judge may find himself in a position to exercise judicial discretion. Naturally, this discretion is limited, but it nonetheless exists. In such situations a judge may act according to his own views. But even in these cases—and they are a tiny minority—the path to full subjectivity is closed. The judge may not resort to his anomalous personal inclinations or to his particular opinions. The judge may not resort to individual values that contradict the values of the legal system but must make the best decision within the framework of objective considerations. The judge cannot return to the point of origin but must march forward. He must try to give the best solution of which he is capable. Indeed, someone who has taken personal stock of himself and who has succeeded in overcoming his particular inclinations will not resort to them. The judge must find the best solution within the confines of the objective data available. Were the legal system not to guide, the judge would be faced with several possibilities. But the legal system limits the scope of the judge's considerations. The judge is never permitted simply to do as he pleases. Even when the judge is "with himself," he is within the framework of society, the legal system, and judicial tradition.

Admittedly, there are some cases in which the judge has discretion that allows him to choose among a limited number of options, according to his views. How should the judge choose? All I can say is that the choice is a product of the judge's personal life experience and the balance he must find between certainty and experimentation, between stability and change, between logic and emotion. The judge's choice is influenced by his concept of the judicial role and attitudes toward the other branches of the state. It is derived from the judge's judicial philosophy.[13] It is the product of a delicate balance in the judge's soul between the specific and the general, between the individual and society, and between the individual and the state. Most judges do not feel comfortable in such situations. They are subject to tremendous internal pressure. They usually display caution and self-restraint.[14] Their sense of personal responsibility

[13] See William H. Rehnquist, "The Notion of a Living Constitution," 54 *Tex. L. Rev.* 693, 697 (1976) (acknowledging that a judge's interpretation of the Constitution "will depend to some extent on his own philosophy of constitutional law").

[14] See, e.g., *Moore v. City of E. Cleveland*, 431 U.S. 494, 502 (1977).

reaches its peak.[15] They feel greatly isolated.[16] In such situations, I try to be guided by my North Star, which is justice. I try to make law and justice converge, so that the Justice will do justice.

SOCIAL CONSENSUS

As a rule, I have always tried to carry out my role as a judge within the framework of social consensus, to the extent that data exist about it.[17] The judge should generally not be the flagbearer of a new social consensus. As a rule, judges should reflect values and principles that exist in their system rather than create them. Justice Traynor rightly stated, "The very responsibilities of a judge as an arbiter disqualify him as a crusader."[18]

Nevertheless, there are cases—and they must naturally be few—in which the judge carries out his role properly by ignoring the prevalent social consensus and becoming a flagbearer of a new social consensus. Consider the case of *Brown v. Board of Education*.[19] I do not know what the consensus was in the United States just before the Supreme Court's decision in *Brown*,[20] but in my opinion, the Court at that time fulfilled its role, even if it ruled against the then prevailing consensus. Naturally, a court will not retain public confidence if it announces a new *Brown* twice a week. Similarly, a court will lose public confidence if it misses an opportunity like *Brown* when faced with it. In the final analysis, everything is a question of degree.

---

[15] *See, e.g.*, William J. Brennan, Jr., "Reason, Passion, and 'The Progress of the Law,'" 10 *Cardozo L. Rev.* 3, 12 (1988) (explaining that "[n]o matter how much one has studied or thought about the Constitution, the weight of responsibility that comes with the job of Supreme Court Justice cannot be fully anticipated").

[16] *See* Brennan, *supra* p. 85, note 153, at 434 ("[T]he process of deciding can be a lonely, troubling experience for fallible human beings conscious that their best may not be adequate to the challenge").

[17] *See* Barak, *supra* p. xiii, note 14 at 213–15.

[18] Traynor, *supra* p. 12, note 21 at 1030.

[19] 347 U.S. 483 (1954).

[20] *See* Charles J. Ogletree, *All Deliberate Speed: Reflection on the First Half Century of* Brown v. Board of Education (2004).

The consensus within which judges usually ought to operate should be a consensus grounded in the fundamental values of the legal system. Judges should not act according to a consensus formed by transient trends that are inconsistent with the society's fundamental values. Judges' social framework must be central and basic, not temporary and fleeting. When society is not being true to itself, judges are not required to give expression to its passing trends. They must stand firm against these trends while giving expression to the social consensus that reflects their society's fundamental principles and tenets: "[They] must reveal what is principled and fundamental, while rejecting what is temporary and fleeting."[21]

Remaining in touch with these views requires a study of social consensus; it requires judicial self-restraint, moderation, and sensitivity. In exceptional situations, judges may depart from the current consensus. Moreover, fundamental principles are the result of modern experience. While even modern experience sprouts from the soil of the past to which it is connected, its horizons are not limited to the horizons of the past. Every generation has its own horizons. This approach to fundamental principles—emphasizing deeply held views and not the temporary and the fleeting, emphasizing history and not hysteria—also provides a proper answer to the criticism that taking into account the fundamental principles of the present may harm individuals in the minority.[22] The answer to this criticism is, *inter alia*, that the fundamental values of the present are not necessarily the values that today's majority accepts. They are the deeply held values of the society that have developed over time. Again, it is precisely judges, enjoying the independence of an appointed position, who are in the appropriate position to ignore passing vogues and give expression to the deeply held values of society.[23] Indeed, judges' nonaccountability is their most precious asset,[24] enabling them to give expression to the deeply held principles of society in its progress through history.

---

[21] H.C. 693/91, *Efrat v. Dir. of Population Register*, 47(1) P.D. 749, 780.

[22] *See* Scalia, *supra* p. xviii, note 33 at 315–17.

[23] *See* Bickel, *supra* p. 96, note 184 at 24.

[24] *See* Atiyah, *supra* p. 96, note 185 at 369.

PUBLIC CONFIDENCE

The Essence of Public Confidence

An essential condition for realizing the judicial role is public confidence in the judge.[25] This means confidence in judicial independence, fairness, and impartiality.[26] It means public confidence in the ethical standards of the judge. It means public confidence that judges are not interested parties to the legal struggle and that they are not fighting for their own power but to protect the constitution and democracy. It means public confidence that the judge does not express his own personal views but rather the fundamental beliefs of the nation.[27] Indeed, the judge has neither sword nor purse.[28] All he has is the public's confidence in him. This fact means that the public recognizes the legitimacy of judicial decisions, even if it disagrees with their content.

The precondition of "public confidence" runs the risk of being misunderstood.[29] The need to ensure public confidence does not

---

[25] *See* Barak, *supra* p. xiii, note 14 at 215–21; Otto Kirchheimer, *Political Justice* 178 (1961) (stating that a court's authority "rests on the community's preparedness to recognize the judge's capacity to lend legitimacy or to withdraw it from an individual's act"); Steyn, *supra* p. 77, note 130 at 388.

[26] For five separate opinions articulating varying notions of judicial impartiality, see *Republican Party of Minnesota v. White*, 122 S. Ct. 2528 (2002).

[27] I noted in one case:

> An essential condition for an independent judiciary is public confidence. This means public confidence that the judiciary is dispensing justice according to the law. It means public confidence that judging is being done fairly, impartially, with equal treatment of both parties and without any trace of a personal interest in the outcome. It means public confidence in the high ethical level of judging. Without public confidence the judiciary cannot operate. . . . [P]ublic confidence in the judiciary is the most precious asset that this branch of government has. It is also one of the most precious assets of the nation. As De Balzac noted, lack of confidence in the judiciary is the beginning of the end of society. (H.C. 732/84, *Tzaban v. Minister of Religious Affairs*, 40(4) P.D. 141, 148)

[28] *See Baker v. Carr*, 369 U.S. 186, 267 (1962) (Frankfurter, J., dissenting) ("The Court's authority—possessed of neither the purse nor the sword—ultimately rests on sustained public confidence in its moral sanction").

[29] *See, e.g.,* Elizabeth Handsley, "Public Confidence in the Judiciary: A Red Herring for the Separation of Judicial Power," 20 *Sydney L. Rev.* 183, 214 (1998)

mean the need to ensure popularity. Public confidence does not mean following popular trends or public opinion polls. Public confidence does not mean accountability to the public in the way that the executive and the legislature are accountable. Public confidence does not mean pleasing the public; public confidence does not mean ruling contrary to the law or contrary to the judge's conscience to bring about a result that the public desires. On the contrary, public confidence means ruling according to the law and according to the judge's conscience, whatever the attitude of the public may be. Public confidence means giving expression to history, not to hysteria. Public confidence is ensured by the recognition that the judge is doing justice within the framework of the law. Inside and outside the court, judges must act in a manner that preserves public confidence in them. They must understand that judging is not merely a job but a way of life. It is a way of life that does not include the pursuit of material wealth or publicity; it is a way of life based on spiritual wealth; it is a way of life that includes an objective and impartial search for truth. It is not fiat but reason; not mastery but modesty; not strength but compassion; not riches but reputation; not an attempt to please everyone but a firm insistence on values and principles; not surrender to or compromise with interest groups but an insistence on upholding the law; not making decisions according to temporary whims but progressing consistently on the basis of deeply held beliefs and fundamental values. Admittedly, judging is a way of life that involves some degree of seclusion, abstention from social and political struggles, restriction on the freedom of expression and the freedom to respond, and a large amount of isolation and internalization. But judging is emphatically not a way of life that involves a withdrawal from society. There should be no wall between the judge and the society in which the judge operates. The judge is a part of the people.

(criticizing the High Court of Australia for shifting back and forth between a perception of public confidence as "an immutable characteristic which can lend legitimacy to an otherwise suspect act" and a perception of public confidence as "fragile" and easily destroyed).

Ways to Maintain Public Confidence

If this view of the judicial role is adopted by judges, we can hope that the public will have and maintain confidence in the judiciary. In this respect, I wish to note several judicial traits that can help the public maintain confidence in its judges.

First, the judge ought to be aware of his power and his limits. A judge has great power in a democracy. Like all power, judicial power can be abused. The judge ought to recognize that his power is limited to realizing the proper judicial role. From my experience, I know that it takes considerable time for a new judge to learn his role on a court. Naturally, the judge knows the law and the power it grants to the judge, but he must also learn the limits imposed on him as a judge;[30] he must know that power should not be abused and that a judge cannot obtain everything he wants.

Second, a judge must recognize his mistakes. Like all mortals, judges err. A judge must admit this. According to the well-known statement of Justice Jackson, "We are not final because we are infallible, but we are infallible only because we are final."[31] In one opinion, citing Justice Jackson's statement, I added, "I think that the learned judge erred. The finality of our decisions is based on our ability to admit our mistakes, and our willingness to do so in appropriate cases."[32] In another case, I wrote an opinion on a matter that was subsequently reargued before an enlarged panel. My decision before the enlarged panel reversed my original ruling. I explained the change as follows:

> This conclusion of mine conflicts with the conclusion that I reached in my ruling, which is the subject of this petition. In other words, I changed my mind. Indeed, since the judgment was given—and

[30] See, e.g., Brian Dickson, supra p. 3, note 1 at 384 (arguing that "the Supreme Court of Canada justice must display sensitivity to the limits of the court's ability to effect major legal change" and that "the legislature is best equipped to set down guiding principles designed to address some of our most complex social problems").
[31] Brown v. Allen, 344 U.S. 443, 540 (1953) (Jackson, J., concurring).
[32] C.A. 243/83, Municipality of Jerusalem v. Gordon, 39(1) P.D. 113, 136–37.

against the backdrop of the further hearing itself—I have not ceased to examine whether my approach is correctly grounded in law. I do not count myself among those who believe that the finality of a decision testifies to its correctness. We all err. Our professional integrity requires us to admit our mistakes, if we are convinced that we have indeed erred . . . in our difficult hours, when we evaluate ourselves, our North Star should be uncovering the truth that brings justice within the limits of law. We should not entrench ourselves in our previous decisions. We must be prepared to admit our mistakes.[33]

I hope that if we admit our mistakes as judges, we will strengthen public confidence in the judiciary.[34]

Third, in our writing and our thinking, judges must display modesty and an absence of arrogance. Statements such as those of Chief Justice Hughes that "we are under a Constitution, but the Constitution is what the judges say it is"[35] are not merely incorrect but also perniciously arrogant.

Fourth, judges should be honest. If they create new law, they should say so. They should not hide behind the rhetoric that judges declare what the law is but do not make it. Judges make law, and the public should know that they do. The public has the right to know that we make law and how we do it; the public should not be deceived. "The right to know the architect of our obligations," wrote Professor Julius Stone, "may be as much a part of liberty as the right to know our accuser and our judge."[36] Public confidence in the judiciary increases when the public is told the truth.

[33] Cr.A. 7048/97, *Anonymous v. Minister of Def.* 54(1) P.D. 721, 743.
[34] *See* Beverley McLachlin, "The Charter of Rights and Freedoms: A Judicial Perspective," 23 *U. B.C. L. Rev.* 579, 589 (1989) (arguing that judges should be flexible and admit their mistakes).
[35] Charles Evans Hughes, Speech at Elmira (May 3, 1907), in *The Autobiographical Notes of Charles Evans Hughes* 144 (David J. Danelski and Joseph S. Tulchin eds., 1973). In defense of this position, see Terri Jennings Peretti, *In Defence of a Political Court* (1999).
[36] Julius Stone, *Social Dimensions of Law and Justice* 678 (1966).

CHAPTER FOUR

The Meaning of Means

THE LEGITIMACY OF THE MEANS

The means of realizing the judicial role must be legitimate; the principle of the rule of law applies first and foremost to judges themselves, who do not share the legislature's freedom in freely creating new tools. The bricks with which we build our structures are limited. Our power to realize our role depends on our ability to design new structures with the same old bricks or to create new bricks.[1] Sometimes there is great similarity between the new structures we build with the old bricks and the old structures we have known in the past. We tend to say that there is nothing new under the sun, and that the legal pendulum swings to and fro before returning to its point of origin. But these analogies are inappropriate. The structures are always new. There is no return to the point of origin; the movement is always forward. Law is in constant motion; the question is merely one of the rate of progress, its direction, and the forces propelling it. Moreover, sometimes we succeed in creating new "tools." Here the genius of law is evident. But such inventions are few. Usually we return to the old tools and use them to resolve new situations.

OPERATIVE LEGAL THEORY

Legal Culture and Tradition

The operative legal theory of a given legal system influences the use of existing tools and the creation of new tools.[2] Indeed, every legal

---

[1] See Moshe Landau, "Case-Law and Discretion in Doing Justice," 1 *Mishpatim* 292 (1965).

[2] See Barak, *Judicial Discretion*, 142 (1987).

system possesses its own legal theory. I do not here refer to a legal philosophy that transcends state borders; rather, I refer to an operative theory of law. This theory determines the jurisprudential key concepts. It is a spring from which law draw its power, and it fashions the common legal experience. When the legal text—especially a constitution or a statute—includes such phrases as "void," "authority," "legal action," "intention," "limitation of action," "good faith," "reasonableness," these words reflect a legal culture and legal tradition. They are not empty vessels into which the judge can simply pour any and all content. Instead, they reflect fundamental legal approaches, derived from the legal tradition to which the legal system and culture belong. All of these give these expressions their conventional jurisprudential meaning in that system. Indeed, when a constitution or a statute employs these terms, it does so against the backdrop of the basic approaches of that society's legal culture and operative legal theory. When judges fulfill their role in a society, they act within the context of those selfsame conceptions. Justice Frankfurter asserted:

> An enactment is an organism in its environment. And the environment is not merely the immediate political or social context in which it is to be placed, but the whole traditional system of law and law enforcement. . . .[3]

Therefore, a statute on property lives and breathes within the framework of the basic jurisprudential concepts regarding the right to property, ownership, and possession. In fact, various theoretical distinctions that characterize our legal discourse—between procedure and substance, between a cogent law (that cannot be stipulated against) and a dispositive law (which is binding as long as not lawfully stipulated against), between a right and a remedy, between a natural legal persona (human being) and a non-natural persona (corporation), between private and public law, between liberty and power—comprise the dogmatism of the legal system. They serve as the infrastructure, providing the framework within

---

[3] Felix Frankfurter, "A Symposium on Statutory Construction: Foreword," 3 *Vand. L. Rev.* 365, 367 (1950).

which the texts of the constitution and the statute are created. Indeed, every statute is legislated within the context of conceptual approaches to liability (criminal or civil) and defenses; within the context of the distinction between defenses and immunities, between different types of rights, and between different types of remedies. These concepts constitute the backdrop against which judges fulfill their role, within the framework of that law and the framework of that society.

Dogmatism as a Tool, Not an Aim

Operative legal theory has an important place in the performance of the judicial role. Any other approach would have ignored centuries of legal thought and judicial experience. The law did not begin with us, nor will it end with us. There is also no need to reinvent the wheel; we must learn from the wisdom of the past. Legal concepts reflect the understanding and experience of generations. They ensure stability and certainty; this is their importance. They refine our thinking. With their strength, legislation does not begin with a clean slate. Nevertheless, legal concepts are merely supporting tools. They are the servant, not the master. Operative legal theory determines the starting point; it must not be transformed into the ending point. We must not return to a legal theory of concepts (*Begriffenjurisprudenz*). The law is not an Eden of concepts but rather an everyday life of needs, interests, and values that a given society seeks to realize in a given time. The law itself is only a tool and an instrument. It is intended to provide solutions for the problems of human beings in society. It is intended to realize the values of the society. And if the law is a tool, then operative legal theory is also a tool. Indeed, the fundamental concepts of the law are legal constructions. They are tools in our hands to understand the law. They are tools in the hands of the judge to realize his role. Therefore, the judge should use the dogmatism of his system and the theoretical tools that it places at his service. He should do so to actualize the values and the principles over which he is entrusted to watch. I emphasized this in one case, stating that we must distance ourselves from the legal theory of concepts in which the theoretical concept forces itself upon the interests and the values that require a normative ordering. We must strive for a legal theory of values, according to which the theoretical concept is the outcome of the balance and ordering of values and interests that require a normative ordering. Legal concepts (e.g., ownership, right, crime) are not a reality that we must accept as fact. Legal concepts are constructions that come to serve human beings.[4]

JUDICIAL PHILOSOPHY

Philosophy as a Judicial Tool

In my treks in the paths of justice, I have found that a good philosophy is a very practical matter. A philosophy of life and a philosophy of law help the judge in understanding his role and in executing that role. It is important that the judge have an understanding of the philosophical discourse. Through it, he can participate in the search for truth, while understanding the limitations of the human mind and the complexity of humankind. With the help of a good philosophy, he will better understand the role of the law in a society and the task of the judge within the law. One cannot accomplish much with a good philosophy alone, yet one cannot accomplish anything without it.

The Judge and the Philosophy of Law

From the outset of our studies in law school until the end of our professional lives, we are exposed to various philosophical approaches to the law: positivism, naturalism, realism, legal process, critical legal studies, law and sociology, law and economics, feminism, and others. I have found these theories to be of great interest, for each has an

[4] FCr.A. 4603/97, *Meshulem v. the State of Israel*, 51(3) P.D. 160, 182.

element of truth. Nonetheless, human experience is too rich to be imprisoned in a single legal theory. The following remarks made by Professor Edwin Patterson more than fifty years ago aptly reflect my approach:

> My own philosophy of law is eclectic because I recognize that each of the major philosophers has begun his system with several appealing self-evident principles, and I cannot reject them as wholly wrong. . . . My eclecticism in legal philosophy is based partly on my belief in tolerance, partly on my belief in pluralism, and partly on the inertia of habit.[5]

Indeed, in my view, only by considering all the theories and giving each of them the appropriate weight is it possible to understand the law and the role of the judge. Law is a tool that is intended to realize social goals. There is no consensus about the content of these goals, which is why it is necessary to find a balance among the various theories *inter se*. Some will regard the eclectic approach as an attempt to avoid a coherent legal theory. There will doubtless be others who regard the eclectic approach as an independent legal theory in itself. Whatever the case, each judge should adopt for himself a position on these questions. It will serve him as a tool for realizing his judicial role. It is unfortunate that in recent years, a widening gap has formed between academics concerned with the philosophy of law and a significant number of judges. I think we should do whatever we can to narrow this gap. Judges need theories of law, and theories of law need judges.

Judicial Philosophy

Situations exist in which the judge is faced with the necessity of choosing between various legal options, without the legal system guiding this choice. The judge has discretion. True, limitations (procedural and substantive) placed upon him limit the options at

[5] See Edwin Patterson, *Jurisprudence: Men and Ideas of the Law* 556 (1953).

his disposal and the considerations that he is allowed to consider. A judge's discretion is never absolute, but within the framework of these limitations, he has the freedom to choose. How should this choice be made? Clearly, there are no rules that would lead in every case to one and only one result. The existence of rules would negate the very existence of judicial discretion; nevertheless, the choice cannot be based on happenstance. The judge must strive for the optimal solution. How will he discover this solution? I believe that each and every judge must create for himself a judicial philosophy about the manner in which he will solve hard cases. This should be a system of nonobligatory considerations that will guide him in exercising his discretion. These are a set of thoughts about how to exercise discretion in hard cases. Judicial philosophy is an organized thought about the way in which a judge is to contend with the problematics of a hard case. From my experience, the majority of judges have such a judicial philosophy. For most, it is an unconscious philosophy. I seek to raise judicial philosophy into the realm of consciousness and subject it to public critique.

One must distinguish between judicial philosophy and legal policy.[6] Judicial philosophy is a system of considerations that the judge takes into account when exercising discretion. One's approach to the judicial role rests on this philosophical basis. Legal policy is the principles, social aims, and standards that lie at the basis of the norm that is employed (e.g., the protection of human dignity, the protection of national security, the proper balance between them.) Legal policy changes from case to case. Judicial philosophy is an all-encompassing philosophy that guides the judge in choosing between legal options at his disposal in hard cases. Certainly, this judicial philosophy takes into account the character of the legal policy that lies at the base of each of the options at the judge's disposal. Employing the judicial policy for solving conflicts in the realm of property is not the same as employing it for solving problems in criminal law.

[6] *See* Barak *supra* p. 113, note 2 at 299.

One must also distinguish between a judge's judicial philosophy and a judge's political opinions. We are not interested in a judge's opinion in various issues of dispute in a state. We are only interested in a judge's opinion regarding the way in which he is to exercise his discretion. These considerations must not take into account judge's political opinions.

Judicial philosophy is closely intertwined with the personal experience of the judge. It is influenced by his education and personality. Some judges are more cautious and others are less cautious. There are judges that are more readily influenced by a certain kind of claim than are other judges. Some judges require a heavy "burden of proof" in order to depart from existing law, while others require a lighter "burden of proof." Every judge has a complex life experience that influences his approach to life, and therefore influences his approach to the law. There are judges for whom considerations of national security or individual freedom are weightier than for other judges. There are judges whose personal makeup obligates order, and as a result, they require an organic development and evolution of the law. There are judges whose personalities place great importance on the proper solution, even if they reach that solution in a nonevolutionary way. There are judges whose starting point is judicial activism; there are judges whose starting point is self-restraint. There are judges who give special weight to considerations of justice in the general sphere, even if it creates injustice in the individual case. Other judges emphasize justice in the individual case even if it does not fit with the general justice at the basis of the norm.

One must always remember that this judicial philosophy—the fruit of the judge's personal experience—is relevant in the realm in which the judge has judicial discretion. It functions only within a range of reasonableness. It works only in those cases where the legal problem has more than one legal solution. It is relevant only in the hard cases, in which the judge strives to achieve the optimal solution. Judicial philosophy aims to bring us to this safe space. It is the principal compass that directs the judge (consciously or unconsciously) in discovering the solution to the hard cases with which he is confronted. Professor Freund wrote that "the most important thing about a judge is his philosophy; and if it be dangerous for him to have one, it is at all events less dangerous than the self-deception of having none."[7]

The Approach to the Judicial Role

At the basis of the judicial philosophy lies the judge's approach to his judicial role. A judge who perceives it as his obligation and right to bridge between the law and life, and strives to do so, is not the same as a judge who sees it as an evil that at times is unavoidable.

His approach to the judicial role influences the manner in which he interprets statutes and the manner in which he is willing to develop the common law. Judge Schaefer, in a discussion on overruling precedent, stated:

> [M]ost depends upon the judge's unspoken notion as to the function of the court. If he views the role of the court as a passive one, he will be willing to delegate the responsibility for change, and he will not greatly care whether the delegated authority is exercised or not. If he views the court as an instrument of society designed to reflect in its decisions the morality of the community, he will be more likely to look precedent in the teeth and to measure it against the ideals and aspirations of his time.[8]

Similarly, a judge who sees it as part of his role to protect the constitution and the democracy will deliberate in a manner differently from a judge who distances himself from such considerations. The judge who sees that balancing between competing values is an essential element in his judicial role is unlike a judge who believes that this balance should be done only by the legislature itself. The perception of the judicial role influences the range of means that

---

[7] Paul Freund, "Social Justice and the Law," *Social Justice* 93, 110 (R. Brandt ed., 1962).
[8] Walter Schaefer, "Precedent and Policy," 34 *U. Chi. L. Rev.* 3, 23 (1966).

the judge uses to fulfill his role and influences his relations with the legislature and the executive branch. His position on questions of judicial activism or self-restraint are determined from his approach to his role, which is determined by his judicial philosophy. Just to reiterate, one must remember that the perception of the judicial role plays an important role only in situations in which the judge has discretion. In the absence of discretion, all judges will act in the same manner, even if the judicial philosophy of one is different from his colleague's. When the judge does have discretion, then and only then does the importance of the perception of the judicial role emerge. Even then its function is limited, as judicial discretion is never absolute. It acts within the framework of the limitations (of substance and of procedure) placed on judicial discretion.

Interpretation

THE ESSENCE OF INTERPRETATION

Interpretation, by which I mean rational activity giving meaning to a legal text (whether it be a will, contract, statute, or constitution),[1] is both the primary task and the most important tool of a court. Interpretation derives the legal meaning from the text. Put another way, interpretation constitutes a process whereby the legal meaning of a text is "extracted" from its semantic meaning. The interpreter

---

[1] My theory of interpretation draws a sharp distinction between interpreting and filling in a gap (lacuna) in a legal text. Interpretation gives meaning to the text. Gap filling subtracts from or adds to the text by way of analogy or by applying the system's fundamental values. Continental jurisprudence has developed this distinction. *See* Claus-Wilhelm Canaris, *Die Feststellung von Lucken in Gesetz* (1983); Bernd Ruthers, *Rechtstheorie* 456 (1999). A gap in a text exists when its interpretation leads to the conclusion that the absence of a solution to the legal problem conflicts with the purpose of the text. It is as if an essential brick is missing from the wall that the text constructs. A gap may be apparent or hidden. An apparent gap exists when the text does not cover a particular case. A hidden gap exists when the text does cover the case but lacks an exception necessary to remove a particular incident from the text's coverage. Continental legal tradition authorizes a judge to fill in the gap, whether it be apparent or hidden. An interesting example of an apparent gap is the absence of an express right to privacy in the American Bill of Rights. It may be argued that in *Griswold v. Connecticut* , 381 U.S. 473 (1965), Justice Douglas filled in this gap. Another example of an apparent constitutional gap may be found in the decisions of the High Court of Australia recognizing "implied" constitutional rights. *See supra* section II.B.2.b. A good example of a hidden gap is the case of the murderous heir: the silence of the law of succession on the question of whether he can inherit is a hidden gap that the judge is authorized to fill in. Such a solution is preferable to the one that denies the heir his inheritance by way of interpretation. *See* Dworkin, *Taking Rights Seriously*, *supra* p. xiii, note 18 at 23. Using gap filling overcomes the accusation of "spurious interpretation." *See* Roscoe Pound, "Spurious Interpretation," 7 *Colum. L. Rev* . 379, 382 (1907). Common law judges would do well to develop

translates "human" language into "legal" language.[2] He changes "static law" into "dynamic law" by transforming a linguistic text into a legal norm.

Many aspire in vain to uncover what the legal meaning of a text "truly" is.[3] This is a fruitless search: a text has no "true" meaning. We do not have the ability to compare the meaning of a text before and after its interpretation, through focus on its "true" meaning. There is no pre-exegetic understanding of a text, for we can only access and understand it through an interpretive process. Only different interpretations of a given text can be compared. The most to which we can aspire is the "proper" meaning, not the "true" meaning.

The key question is, what is the proper system of interpretation? There are indeed many systems of interpretation. Legal history is the history of the rise and fall of different systems of legal interpretation. All interpretive systems struggle with the limitations of language and generalizations. All interpretive systems must resolve the relationship between text and context, between the word (*verba*) of the text and its spirit (*voluntas*). All interpretive systems must adopt a position on the relationship between the real and hypothetical intention of the author, between the author's declared intent, which is learned from the text, and his real intent, which is learned from the text and from sources outside the text. How can we determine the proper system of interpretation?

The answer to this question is critical, for every individual in the legal system and every branch of the state engages in interpretation and should know how to do it properly. The answer is especially important for the judge, particularly the supreme court judge, the vast majority of whose work is interpretive. How is he to carry it out? Indeed, this question has occupied me since the moment of

---

the doctrine that deals with these lacunae. With it, and by using analogy from the provisions of similar statutes, a statute, like the common law, projects itself into the system and can be developed beyond its language.

[2] *See* Aharon Barak, *Purposive Interpretation in Law* (2005).

[3] *See* Aharon Barak, "Hermeneutics and Constitutional Interpretation," 14 *Cardozo L. Rev.* 767, 769 (1993).

my appointment to the bench. I discovered—as many better than I discovered before me—that neither common law systems[4] nor civil law systems[5] have satisfactory answers to these questions. This is troubling. Interpretation is the judge's primary tool for realizing his role in a democracy. How can we have failed to agree on a theory of interpretation?

I do not know the answer to this simple question.[6] In any event, it seems to me that the solution lies in answering another simple question: What is the purpose of interpretation? Indeed, you cannot know how to interpret without knowing why you are interpreting. In my worldview, the answer to the question, for what reason? is the following: The aim of interpretation in law is to realize the purpose of the law; the aim in interpreting a legal text (such as a constitution or statute) is to realize the purpose the text serves. Law is thus a tool designed to realize a social goal. It is intended to ensure the social life of the community, on the one hand, and human rights, equality, and justice on the other. The history of law is a search for the proper balance between these goals, and the interpretation of the legal text must express this balance. Indeed, if a statute is a tool for realizing a social objective, then interpretation of the statute must be done in a way that realizes this social objective. Moreover, the individual statute does not stand alone. It exists

---

[4] *See* Henry M. Hart, Jr., and Albert M. Sacks, *The Legal Process: Basic Problems in the Making and Application of Law* 1169 (William N. Eskridge, Jr., and Philip P. Frickey eds., 1994) ("American courts have no intelligible, generally accepted, and consistently applied theory of statutory interpretation").

[5] *See* Konrad Zweigert and Hans-Jürgen Puttfarken, "Statutory Interpretation—Civilian Style," 44 *Tul. L. Rev.* 704, 715 (1970) ("Conspicuously lacking in civil law jurisprudence is a methodology of the judicial development of the law . . . which would analyze, rationalize, and systematize the specific role of the judge in the process of finding and making law").

[6] For an excellent attempt to answer the question, see William N. Eskridge, *Dynamic Statutory Interpretation* (1984). For the current debate in the United States, see Timothy Terrell, "Statutory Epistemology: Mapping the Interpretation Debate," 53 *Emory L.J.* 523 (2004). On the comparative law of interpretation, see *Legal Interpretation in Democratic States* (Jeffrey Goldsworthy and Tom Campbell eds., 2002); *Interpreting Statutes: A Comparative Study* (D. Neil MacCormick and Robert S. Summers eds., 1991).

in the context of society, as part of general social activity. The purpose of the individual statute must therefore also be evaluated against the backdrop of the legal system. This approach underlies the system of interpretation that I think is proper: purposive interpretation.[7] Let us now turn to a discussion of that system.

PURPOSIVE INTERPRETATION

What Is Purposive Interpretation?

Purposive interpretation[8] is not a new system. Continental law has long recognized teleological interpretation, which is interpretation according to *telos*, or objective.[9] Common law systems also accept purposive interpretation,[10] although there is some uncertainty about whether the purpose is subjective, reflecting authorial intent at a high level of abstraction, or objective, or a blend of the two.[11] The purposive interpretation I discuss attempts to clarify this issue by setting out a comprehensive interpretive system.

Purposive interpretation is based, of course, on the concept of purpose. Purpose is a normative concept that the law constructs. The purpose of a given legal norm has both subjective and objective elements. The real intent of the author (the subjective purpose)

---

[7] On purposive interpretation, see Barak, *supra* p. 123, note 2.

[8] See Barak, *supra* p. 123, note 2.

[9] *See, e.g.*, Karl Larenz, *Methodenlehre der Rechtswissenschaft* (5th ed. 1983); Zweigert and Puttfarken, *supra* p. 124, note 5.

[10] *See, e.g.*, Francis Bennion, *Statutory Interpretation* 731 (3d ed. 1997); Pierre-André Côté, *The Interpretation of Legislation in Canada* 381–92 (3d ed. 2000); Rupert Cross, *Statutory Interpretation* 92 (3d ed. 1995); Eskridge, *supra* p. 18, note 43 at 24–35; Ruth Sullivan, *Dreidger on the Construction of Statutes* 35–77 (3d ed. 1994).

[11] This lack of certainty surfaced in the writings of the American realists and scholars of the legal process. *See, e.g.*, Hart and Sacks, *supra* p. 124, note 4 at 1124–25; Karl N. Llewellyn, "Remarks on the Theory of Appellate Decision and the Rules or Canons about How Statutes Are to Be Constructed," 3 *Vand. L. Rev.* 395, 395 (1950); Max Radin, "A Short Way with Statutes," 56 *Harv. L. Rev.* 388, 398–99 (1942).

is always relevant. The subjective purpose acts on different levels, for every author usually wishes to realize multiple intentions at various levels of abstraction. Objective elements also influence purpose (the objective purpose), again operating at various levels of abstraction. At a low level of abstraction, objective purpose is the hypothetical intent that a reasonable author would want to realize through the given legal text or a type of legal text. At a high level of abstraction, the objective purpose of a text is to realize the fundamental values of the legal system. The (ultimate) purpose of every text is determined by the relationship among the various subjective elements (the author's real intent) and the various objective elements (the hypothetical intent of the author or the "intent" of the legal system).

Constitutional Considerations in Purposive Interpretation

The critical question then becomes, how do we determine the proper relationship between the subjective and the objective? We will not find this answer in linguistics or general hermeneutics. The interpretation of literature or music is interesting by way of comparison, but it does not answer the question. Rather, the answer to this question depends on constitutional considerations.[12] Constitutional law is the appropriate place in which to seek an answer to the question of how to balance authorial intent with the fundamental values embedded in the legal system. However, the constitution does not necessarily give a single, unique resolution to the proper balance between objective and subjective elements. Sometimes, constitutional law leaves that resolution to the discretion of the judge;[13] indeed, proponents of purposive interpretation

---

[12] *See* Jerry Mashaw, "As If Republican Interpretation," 97 *Yale L.J.* 1685, 1686 (1988) (arguing that "[a]ny theory of statutory interpretation is at base a theory about constitutional law").

[13] *See generally* Akhil Reed Amar, "Intratextualism," 112 *Harv. L. Rev.* 747 (1999) (urging interpreters to read words and phrases in a constitution in light of identical words and phrases within the same document); Akhil Reed Amar, "The Supreme Court, 1999 Term—Foreword: The Document and the Doctrine,"

view judicial discretion as an indispensable element of any theory of interpretation. Interpretive theories vary only in the extent of judicial discretion they permit.

I will now briefly consider how purposive interpretation applies to the interpretation of constitutions and statutes. I should point out, however, that in my view, purposive interpretation applies to the interpretation of all legal texts, including contracts and wills.

PURPOSIVE INTERPRETATION OF A CONSTITUTION

What Does Purposive Interpretation of a Constitution Mean?

In interpreting a constitution,[14] as in interpreting every other legal text, a judge extracts the legal meaning along the range of the text's various semantic meanings. One should not give the constitution a meaning that its express or implied language cannot sustain. The express language conveys to the reader the dictionary meaning of the text. The implied language conveys to the reader a meaning that is not derived from the dictionary meaning of the language. It is a language written in invisible ink, between the lines, and derived from the structure of the constitution.[15] Any interpretation of the constitution must be grounded in its own language.

From among the range of semantic meanings of the constitution, the interpreter must extract the legal meaning that best realizes the purpose of the constitution. This purpose strikes the proper internal balance between subjective and objective aspects, namely,

---

114 *Harv. L. Rev.* 26 (2000) (emphasizing the importance of constitutional text). Note, however, that I do not wish to establish a two-step process, the first examining the text and the second examining "doctrine," or according to my theory, purpose. Rather, I am looking for a single step allowing for fluid movement back and forth between the doctrine and the text.

[14] *See* Jeffrey Goldsworthy and Tom Campbell, *supra* p. 124, note 6 at 173–267.

[15] *See* 1 Laurence H. Tribe, *American Constitutional Law* § 1–13 at 40–41 (3d ed. 2000). *See generally* Charles L. Black, Jr., *Structure and Relationship in Constitutional Law* (1985) (arguing that there is a close relationship between textual and structural interpretation).

between the intent of the framers of the constitution (at various levels of abstraction) and fundamental contemporary values. The judge gleans these aspects from the text of the constitution, from its history, and from precedent. Comparisons with other national systems and from international law can also assist him. It is constitutional theory, grounded in constitutional law, that determines this balance between subjective and objective purpose.[16]

The Unique Nature of a Constitution

A constitution is a unique legal document. It enshrines a special kind of norm and stands at the top of the normative pyramid. Difficult to amend, it is designed to direct human behavior for years to come. It shapes the appearance of the state and its aspirations throughout history. It determines the state's fundamental political views. It lays the foundation for its social values. It determines its commitments and orientations. It reflects the events of the past. It lays the foundation for the present. It determines how the future will look. It is philosophy, politics, society, and law all in one. The performance of all these tasks by a constitution requires a balance of its subjective and objective elements, because "it is a constitution we are expounding."[17] As Chief Justice Dickson of the Supreme Court of Canada noted:

> The task of expounding a constitution is crucially different from that of construing a statute. A statute defines present rights and obligations. It is easily enacted and as easily repealed. A constitution, by contrast, is drafted with an eye to the future. Its function is to provide a continuing framework for the legitimate exercise of governmental power and, when joined by a Bill or Charter of rights, for the unremitting protection of individual rights and liberties. Once

[16] *See* Laurence H. Tribe and Michael C. Dorf, *On Reading the Constitution* 97–117 (1991).
[17] *McCulloch v. Maryland*, 17 U.S. (4 Wheat.) 316, 407 (1819) (Marshall, C.J.).

enacted, its provisions cannot easily be repealed or amended. It must, therefore, be capable of growth and development over time to meet new social, political and historical realities often unimagined by its framers. The judiciary is the guardian of the constitution and must, in interpreting its provisions, bear these considerations in mind.[18]

How does a constitution's unique character affect its interpretation? In determining the purpose of a constitution, how does its distinctive nature affect the relationship between its subjective and objective elements? Naturally, different judges and scholars of constitutional law answer this question differently. My answer is this: one should take both the subjective and objective elements into account when determining the purpose of the constitution. The original intent of the framers at the time of drafting is important. One cannot understand the present without understanding the past. The framers' intent lends historical depth to understanding the text in a way that honors the past. The intent of the constitutional authors, however, exists alongside the fundamental views and values of modern society at the time of interpretation. The constitution is intended to solve the problems of the contemporary person, to protect his freedom. It must contend with his needs. Therefore, in determining the constitution's purpose through interpretation, one must also take into account the values and principles that prevail at the time of interpretation, seeking synthesis and harmony between past intention and present principle.

The key question then becomes, what is the proper relationship between the subjective and objective elements in determining the purpose of the constitution when the two elements conflict? To this question there is no "true" answer. But that does not mean that *any* interpretation is appropriate. We must construct a system to evaluate different understandings of the relationship. I accept that there is no absolute proof that one understanding is better than another. Professor Laurence Tribe rightly points out that there are no criteria external to the constitution that determine the proper

---

[18] *Hunter v. Southam Inc.*, [1984] 2 S.C.R. 145, 156.

order of priorities among the different considerations.[19] That does not mean, however, that we cannot construct constitutional arguments showing that one understanding is preferable to another. These arguments may not be based on a "true" revelation that allows no alternative, but they nevertheless help us to arrive at a proper meaning.

The Interpretation of the Constitution in Light of Its Uniqueness

We return, then, to the original question: What is the proper (as opposed to "true") relationship between the subjective and objective elements in determining the purpose of the constitution when the subjective and the objective pull in different directions? In my opinion, greater weight should be accorded to the objective purposes. This is particularly true for constitutions like that of the United States, which are very difficult to amend and change, and for which a long time has passed between the creation of the constitution and its interpretation. Only by giving preference to the objective elements can the constitution fulfill its purpose. Only thus is it possible to guide human behavior over generations of social change. Only thus is it possible to balance among the past, present, and future. Only thus can the constitution provide answers to modern needs. Admittedly, the past influences the present, but it does not determine it. The past guides the present, but it does not enslave it. Fundamental social views, derived from the past and woven into social and legal history, find their modern expression in the old constitutional text. Justice Brennan expressed this idea well in the following remarks:

> We current Justices read the Constitution in the only way that we can: as Twentieth Century Americans. We look to the history of the time of framing and to the intervening history of interpretation. But the ultimate question must be, what do the words of the text mean in our time?

[19] See 1 Tribe, *supra* p. 35, note 57, § 1–18 at 89. *See also* Philip Bobbitt, *Constitutional Interpretation* 179 (1991).

For the genius of the Constitution rests not in any static meaning it might have had in a world that is dead and gone, but in the adaptability of its great principles to cope with current problems and current needs. What the constitutional fundamentals meant to the wisdom of other times cannot be their measure to the vision of our time. Similarly, what those fundamentals mean for us, our descendants will learn, cannot be their measure to the vision of their time.[20]

The same idea was advanced by Justice Michael Kirby of the High Court of Australia, who said that "[o]ur *Constitution* belongs to the 21st century, not to the 19th."[21]

Various courts have issued opinions in the same spirit, including the Canadian Supreme Court[22] and the German Constitutional Court.[23] This is the purposive interpretation that I espouse. It does not ignore the subjective purpose in constitutional interpretation, but it does not give it controlling precedence either. The weight of the subjective purpose decreases as the constitution becomes older and more difficult to change. In interpreting such constitutions, preference should be given to the objective purpose that reflects deeply held modern views in the movement of the legal system through history. The constitution thus becomes a living norm and not a fossil, preventing the enslavement of the present to the past.

[20] William J. Brennan, Jr., "Constructing the Constitution," 19 *U.C. Davis L. Rev.* 2, 7 (1985).

[21] Michael Kirby, "Constitutional Interpretation and Original Intent: A Form of Ancestor Worship?" 24 *Melb. U. L. Rev.* 1, 14 (2000).

[22] *See* in *Re B.C. Motor Vehicle Act* [1985] 2 S.C.R., 504: "If the newly planted 'living tree' which is the *Charter* is to have the possibility of growth and adjustment over time, care must be taken to ensure that historical materials do not stunt its growth" (Lamer, J.); Hogg, *supra* p. 82, note 145 at 1393–94.

[23] See the Life Imprisonment Case, (1977) 45 BVerfGE187: "Neither original history nor the ideas and intentions of the framers are of decisive importance in interpreting particular provisions of the Basic Law. Since the adoption of the Basic Law, our understanding of the content, function, and effect of basic rights has deepened. Additionally, the medical, psychological, and sociological effects of life imprisonment have become better known. Current attitudes are important in assessing the constitutionality of life imprisonment. New insights can influence and even change the evaluation of this punishment in terms of human dignity and the principles of a constitutional state." *See* Kommers, *supra* p. 22, note 9 at 307.

Indeed, constitutional interpretation is a process by which each generation expresses its fundamental views, as they have been formed against the background of its past. The interpreter honors the past through his desire to maintain a link with it. Nonetheless, the ultimate purpose is modern. A very clear expression of this approach was offered by Justice Deane of the Australian High Court. He was asking himself if the Australian Constitution, being silent on the subject of a bill of rights, could be construed to include implied human rights. It had been noted that there was no evidence that the framers of the Australian Constitution intended to preclude the implication of constitutional rights by drafting the constitution without a bill of rights. Here is what Justice Deane observed:

> [E]ven if it could be established that it was the unexpressed intention of the framers of the Constitution that the failure to follow the United States model should preclude or impede the implication of constitutional rights, their intention in that regard would be simply irrelevant to the construction of provisions whose legitimacy lay in their acceptance by the people. Moreover, to construe the Constitution on the basis that the dead hands of those who framed it reached from their graves to negate or constrict the natural implications of its express provisions or fundamental doctrines would deprive what was intended to be a living instrument of its vitality and adaptability to serve succeeding generations.[24]

Some argue that giving a modern meaning to the language of the constitution is inconsistent with regarding the constitution as a source of protection of the individual from society.[25] Under this approach, if the constitution is interpreted in accordance with modern views, it will reflect the views of the majority to the detriment of the minority. My reply to this claim is, *inter alia*, that a modern conception of human rights is not simply the current

---

[24] *Theophenous v. Herald Weekly Time Ltd.*, (1995) 182 CLR 104, 106.
[25] *See generally* Antonin Scalia, "Originalism: The Lesser Evil," 57 *U. Cin. L. Rev.* 849, 862–63 (1989).

majority's conception of human rights. The objective purpose refers to fundamental values that reflect the deeply held beliefs of modern society, not passing trends. These beliefs are not the results of public opinion polls or mere populism; they are fundamental beliefs that have passed the test of time, changing their form but not their substance.[26]

The American Dilemma

The interpretation of the Constitution is a central issue in United States constitutional law, with a vast literature on the subject.[27] The justices of the United States Supreme Court are divided on how to approach this task.[28] Some justices give precedence to the subjective element (intentionalism, framers' intent), while others oppose privileging the subjective element. Among these opponents, some wish to give the Constitution a meaning that does not necessarily accord with the will of its authors, but rather reflects the understanding at the time the Constitution was written (originalism). Others emphasize contemporary objective elements. This split in American constitutional viewpoints is regrettable. Why can some enlightened democratic legal systems (such as those of Canada, Australia, and Germany) extricate themselves from the heavy hands of intentionalism and originalism in interpreting the constitution, while constitutional law in the United States remains mired in these difficulties?[29]

---

[26] See supra p. 58.

[27] See, e.g., 1 Tribe, supra p. 35, note 57, § 1–11, at 30–32.

[28] See W. Va. Univ. Hosps. Inc. v. Casey , 499 U.S. 83, 112 (1991) (Stevens, J., dissenting) (noting that the Court vacillates between a "purely literal approach" and one that "seeks guidance from historical context"). See also Dorf, supra p. 16, note 39 at 14–26 (1998) (discussing the Court's struggle between textualism and purposivism).

[29] See Claire L'Heureux-Dubé, "The Importance of Dialogue: Globalization, The Rehnquist Court, and Human Rights in," The Rehnquist Court: A Retrospective 234 (Martin H. Belsky ed., 2002) at 242:

> [T]here is generally less debate . . . over whether the intent of the framers of a constitution is what should govern its interpretation. Originalism, an

Constitutional Interpretation and Fundamental Principles

A constitution is a text that shapes the character of the state. What underlies the constitution is the will of the people. But the will of the people underlying the constitution is different from the will of the people underlying ordinary legislation.[30] The former is the deeply held view that justifies the constitutional nature of the democracy. This view establishes the branches of the state and expresses the fundamental values and principles of the people. Foremost among these values and principles are human rights. These elements of the constitutional structure act as a basis for judicial review of the constitutionality of statutes. The values and principles underlying the constitution are also the basis for constitutional interpretation, in which the judge must give expression to the constitution's fundamental values.[31] They form a normative umbrella that extends over the constitution itself. The constitution does not operate in a normative vacuum; outside and around the

---

extremely controversial question in the United States, is usually simply not the focus, or even a topic, of debate elsewhere. Not that there are not heated differences of opinion about "judicial activism" or whether judging can be merely the interpretation of words on a page, but this is for the most part not as focused on textualism and originalism as that in the United States. . . . In Canada, there are few judges or commentators who would dispute the notion that the rights and other provisions in our Constitution should be interpreted "as a living tree capable of growth and expansion within its natural limits" in the words of Lord Sankey in a 1930 Privy Council case from Canada about whether the term "persons" in our Constitution included women. (*Id.* [citations omitted]).

The judgment referred to above is *Edwards v. A.G. Canada*, [1930] A.C. 114, 136, in which Lord Sankey decided that women were "persons," even if the intention of the framers did not include women.

[30] For a discussion of this point, see generally Bruce Ackerman, "Constitutional Politics/Constitutional Law," 99 *Yale L.J.* 453 (1989).

[31] *See* Robert C. Post, *Constitutional Domains: Democracy, Community, Management* 24–26 (1995).

constitution there are values and principles that the constitution must realize.[32]

These values are not the personal values of the judge. They are the national values of the state: "It is a well-known axiom that the law of a people must be studied in the light of its national way of life."[33] The "national way of life" constitutes a source for the values and principles that the constitution ought to realize. These principles and values reflect the social consensus that underlies the legal system. They enshrine fundamental social outlooks. They are derived in part from the constitutional text and its history. They are derived in part from the historical experience of the people, their social and religious views, and their tradition and heritage.[34] Naturally, not all the values and principles constituting the normative umbrella over the constitution are mentioned (expressly or even implicitly) in the constitution. If they are not mentioned, they should not be forced into the constitution artificially. Nonetheless, these unmentioned values and principles constitute a point of reference for understanding the values and principles that *are* mentioned in the constitution. Only with the help of these unmentioned values and principles can the constitution realize its purpose.

Purposive interpretation of the constitution is based on the status of the judge as an interpreter of the constitution. A judge who interprets the constitution is a partner to the authors of the constitution. The authors establish the text; the judge determines its meaning. The authors formulate a will that they wish to realize; the judge locates this will within the larger picture of the constitution's role in modern life. The judge must ensure the continuity of the constitution. He must strike a balance between the will of the authors of the constitution and the fundamental values of those living under it.

---

[32] *See generally* Thomas C. Grey, "Do We Have an Unwritten Constitution?" 27 *Stan. L. Rev.* 703 (1975).

[33] H.C. 73/53, *"Kol Ha'am" Co. Ltd. v. Minister of Interior*, 7 P.D. 871, 874 (Agranat, J.) (English translation available at www.court.gov.il).

[34] *See generally* Terrance Sandalow, "Constitutional Interpretation," 79 *Mich. L. Rev.* 1033 (1981).

PURPOSIVE INTERPRETATION OF STATUTES

The Purpose of a Statute

Purposive interpretation applies not only to the interpretation of constitutions but also to the interpretation of all other legal texts, including statutes.[35] Every statute has a purpose, without which it is meaningless. This purpose, or *ratio legis*, is made up of the objectives, the goals, the interests, the values, the policy, and the function that the statute is designed to actualize. It comprises both subjective and objective elements. The judge must give the statute's language the meaning that best realizes its purpose.

The Subjective Purpose

The subjective purpose reflects the actual intention of the legislature, in contrast to the intention of the *reasonable* legislature, which forms a part of the objective purpose. The subjective purpose is not the interpretive intention of the legislature.[36] The subjective purpose

---

[35] *See* Barak, *supra* p. 123, note 2.
[36] For a description of "interpretive" intention, "concrete" intention, or "result-oriented" intention, see Ronald Dworkin, *A Matter of Principle* 48–50, 52–55 (1985); Ronald Dworkin, "Comment," in Scalia, *supra* p. 18, note 41 at 116–17. *See also* H.C. 547/84, *Off HaEmek Registered Agric. Coop. Ass'n v. Ramat-Yishai Local Council,* 40(1) P.D. 113, 143–44 (Isr.) ("The judge does not look to the legislative history for a concrete answer to the practical problem that he must decide. The court is not interested in the specific scenarios and concrete examples that the legislator considered. We seek the purpose of the legislation in the legislative history. We seek the interests and purposes that, after compromising and balancing among them, lead to the policy underlying the norm we must interpret. We seek the principled viewpoint, not the individual application. We seek the abstract, the principle, the policy, and the objective. We are interested in the legislator's conception of the purpose of the law, and not in his conception of the solution to a specific dispute that is to be decided by the court" (citations omitted).

consists of the policies the legislature sought to actualize. This aspect of purpose deals with the legislature's "real" intention, which all credible sources, internal and external, help reveal.[37]

The Objective Purpose

Subjective purpose is not the only purpose relevant to statutory interpretation, especially in situations where we lack information about that purpose. Even when we do have such information, it does not always help us in the interpretive task. Moreover, even when we do find useful information about the subjective purpose, we must keep in mind that focusing on legislative intent alone fails to regard the statute as a living organism in a changing environment. It is insensitive to the existence of the system in which the statute operates. It is not capable of integrating the individual statute into the framework of the whole legal system. It makes it difficult to bridge the gap between law and society. Thus, it does not allow the meaning of the statute to be developed as the legal system develops. Rather, it freezes the meaning of the statute at the historical moment of its legislation, which may no longer be

[37] Many scholars have argued that a multimember body like a legislature has no identifiable intention. For example, Jeremy Waldron points out that, although each member of the legislature has a will, this fact does not imply the existence of a similar will behind the product of the collective body. The collective body only creates the statute itself. Because the legislators' shared views and sense of common purpose do not exist beyond the meanings embodied in a statutory text, interpreters must recognize the primacy of the language of the statute. *See* Jeremy Waldron, "Legislators' Intentions and Unintentional Legislation," in *Law and Interpretation: Essays in Legal Philosophy* 353 (Andrei Marmor ed., 1995). Indeed, I accept that a collective body such as a legislature does not have a will in the same sense that an individual does. Instead of the will of any given individual, one should consider the purposes, social changes, and goals upon which the members of the legislature agreed. Such agreement does exist and can be identified, although it is not a part of the statute. Instead, it serves as a criterion for understanding the statute. Similarly, although the intention of a testator is also not part of his will, no one seriously argues that a will should not be interpreted according to the intention of the testator. Justice Breyer has rightly stated that even though the dictionary is not part of the statute, judges may certainly use it to interpret statutory language. *See* Stephen Breyer, "On the Uses of Legislative History in Interpreting Statutes," 65 *S. Cal. L. Rev.* 845, 863 (1992).

relevant to the meaning of the statute in a modern democracy. If a judge relies too much on legislative intent, the statute ceases to fulfill its objective. As a result, the judge becomes merely a historian and an archaeologist[38] and cannot fulfill his role as a judge. Instead of looking forward, the judge looks backward. The judge becomes sterile and frozen, creating stagnation instead of progress.[39] Instead of acting in partnership with the legislative branch, the judge becomes subordinate to a historical legislature. This subservience does not accord with the role of the judge in a democracy.

The objective purpose of the statute means the interests, values, objectives, policy, and functions that the law should realize in a democracy. Objective criteria at the time of interpretation determine the objective purpose. The objective purpose is not a guess or conjecture about the original intent of the legislature; in fact, sometimes it is the opposite, because the objective purpose applies even when it is clear that the legislature could not possibly have intended such a purpose. Therefore, the objective purpose does not necessarily reflect the real intent of the legislature. It is not an expression of a psychological-historical reality. At low levels of abstraction, objective purpose reflects the intent the legislature would have had if it had thought about the matter, or the intent of a reasonable legislature.[40] At a higher level of abstraction, it reflects the purpose that should be attributed to a statute of that nature. From the nature of the matter regulated by the statute, we can learn of its objective purpose. The nature of the "legal institution"— for example, sale, lien, agency, licensing regime—indicates its purpose. Finally, at the highest level of abstraction, the objective purpose of the statute is to realize the fundamental values of democracy.

---

[38] *See* T. Alexander Aleinikoff, "Updating Statutory Interpretation," 87 *Mich. L. Rev.* 20, 21 (1988) (discussing the "archaeological" approach to statutory interpretation).

[39] *See* Eskridge, *supra* p. 18, note 43.

[40] *See* Stephen Breyer, "Our Democratic Constitution," 77 *N.Y.U. L. Rev.* 245, 266 (2002); Stephen Breyer, *Active Liberty: Interpreting Our Democratic Constitution* 87 (2005).

This purpose is not unique to one statute or another; it applies to all statutes, constituting a kind of normative umbrella that extends over all legislation.

The judge can learn the objective purpose of the statute first and foremost from its language. From the subject regulated by the statute and from the nature of the arrangement, by exercising common sense the judge can further grasp the objective purpose underlying the statute. An interpreter may derive the objective purpose of a statute not only from the statute itself but also from closely related statutes addressing the same issue (*in pari materia*). Moreover, the whole body of legislation provides information about the objective purpose of the statute. The individual statute becomes part of a body of legislation, thereby creating a reciprocal relationship, with the statute and the body influencing one another. As I expressed in one of my judgments:

> [A] piece of legislation does not stand on its own. It constitutes a part of the legislative body. It integrates into it, with the objective of legislative harmony. . . . [W]hoever interprets one statute interprets legislation as a whole. The isolated statute is related to the body of legislation by a system of interconnected vessels. The whole body of legislation influences the purpose of the individual statute. An earlier statute influences the purpose of a later statute. A later statute influences the purpose of an earlier statute.[41]

Moreover, a statute's social and historical background influences its purpose. Social needs drove the creation of the statute; therefore, it is relevant to consider them. Also relevant are the social and cultural premises upon which the statute was based. The operative legal theory[42] of the system and its legal culture influence the process by which judges determine the purpose of every statute.[43] This theory serves as a well from which statutes draw their strength; it shapes common legal experience. Indeed, as every statute is

---

[41] H.C. 693/91, *Efrat v. Dir. of Population Register*, 47(1) P.D. 749, 765–66.
[42] *See supra* p. 115.
[43] *See* Felix Frankfurter, "Some Reflections on the Reading of Statutes," 47 *Colum. L. Rev.* 527, 533, 537, 542–43 (1967).

created by a legal community, the community's fundamental views of culture, law, and operational legal theory inevitably imprint themselves on the statute's purpose. Thus, the exact same statute in different legal systems may give rise to different objective purposes.

Last, the fundamental principles of the democratic legal system constitute the "spirit" (the purpose) that encompasses the "material" (the statute). Every statute springs from the backdrop of these principles, which serve as part of the objective purpose.[44] Purposive interpretation translates these principles into presumptions about the general purpose of every statute.[45] These presumptions become part of every statute's objective purpose. They are not limited to a particular type of legislation or merely to "unclear" legislation; they apply always and immediately. They accompany the interpretive process from beginning to end. They constitute what Sunstein calls the "background norms"[46] that assist the interpreter. Purposive presumptions change the interpretative canons into presumptions. At the base of purposive presumptions lie constitutional considerations. They express constitutional assumptions about democracy (formal and substantive). They vary from legal system to legal system, and even within a given legal system, they vary over time.

Statutory Interpretation and Democracy

As in the interpretation of a constitution, the key question in the interpretation of statutes is the relationship between the subjective and the objective in determining the statute's ultimate purpose.

---

[44] See *Regina v. Sec'y of State for the Home Dep't,* ex parte *Pierson* [1998] A.C. 539, 587–88.

[45] For a discussion of this point, see Cross, *supra* p. 125, note 10; Lourens M. du Plessis, *Reinterpretation of Statutes* 148 (2002). Pierre-André Côté, *The Interpretation of Legislation in Canada* 326 (3d ed., 2000).

[46] Cass R. Sunstein, "Interpreting Statutes in the Regulatory State," 103 *Harv. L. Rev.* 405, 460 (1989). *See also* Jonathan R. Siegel, "Textualism and Contextualism in Administrative Law," 78 *B.U. L. Rev.* 1023, 1060 (1998).

Naturally, interpreters strive for synthesis and integration. The purposive interpreter does not look for conflicts; he aims for harmony. Nevertheless, conflicts and inconsistencies among the various purposes exist. How are they to be resolved? What I said with regard to the interpretation of constitutions[47] also applies to statutes. The interpreter resolves the subjective purpose (the intention of the legislature) and the objective purpose (the "intention" of the system) on the basis of constitutional criteria, of which the central one is democracy. As we have seen,[48] we must distinguish between formal democracy and substantive democracy. Formal democracy in this context means the rule of the people through their representatives in the legislature, from which the principle of legislative supremacy arises. Substantive democracy in this context means the separation of powers, the rule of law, independence of the judiciary, fundamental principles, and human rights. From this rich concept of democracy, what can we deduce about statutory interpretation? In my opinion, we can derive two conclusions.

First, in interpreting statutes, the judge must attach considerable weight to the subjective purpose that underlies the statute. In this way the judge gives effect to legislative supremacy,[49] thereby recognizing that the legislature does not enact statutes merely for the sake of legislation. Indeed, through legislation, the legislature determines social policy, allocates national resources, and orders national priorities. A statute is a tool for realizing these goals. The legislature does not produce a statute unless it wants to achieve a particular social goal. Legislative supremacy requires that the interpreter give effect to the (abstract) intention of the legislature. Indeed, where the judge has reliable information about the abstract

---

[47] *See supra* p. 127.

[48] *See supra* p. 24.

[49] For various arguments regarding statutory interpretation and legislative supremacy, see Eskridge, *supra* p. 32, note 46 at 319 (1989); Daniel A. Farber, "Statutory Interpretation and Legislative Supremacy," 78 *Geo. L.J.* 281 (1989); Earl M. Maltz, "Rhetoric and Reality in the Theory of Statutory Interpretation: Underenforcement, Overenforcement, and the Problem of Legislative Supremacy," 71 *B.U. L. Rev.* 767 (1991).

intention of the legislature, and this intention is relevant to solving the questions that the judge faces, the judge should give weight to the subjective purpose in interpreting the legislation.

Second, in interpreting a statute, the judge should attach significant weight to its objective purpose. There is no democracy without a recognition of the values and principles that shape it. Just as the supremacy of fundamental values, principles, and human rights justifies judicial review of the constitutionality of statutes, so too must that supremacy assert itself in statutory interpretation. The judge must reflect these fundamental values in the interpretation of legislation. The judge should not narrow interpretation to the exclusive search for subjective legislative intent. He must also consider the "intention" of the legal system, for the statute is always wiser than the legislature.[50] By doing so the judge gives the statute a dynamic meaning and thus bridges the gap between law and society.

Subjective versus Objective

So we return to the original question: What is the proper relationship between abstract subjective purpose and objective purpose in the interpretation of statutes? In this regard, do we assume that the judge faces a clear and reliable subjective purpose and that it conflicts with the objective purpose? The reply of purposive interpretation is that one cannot view all statutes monolithically. Purposive interpretation distinguishes among different types of statutes. The age of the statute influences the relationship between the different purposes it contains. The older the statute, the greater the weight the judge should attach to its objective purpose. Conversely, the

---

[50] *See* Gustav Radbruch, "Legal Philosophy," in *The Legal Philosophies of Lask, Radbruch and Dabin* 47, 141–42 (1950) ("The interpreter may understand the law better than its creators understood it. The law may be wiser than its authors—indeed, it must be wiser than its authors").

younger the statute, the greater the weight the judge should attach to its (abstract) subjective purpose. As Francis Bennion rightly points out:

> Each generation lives under the law it inherits. Constant formal updating is not practicable, so an Act takes on a life of its own. What the original framers intended sinks gradually into history. While their language may endure as law, its current subjects are likely to find that law more and more ill-fitting. The intention of the originators, collected from the Act's legislative history, necessarily becomes less relevant as time rolls by.[51]

Purposive interpretation also distinguishes among various statutes according to the scope of the issues they regulate. A specific statute that deals with a narrow and defined issue, for instance, cannot be compared to the codification of a broad subject. The more specific and narrow the statute, the greater the weight the judge should attach to the subjective purpose the legislature wanted to achieve. By contrast, the more general and comprehensive the statute, the greater the weight the judge should attach to its objective purpose. It is possible to describe precisely the human behavior that a more specific or narrow statute is intended to regulate. It is possible to foresee future developments more precisely and thus to regulate them. In such circumstances, the justification for referring to the intention of the legislature increases and the need to refer to the general values of the system decreases. This is not the case with a general statute that regulates a large area of human activity, such as a codification. It is harder to describe precisely the modes of human behavior such a statute is meant to regulate. It is also more difficult to foresee future developments. Naturally, this type of statute must be couched in general language that describes the social behavior regulated. In such circumstances, there is a greater need to refer to the general values of the system

---

[51] F.A.R. Bennion, *Statutory Interpretation* 687 (3d ed. 1997).

and less need to refer to legislative intent, which in any event ceases to be helpful as time passes.[52]

It is also important to distinguish between a statute based on rules and a statute based on principles or standards.[53] My approach is to give great weight to the intention of the legislature in interpreting a rule-based statute and great weight to the principles of the system in a more policy-oriented statute. The reason for this approach is that under a statute establishing rules, adjudication usually must draw a clear line between what the statute forbids and what it permits, and that distinction can be derived from legislative intent. By contrast, a statute that formulates principles or policies prescribes an ideal to be achieved. This ideal operates within the framework of the legal system, is shaped by it, and in turn influences it. Naturally, significant weight should be attached to the fundamental values of the legal system in order to shape the ideal according to the current thinking of members of society at the time of interpretation. Therefore, for a statute forbidding "unreasonable" behavior, legislative intent is of little help in defining reasonableness. The question is not what the legislature understood by the word "reasonable" at the time of the legislation. Rather, it is how do members of society to whom the provision applies understand reasonableness at the time of interpretation?

Another relevant distinction is between statutes enacted by stable democratic social regimes and statutes enacted by undemocratic regimes that nonetheless remain in force after the state's transition to democracy. For statutes enacted during the undemocratic period, little weight should be attached to the intention of the undemocratic legislature. Indeed, consideration of legislative intent in statutory interpretation is based on the need to give expression to the intent

---

[52] *See* Julian B. McDonnell, "Purposive Interpretation of the Uniform Commercial Code: Some Implications for Jurisprudence," 126 *U. Pa. L. Rev.* 795 (1978). *Cf.* Bruce W. Frier, "Interpreting Codes," 89 *Mich. L. Rev.* 2201, 2214 (1991) (arguing that codes such as the UCC become integrated into the national legal heritage over time, making general principles and clauses more salient).

[53] *See* Kathleen M. Sullivan, "The Supreme Court, 1991 Term—Foreword: The Justices of Rules and Standards," 106 *Harv. L. Rev.* 22, 57–69 (1992).

of the *democratic* legislator. When the legislator is not democratic, there is no reason to give expression to his intent. Professor David Dyzenhaus expressed this well in addressing the argument in favor of interpreting statutes enacted by the white parliament in South Africa during apartheid according to the intent of the legislature:

> [T]he legitimacy of that approach depends on a democratic theory which says that the people speak through their elected parliamentary representatives, and thus the statutes enacted by the legislature must be applied by judges so as best to approximate what those representatives actually intended. In others words, the legitimacy of an approach which requires judges to ignore in their interpretation of the law their substantive convictions about what the law should be requires a substantive commitment at a deeper level to the intrinsic legitimacy of that law. However, the Parliament whose statutes they interpreted was illegitimate by the criteria of any democratic theory and so the substantive justification for their approach was absent.[54]

Dyzenhaus notes that giving expression to legislative intent during apartheid led to results disastrous for civil liberties. Indeed, in that type of regime, one should give statutes a narrow semantic interpretation. Once the corrupt regime ends, and the statute is interpreted in the context of a democratic regime, the intent of the undemocratic legislature should be given no weight. Instead, weight should be attached to the fundamental democratic values in whose framework the old legislation now operates. An example of this interpretive principle is the interpretation of legislation enacted in Palestine during the period of the British Mandate. In a long line of cases, the Supreme Court of Israel has ruled that it should interpret this legislation in accordance with the fundamental values of the new, democratic state, and not according to the intention of the undemocratic legislature.[55]

---

[54] Dyzenhaus, *Judging the Judges, supra* p. xvi, note 28 at 166.
[55] *See, e.g.,* H.C. 680/88, *Schnitzer v. Chief Military Censor* , 42(4) P.D. 617, 628 (English translation available at www.court.gov.il); H.C. 2722/92, *Alamarin v. IDF Commander in Gaza Strip,* 46(3) P.D. 693, 705 (English translation available at www.court.gov.il).

Finally, the content of the legislative arrangement may influence the relationship between the subjective purpose and the objective purpose. For example, in criminal law, great weight may be attached—for rule-of-law reasons like the need for publicity and certainty—to the objective purpose that is evident from the express language of the statute. This language is what is seen by members of society, and the purpose that is evident from it should be given great weight.

PURPOSIVE INTERPRETATION
AND JUDICIAL DISCRETION

In both constitutional and statutory interpretation, a judge must sometimes exercise discretion in determining the proper relationship between the subjective and objective purposes of the law. Indeed, a theory of interpretation cannot be constructed without interpretive discretion as its foundation. Interpretation without judicial discretion is a myth. Any theory of interpretation—intentionalism, originalism, purposivism, and so on—must be based on an inherent internal element of interpretive discretion.[56] Discretion exists because there are laws with more than one possible interpretation.[57] In such circumstances, the judge undertakes "the sovereign prerogative of choice,"[58] bounded by the fundamental views of the

---

[56] See Barak, *supra* p. 113, note 2. *See also* Farber and Sherry, *supra* p. 91, note 169 at 155 ("[T]he grand theorists' desire to restrain judicial discretion is an impossible dream based on an unwillingness to tolerate uncertainty"); Aharon Barak, "The Role of the Supreme Court in a Democracy," 33 *Isr. L. Rev.* 1, 2–3 (1999).

[57] See Barak, *supra* p. 113, note 2 at 7; William Twining and David Miers, *How to Do Things with Rules* 179 (4th ed. 1999); *The Uses of Discretion* (K. Hawkins ed., 1992); Vila, *supra* p. xiii, note 17 at 12–13. *See generally* Jose Juan Moreso, *Legal Indeterminacy and Constitutional Interpretation* (1998) (using formal logical analysis to determine the truth-conditions of alternative interpretations of legislation).

[58] Oliver Wendell Holmes, "Law in Science and Science in Law," in *Collected Legal Papers* 210, 239 (1952).

legal community.[59] This conceptualization of the view of the legal community is, by its nature, imprecise. There are many borderline cases with no clear resolution. Still, judicial discretion is always limited, never absolute.[60] The limitations imposed on interpretive discretion are procedural and substantive. The procedural limitations guarantee the fairness of the exercise of judicial discretion. The judge must treat the parties equally. He must base his decision on the evidence presented to the court, and he must give reasons for that decision. Above all, the judge must act impartially, without appeal to personal biases or prejudices. The substantive limitations mean that the exercise of discretion must be rational, consistent, and coherent. The judge must act reasonably, taking into account the institutional constraints imposed by other parts of the legal system.

What will the judge who is aware of all these responsibilities and limitations do? Beyond the aforementioned procedural and substantive boundaries, there are no rules for exercising discretion, except that the judge must choose the solution that seems to him the best accommodation of the competing purposes he has considered.[61] Within this scope, pragmatism operates. My advice is that, at this stage of the interpretive activity, the judge should aspire to achieve justice. This means justice for the parties before the court and with regard to the whole legal system. Justice guides the entire interpretive process, for indeed, justice is one of the core values of the legal system. Within the bounds of judicial discretion, justice becomes a "residual" value that can decide hard cases. Of course, it is only natural that different judges have different conceptions of justice, for justice is a complex concept. Despite all its theoretical complexity, however, each of us has an intuitive feeling about the just solution of a dispute. This feeling must guide us at all stages of the interpretive process. It must direct our decisions in hard cases, when judicial discretion becomes our most essential tool.

[59] *See* Owen M. Fiss, "Objectivity and Interpretation," 34 *Stan. L. Rev.* 739, 744–45 (1982).
[60] *See* Benjamin N. Cardozo, *The Growth of the Law* 61 (1924).
[61] *See* Joseph Raz, *The Authority of Law* 197 (1979).

PURPOSIVE INTERPRETATION AND INTENTIONALISM
(OR SUBJECTIVE PURPOSE)

Many criticize intentionalism, claiming that a body made up of many people, such as a legislature, cannot have a will. I do not accept this criticism. In my opinion, it is sometimes possible, at a high level of abstraction, to identify the joint (subjective) intent of the members of the legislature.[62] My criticism of intentionalism is different. It focuses on the following three issues:[63]

First, most of the intentionalist methods are not truly subjective. Their rhetoric focuses on the intent of the legislator, but their methodology does not reflect this intent; it reflects the estimated and hypothetical intent of the reasonable author. In my view, when considering the intent of the author, the consideration should be of the "true" intent of the author and not of the estimated intent of the reasonable author.

Second, intentionalism is not capable of providing solutions for all the interpretive problems that confront us. In many cases it is not possible to know what the author's intent was. At times the author's intent cannot solve the interpretive problem. In these and other situations, a subjective standard is not sufficient for the completion of the interpretive process. An additional standard is needed, one that intentionalism does not provide.

Third, and most important, focusing on the intent of the author does not treat the interpreted text as a creation living in a changing environment. Intentionalism is insensitive to the existence of the system in which the text operates. It is incapable of integrating the individual text into the legal system as a whole. It does not allow the meaning of the text to develop along with the development of the legal system. It freezes the meaning of the text at the historic moment of its creation, a meaning that at times is no longer relevant to its meaning in a modern democratic society. The text in this

---

[62] See Barak, *supra* p. 123, note 2 at 132.
[63] *Id.* at 265.

situation has stopped fulfilling its purpose. The judge turns into a historian and an archeologist, and does not fulfill his role in society as a bridge builder between law and life. Instead of looking ahead, he looks backward. The judge becomes sterile and frozen. Instead of being dynamic, all is static. The text provides solutions for the problems of the past. The judge is incapable of confronting the problems of the future. The judge no longer confronts the need to bridge between law and life. A distance is created between the judge and the fundamental values of the system and its principles. Instead of a partnership between author and judge there is a judicial subordination to the historic author. This subordination does not fit the role of a judge in a democratic society.

PURPOSIVE INTERPRETATION AND OLD TEXTUALISM

There is not only one method of objective interpretation. There are a number of methods of objective interpretation. They all share the focus on the understanding of the reasonable reader, not on the intent of the text's author. Some call this common denominator by the unfortunate name—for we are all restricted by the text—of textualism. Within textualism, there are two different views, "old" and "new."

The first method, which in the American literature is called old textualism and is used primarily in the interpretation of statutes, focuses on the intent of the reasonable author as clearly expressed in the language of the text itself (the plain meaning rule, or the literal rule). Only when the language of the text is unclear or when the clear language leads to an absurd result may one go beyond the boundaries of the text to discover the intent of the reasonable author (the golden rule). This textual approach is based on a two-stage process of interpretation. During the first stage, the judge-interpreter must determine whether the text is clear and the result not absurd. If the answer to this question is positive, the first stage is also the last. If the answer is negative, the interpreter advances to the second stage.

My criticism of this interpretative approach is as follows.[64] First, why does it ignore the true intent of the author, even when there is certain and reliable evidence of it? If the desire of the reasonable author is decisive, why is the true intent of the author not considered, even when it is reliably determinable?

Second, old textualism is based on a differentiation between clear and unclear text. This differentiation is incorrect. Text becomes clear only at the end of the interpretive process. As long as the purpose of the text has not been realized, the text is unclear. The clarity old textualism embraces is "initial" clarity, the result of a linguistic "feeling." But this feeling must be tested and examined against the background of the totality of data regarding the author's intent. There are no words that are, by themselves, "clear." Indeed, nothing is less clear than the determination that words are "clear." The meaning of a statute is not clear as long as it does not sit well with the clear statutory purpose. The feeling of clarity that arises at the first reading of the statute is only initial and momentary. It fades away as it becomes clear that this "clear" meaning does not fulfill the purpose of the statute. Indeed, old textualism is based on the incorrect view of linguistics and jurisprudence by which the text can be clear without examining its context. Judge Learned Hand was right in saying, "There is no surer way to misread any document than to read it literally."[65]

Third, old textualism claims security and certainty, but security and certainty are beyond it. The decision of whether the text is clear or not is made on the basis of feeling. Each judge has his own feeling. Security and certainty are not attained. The same applies to the question of whether the clear text leads to an absurd result. What one judge sees as absurd, another sees as a reasonable result. How can it be determined whether an interpretation leads to an absurd result if it is not examined against the background of the purpose that the text is intended to fulfill? Moreover, when the judge is permitted to go beyond the boundaries of the text, where

[64] *Id.* at 325.
[65] *See Guiseppi v. Walling*, 144 F. 2d 608, 624 (2nd Cir. 1944).

shall he turn? Old textualism, by concentrating on the clear language of the text, refrains from developing clear rules regarding the sources to which the judge is permitted to turn. May the judge turn to the history of the text? Is the judge permitted to turn to the fundamental values of the system? Indeed, old textualism does not lead to security and certainty. For law it substitutes emotion; for the true intent of the author it substitutes the intent of the interpreter. The judge wears the rhetorical garb of authorial intent. Beneath this rhetoric there often hides the intent of the judge. It seems that out of a desire for self-defense against criticism, the judge betrays his inner truth.

Fourth, the result of old textualism is encouragement of judicial shallowness and avoidance of an attempt to understand the depth of the text. The following words of Zander are sharp, but they have some truth to them:

> A final criticism of the literal approach to interpretation is that it is defeatist and lazy. The judge gives up the attempt to understand the document at the first attempt. Instead of struggling to discover what it means, he simply adopts the most straightforward interpretation of the words in question—without regard to whether this interpretation makes sense in the particular context. It is not that the literal approach necessarily gives the wrong result but rather that the result is purely accidental. It is the intellectual equivalent of deciding the case by tossing a coin. The literal *interpretation* in a particular case may in fact be the best and wisest of the various alternatives, but the literal *approach* is always wrong because it amounts to an abdication of responsibility by the judge. Instead of decisions being based on reason and principle, the literalist bases his decision on one meaning arbitrarily preferred.[66]

The judge in this situation has washed his hands clean. The judge has succeeded in avoiding judicial responsibility. The judge has found a fitting substitute for tossing a coin.

---

[66] *See* Michael Zander, *The Law-Making Process* 125 (5th ed. 1999).

PURPOSIVE INTERPRETATION AND NEW TEXTUALISM

The second textualist method—for some reason called new textualism—is a textual-objective method.[67] This method was developed in the United States for the interpretation of the Constitution and of statutes. It is not used in the interpretation of private law texts. This method proposes that the text should be understood according to a reasonable reader's reading at the time of its authorship (originalism).[68] In order to attain such understanding, it is permissible to view the language of the text as a whole. One may also turn to linguistic aids in order to gain knowledge of the way the text's language was understood at the time of its authorship. One may also make use of the various interpretative maxims, such as *expression unius est exclusion alterius* (expression of the one is the exclusion of another), since they indicate the way that a reasonable reader would have understood the text at the time of its authorship. In addition, one may turn to other statutes enacted by the same legislature to discover its use of similar wording. Neither statutory history nor fundamental values of the system may be turned to. This method is characterized by the view that the goal of interpretation is not to discover legislative intent. The question is not what the legislature intended; the question is what the legislature said. Justice Antonin Scalia wrote:

> It is the *law* that governs, not the intent of the lawgiver . . . the objective indication of the words, rather than the intent of the legislature, is what constitutes the law . . . I object to the use of legislative history on principle, since I reject intent of the legislature as the proper criterion of the law.[69]

New textualism's advantage over old textualism is that new textualism tells the truth. Its rhetoric and its practice are identical. This is, in my opinion, the only advantage of this interpretive method.[70]

[67] *See* Barak, *supra* p. 123, note 2 at 331.
[68] *See* Antonin Scalia, *A Matter of Interpretation: Federal Courts and the Law* (1997).
[69] *Id.* at 17, 29, 31.
[70] For criticism of this method see Barak, *supra* p. 123, note 2 at 335.

Indeed, to the extent that this method is based on the view that it is utterly impossible to discover the real intent of the legislature, it is wrong. Even though it is impossible to discover the true intent of the legislature in all cases, it would be incorrect to say that it is always impossible to discover it. To the extent that this interpretive method is based on the view that the intent of the legislature is irrelevant and that its consideration contradicts democracy, my opinion is that giving text meaning according to the intent of the legislature sits perfectly well with formal democracy's value regarding the legislature's exclusive realm of authority. It is indeed the ignoring of legislative intent that contradicts formal democracy. Indeed, new textualism's attitude toward the legislature's decree as a decision void of intent contradicts formal democracy. When the legislature passes a new statute, it attempts to realize policy. This policy is to be considered in the interpretation of that law. Furthermore, new textualism's ignoring of the fundamental values of the system contradicts substantive democracy. The textual interpretation detaches the statute from the fundamental values of society as a whole, and specifically from human rights. Moreover, new textualism does not fulfill the judicial role. The interpretation of the statute is no longer a device for bridging the gap between law and life; the judge no longer fulfills his role in the protection of democracy. Instead, the judge focuses on the language and on the reader's understanding at the time the law was passed. Thus, the judge increases judicial discretion and the lack of certainty and security in the law.

New textualism does not sit well with the idea of democracy. No aspect of democracy justifies it. True, formal democracy claims that the legislature, and not the intent of the legislature or the intent of the system, created the statute. But the judge who considers the intent of the legislature or the intent of the system doesn't claim that they are the legislative text. One must differentiate between the text—which was enacted by the legislature—and the standard for its understanding. As for substantive democracy, it surely doesn't sit well with new textualism, which does not consider the fundamental values of the system at the time of interpretation. Nor is it called for by the principle of separation of powers. This principle recognizes the judge's authority to interpret the law. This interpretation is based on a partnership, in the framework of which it is possible to recognize the need to examine both the intent of the legislature and the intent of the system.

As shown, new textualism is not an appropriate interpretive method. However, it is likely to provide the basis for an appropriate interpretive method. New textualism's view of the text as the basis for interpretation is appropriate. A statute preventing a vehicle from entering a park cannot be interpreted as preventing an elephant from entering a park. Language restricts the interpretation. The negative attitude toward legislative intent has positive aspects. At times, one cannot know what that intent is; at times there are no reliable data regarding that intent; at times no weight is to be given to that intent. New textualism's consideration of all legislation as a source for understanding a single statute is to be encouraged. However, for new textualism to become an appropriate interpretive method, the interpreter's horizons must be widened. The context of the statute, which new textualism considers important, should be not only other statutes but also principles, values, and the fundamental views of society, not only as they were on the day of its enactment but also as they are on the day of its interpretation. If these and other corrections are made, new textualism will be able to become an appropriate interpretive method. If that should happen, however, it will no longer be new textualism; it will be purposive interpretation.

CHAPTER SIX

The Development of the Common Law

THE COMMON LAW AS JUDGE-MADE LAW

Judges not only interpret statutes created by the legislature, they also create law. This applies to all legal systems. There is no judging without creation of law. It is most strongly manifested in common law systems. The common law is judge-made law. It has been created by judges for hundreds of years. "The history of the common law is a history of continuous, gradual development over a period of many centuries."[1] The common law may develop and provide new solutions to new problems without the need for any legislative authorization. A judge's power to create the common law is inherent to a common law legal system. English judges have done so for almost a thousand years; that is what judges do in the United States, Canada, Australia, India, Israel, and the other common law countries.

The "classic" common law operates where there is no legislation.[2] It provides case law to govern matters that have not been regulated

---

[1] Goff, "Judge, Jurist and Legislature," *The Denning L.J.* 79,80 (1987).
[2] On the nature of the common law, see Oliver Wendell Holmes, *The Common Law* (1881); Karl Llewellyn, *The Common Law Tradition: Deciding Appeals* (1960); Frederick Pollock, *The Genius of the Common Law* (1912); M.A. Eisenberg, *The Nature of the Common Law* (1988); Brian Simpson, "The Common Law and Legal Theory," in *Oxford Essays in Jurisprudence* (2d ser.) 77 (B. Simpson ed., 1973); Gerald Postema, "Philosophy of the Common Law," in *The Oxford Handbook of Jurisprudence and Philosophy of Law* 588 (Jules Coleman and Scott Shapiro eds, 2002). On the history of the common law, see S.F.C. Milson, *Historical Foundations of the Common Law* (2d ed., 1981); S.F.C. Milson, *Studies in the History of the Common Law* (1985); Brian Simpson, *Legal Theory and Legal History: Essay in the Common Law* (1987).

through legislation. As the amount of legislation increases—and it is increasing in every common law country[3]—the role of the classic common law diminishes and becomes limited to the areas that have not yet been covered by legislation.[4] Judicial creation has not, however, decreased. One reason is that the legislative text is sometimes very general, providing little guidance for the judge who interprets it. Expansive judicial case law hangs on a narrow legislative hook. As a matter of dogma, judges interpret the statute. As a matter of practice, they develop the common law within the framework of the statute. This phenomenon exists whenever a statute uses value-laden phrases (such as justice and morality) and open-ended phrases (reasonableness, good faith, public policy). In these cases, judicial activity is interpretive, but in light of the absence of legislative guidance, it approaches the "classic" judicial activity.

Judge-made law is often called "judicial legislation."[5] This is not an apt phrase. It is sometimes substituted by "judicial lawmaking," which is better. "Judicial legislation" is inappropriate because the term legislation is closely related to the way in which the legislature creates law, which is distinct from the way judges create law. Despite its drawbacks, this phrase has caught on, and it is difficult to supplant it. It is therefore appropriate to clarify and reiterate that a judge is not authorized to enact statutes and that judicial legislation means creating law (legislation) by judges, either through the common law or through interpreting written law such as a constitution, statute, or regulation. The legislation within the phrase "judicial legislation" therefore refers to the functional aspect, not the institutional aspect.

---

[3] Francis Bennion calls these statutes "common law statutes." *See* Francis Bennion, *Understanding Common Law Legislation: Drafting and Interpreting* (2001).

[4] *Southern Pacific Co. v. Jensen*, 244 U.S. 205, 221 (1917) ("I recognize without hesitation that judges do and must legislate, but they can do so only interstitially; they are confined from molar to molecular motions"). On the relation between common law and legislation, see Roscoe Pound, "Common Law and Legislation," 21 *Har. L. Rev.* 383 (1908); Patrick Atiyah, "Common Law and Statute Law," 48 *Mod. L. Rev.* 1 (1985); T.R.S. Allan, *Law, Liberty, and Justice* 79 (1993); William Gummow, *Changes and Continuity: Statute, Equity, and Federalism* 1 (1999).

[5] Guido Calabresi, *A Common Law for the Age of Statutes* (1982).

JUDICIAL LAWMAKING

Much has been written about judicial lawmaking within the context of the common law. This creation is grounded in the facts of the case. Judges identify the facts and generalize from them to provide a normative resolution to the dispute before them. Law is extracted from among the facts. The thought process at this stage is inductive. Through judicial lawmaking, an issue of fact becomes an issue of law. When a new case arises that shares similar facts with previous cases, the generality decided in the past will be used. At this stage, we use both induction and deduction. The previous law will only be applied if the facts are similar. What, then, are similar facts? At what level of abstraction are they determined? To take a well-known case,[6] a woman acquires a bottle of beer. She drinks from it. As she is drinking, to her amazement, she discovers a snail inside the beer. She suffers from shock. She incurs damage. The court imposes liability on the beer manufacturer. What general rule may be extrapolated from this case? Certainly, it is not limited to women drinking beer. But does liability attach if the victim received the beer as a present? Does liability attach if, prior to consuming the product, the victim could have seen that there was a snail in the bottle? Who bears liability? Is it the manufacturers of the damaged product? Or, perhaps, is the general rule more abstract, applying to anyone who creates a risk, where it is foreseeable that his negligence would cause damage? What kind of damage creates liability? There are no rigid rules on this issue. Indeed, the law is extrapolated from the facts; the law is imposed on new and similar[7] fact patterns; from those new facts, occasionally, a new law is extrapolated, at a different level of abstraction, that in turn applies to other facts. This is how the common law is developed: induction and

[6] *Donoghue v. Stevenson* [1932] A.C. 562.
[7] It is based to some extent on reason by analogy: *see* Edward Levi, *An Introduction to Legal Reasoning* (1949); Cass Sunstein, "On Analogical Reasoning", 106 *Harv. L. Rev.* 741 (1993); Scott Brewer, "Exemplary Reasoning: Semantics, Pragmatics, and the Rational Force of Legal Argument by Analogy," 109 *Harv. L. Rev.* 923 (1996).

deduction are used in combination. In the words of an English judge, this is the "genius" of the common law.[8] Different judges view the level of abstraction differently. Different precedents are created.

In exercising authority to develop the common law, judges fulfill their role: they bridge the gap between law and life, they protect the constitution and its values. This is the theory of the common law in a nutshell. This is how it is integrated into law, as a primary limb of the body politic. The common law, like judicial interpretation, is a primary tool in realizing the judicial role. It is an important tool. Its latent potential to change and rejuvenate facilitates the law's adaptation to changing social needs. Its characteristic sensitivity to fundamental values and fundamental perspectives guarantees appropriate protection for the constitution and its values.

OVERRULING PRECEDENT

Deviation from Precedent—When?

A judge stands before a dilemma: to follow precedent previously determined by his court, or deviate from it? The judge must use his discretion reasonably. What should the judge do?[9] The reasonableness test requires the judge to consider, on the one hand, all considerations supporting the honoring and following of the precedent. On the other hand, the judge must consider the full scope of considerations pointing toward deviation from the precedent and choosing new law. The judge must assign each one of these systems

---

[8] See Justice Simonds' comments in *Scruttons v. Midland Silicones* [1962] 1 All E.R. 1.

[9] *See* Rupert Cross and J.W. Harris, *Precedent in English Law* (4th ed. 1991); *Precedent in Law* (Laurence Goldstein ed., 1987); Julius Stone, *Precedent and Law: Dynamics of Common Law Growth* (1985); *Interpreting Precedents: A Comparative Study* (D. Neil MacCormick and Robert S. Summers eds., 1997); Barak, *supra* p. 113, note 2 at 398; Harold J. Spaeth and Jeffrey A. Segal, *Majority Rule or Minority Will: Adherence to Precedent on the U.S. Supreme Court* (1999).

of considerations its proper weight. Having done that, the judge must place both on the scale. The judge must choose the prevailing ruling; the judge must choose the ruling whose utility is greater than the damage caused by it. The guiding principle should be this: it is appropriate to deviate from a previous precedent if the new precedent's contribution to the bridging of the gap between law and society and to the protection of the constitution and its values, after setting off the damage caused by the change, is greater than the contribution of the previous precedent to the realization of those goals. The judge must ask himself if the damage from preserving the present law is greater than the damage from changing it judicially. The question is whether the considerations supporting the new ruling are of greater weight than the considerations supporting the old ruling, and how great is the damage caused by the change itself. The judge must consider whether the previous precedent is so unworthy that its replacement by a new and better precedent is justified, despite the damage caused by the change. I want to stress that the problem of deviation from precedent exists both regarding precedents that interpreted constitution, basic law, statute, or any other legislation and regarding common law precedents.[10]

Deviation from precedent, particularly a precedent of the highest court, is a serious matter. Great sensitivity is needed to weigh all the considerations. Judicial discretion reaches its full manifestation when the judge confronts the dilemma of whether or not to deviate from a precedent. This is part of the judge's craft. The dilemma brings to the fore the judge's view regarding judicial activism or restraint.[11] It should be noted, however, that the confrontation with the problem of the weight to be given to the different considerations engages the judge's rationality, not emotions. Precedent is not holy, but there is no reason to such to deviate from it. The considerations that the judge must entertain are complex.

---

[10] *See* Colin Manchester, et al., *Exploring the Law: The Dynamics of Precedent and Statutory Interpretation* (1966).
[11] *See infra* p. 275.

The judge should aspire to bridge the gap between law and life, making sure that the damage caused by this bridging does not surpass its utility. The same applies to the protection of the constitution and its values.

In considering whether to deviate from precedent, I begin by assuming that, had I been a member of the panel that wrote the previous judgment, I would have come to a different conclusion. The precedent set, even if it is legally within the zone of reasonableness, does not seem to me to be a proper one. I prefer a different ruling, a better one, which I am now permitted to give. I am "authorized" to deviate from the previous precedent. The problem before me is one of assessing the change. Do the advantages of the change surpass their disadvantage? The problem may also arise in a different situation: if I had been a member of the panel that wrote the previous judgment, I would have decided as they did. The precedent set in the past was good for its time. The times, however, have changed. Years have passed. The old precedent is still legal, but it is possible today to set a new precedent, a better one. In these situations and others, the question is only this: Do the advantages of the change surpass the damage caused by it?

The Damage Caused by the Change Itself

One must always consider that the change itself causes damage. It is not appropriate to deviate from precedent if this damage surpasses the utility stemming from the change. The importance of assessing this damage is now clear. The question arises, what is this damage?[12]

Deviation from precedent causes damage to the legal system. It detracts from stability, certainty, and the reliance of the public on the old precedent. It obstructs the possibility of planning future activity. Deviation from precedent detracts from consistency, which is an important value in any legal system. This consistency is based

---

[12] For expansion on this topic *see* Barak, *supra* p. 113, note 2 at 234.

on justice, fairness, and equality. It reflects the view that similar cases should be decided in a similar way. Deviation from precedent creates a state of affairs in which similar cases receive different solutions. Beyond that, deviation from precedent damages the continuity of the system and stands in opposition to the need for the present to be integrated with the past in order to greet the future. Rather than being integrated into the existing legal fabric, the deviating judge breaks his own ground, and as a result raises concern that "in time this judicial institution will turn from a 'court of law' to a 'court of judges,' in which the number of members is the same as the number of opinions."[13] I summarized these considerations in one case in the following words: "this approach derives from the honor we owe our brethren, whose law arises from the books, from the need to ensure security and stability, and out of the recognition that we must realize reasonable expectations of the members of the public, based on the case law of this court."[14] In another case, in which I emphasized the need to balance between the damage caused by the change and the utility stemming from it, I placed the following considerations on the "damage" side of the scale:

> on the one side of the scale one must place the existing law and the considerations supporting its continued existence. Among these considerations, the need to maintain stability, certainty, consistency and continuity should be mentioned . . . deviation from precedent sends shock waves through the normative system, and injures it. The public and the government have relied on the existing law, and have made their plans around it. Deviation from precedent contradicts the principle of reliance and the need to maintain certainty and security. Existing and known law is preferable to the uncertainty bound up in changes in it for the sake of improvement.[15]

Moreover, changes in the law make providing legal services more difficult. A court acting according to known and tried precedents

[13] C.F.H. 23/60 *Balan v. Executors of the Litvinsky Will*, 15 P.D. 70, 75 (Silberg, J.).
[14] H.C. 547/84 *Off HaEmek Registered Agric. Coop. Ass'n v. Ramat-Yishai Local Council*, 40(1) P.D. 113, 145.
[15] C.A. 1287/92, *Buskila v. Tzemach*, 46(5) P.D. 159, 172.

works efficiently. Such a court need not invest effort in renewed verification of its assumptions. Judicial work would be impossible and the effort of generations would go to waste if every judicial decision were subject to review every time. Such a situation would encourage going to court anew each time the panel of justices changed. Finally, too frequent deviation from precedents is likely to damage public confidence in the judiciary. Precedent need not be like a ticket that is valid only on the day of issue.[16] Such a situation would also burden the lower courts, which are required to follow higher court precedents. How should they behave when the higher courts deviate so often from their precedents? What should they do when they encounter conflicting precedents?

Assessing the Damage Caused by the Change, Compared to Its Utility

In assessing the damage likely to be caused due to a change, compared to its utility, one must take three considerations of special interest into account.[17] First, one must take into account the level of reliance on the old precedent. When the public and the other branches rely comprehensively and deeply on the existing law in the execution of their affairs, it is proper to deviate from this law only when important legal policy considerations justify the frustration of such reliance. Second, one must take note of the "age" of the precedent from which deviation is being considered. In this regard, the body of a judicial precedent is similar to the human body. At its birth it is very young. It does not yet stand on its own two feet. The damage done by changing it is not great. With the passing years, the precedent grows stronger. The damage resulting from deviating from it at this point is likely to be great. After additional years, old age creeps up on the precedent. It no longer fits the conditions of the time and place. Its hold on reality weakens.

---

[16] *See* the opinion of Roberts, J., in *Smith v. Allwright*, 321 U.S. 649 (1944).
[17] *See* Barak, *supra* p. 113, note 2 at 242.

Deviation from it is expected and will not cause much damage. Third, one must check whether it is possible to bring about the change in the previous law by way other than judicial change of precedent. Thus, for example, when a judicial precedent interprets a constitutional provision, unless one changes the precedent judicially, it can only be changed by amending the constitution. Such a change is an inherently tangled proposition. In this situation, judicial change of precedent should be made less hesitantly. When the previous precedent interpreted a statute, on the other hand, it is possible to change it by changing the statute, which is a simpler process than changing the constitution.

CHAPTER SEVEN

Balancing and Weighing

THE CENTRALITY OF BALANCING AND WEIGHING

From my judicial experience, I have learned that "balancing" and "weighing," though neither essential nor universally applicable, are very important tools in fulfilling the judicial role. Even where applicable, however, they do not produce singular, unambiguous legal solutions. Indeed, the main significance of balancing and weighing is the order they lend to legal thinking rather than the particular legal judgments they produce. To apply these tools, one must first identify the relevant values and principles whose framework provides a necessary context for balancing and weighing.[1] These tools express the complexity of the human being and of human relationships. They also express my eclectic approach,[2] which takes the entirety of the values and interests into consideration and seeks to balance them according to society's changing needs. I do not believe that one comprehensive theory can explain the complicated relationship between an individual and society.[3] Rather, I believe that jurists should balance various theories and approaches, in

---

[1] *See* T. Alexander Aleinikoff, "Constitutional Law in the Age of Balancing," 96 *Yale L.J.* 943, 946–47 (1987); Frank M. Coffin, "Judicial Balancing: The Protean Scales of Justice," 63 *N.Y.U. L. Rev.* 16, 23 (1988); Louis Henkin, "Infallibility Under Law: Constitutional Balancing," 78 *Colum. L. Rev.* 1022, 1025 (1978); Gerard V. La Forest, "The Balancing of Interests Under the Charter," 2 *Nat'l J. Const. Law* 133, 134 (1992); Robert F. Nagel, "Liberals and Balancing," 63 *U. Colo. L. Rev.* 319, 321 (1992); Kathleen M. Sullivan, "Post-Liberal Judging: The Roles of Categorization and Balancing," 63 *U. Colo. L. Rev.* 293, 293–94 (1992).
[2] *See supra* p. 117.
[3] *See* Farber and Sherry, *supra* p. 91, note 169 (arguing that no single, all-encompassing theory can successfully guide judges or provide definitive (or even sensible) answers to every constitutional question).

recognition of the fact that law is not all or nothing. Bridging the gap between law and society and protecting democracy demand accounting for this complexity. An expression of it can be given by means of the tools of "balancing" and "weighing." Balancing and weighing, themselves metaphors,[4] reflect the need to decide a conflict between values and principles that are accepted in the legal system.[5] The result of the balance is important both to the development of common law and to the determination of objective purpose in a legal text (such as statutes and constitutions). The concept of balancing recognizes that fundamental principles may conflict with one another, and that the proper resolution of this conflict lies not in the elimination of the inferior value but in determining the proper boundary between the conflicting values. Similarly, the concept of "balance" reflects the recognition that fundamental principles have "weight" and that it is possible to classify them according to their relative social importance. The act of "weighing" is merely a normative act designed to give the principles their proper place in the law.[6]

Naturally, acts of balancing and weighing are not scientific in nature. They do not negate the existence of judicial discretion.[7] Nonetheless, they confine such discretion to those situations in which the legal system fails otherwise to clarify the relative social status of the conflicting values and principles. In this respect, one should not trade one extreme for the other. Just as balancing and weighing do not negate judicial discretion entirely, these techniques also do not constitute an open invitation for judicial discretion in every case. I should point out that the doctrine of balancing has not been sufficiently developed in the law.[8] This is regrettable, since balancing is so central to fulfilling the judicial role.[9]

[4] See William J. Winslade, "Adjudication and the Balancing Metaphor," in *Legal Reasoning* 403 (Hubert Hubien ed., 1971).

[5] See Robert Alexy, *A Theory of Constitutional Rights* 100 (Julian Rivers trans., 2002).

[6] *Id.* at 408.

[7] See Hans Kelsen, *Pure Theory of Law* 352 (Max Knight trans., 1967) (1960).

[8] With the exception of Alexy, *supra* p. 165, note 5.

[9] Alexy, *supra* p. 165, note 5 at 100.

BALANCING AND CATEGORIZATION

Balancing

Balancing is a normative process by which one attempts to resolve a clash between conflicting values. The solution is not one of "all or nothing." The losing value is not removed from the law. The decision is made by assigning weight to the conflicting values and preferring the prevailing value. In balancing, the various values preserve their place in the legal system. One cannot balance without a scale, and one cannot use a scale unless the relative weight of the various values is determined. One example of this is the conflict between the value of public peace and the freedom of speech. The system of balancing assigns each of the conflicting values weight and determines when it is permissible to infringe upon freedom of speech.

Categorization

Categorization, like balancing, is also a normative process that attempts to resolve conflicts between values and rights. The solution, according to this process, lies in the creation of normative categories. The categorization of an event within the boundaries of the relevant normative category leads to the solution of the conflict. Thus, for example, if one categorizes an event as belonging to property rules and not to contract rules, one will apply to rules concerned with such a categorization, without the need for balancing.

The Relativity of the Differentiation between Balancing and Categorization

The difference between balancing and categorization is a relative one.[10] Categorization can be seen as a balancing in which full weight is given to one of the conflicting values and the other is

---

[10] *See* Sullivan, *supra* p. 164, note 1.

given a weight of zero. Indeed, on the one hand, the balancing equation is its own category, for all that falls within its framework receives the solution determined in it. On the other hand, categorization is the product of a balance between competing values. Often, both of the techniques are used. However, it is correct to differentiate between the two techniques. The difference is not that one of the techniques (balancing) grants greater discretion to the judge than the other (categorization). In both categories there is judicial discretion, and in both it is limited. It is difficult to assess the difference in the scope of discretion. Nor is the difference that someone who wishes to protect human rights will use the balancing technique, whereas someone who wishes to protect the interests of society at large will use the categorization technique. Each of the techniques will protect values in accordance with the content of the balancing or the categorization, and not according to their technical character.[11] The difference between these two methods is in the different lines of thought, different lines of argument, and different rhetoric. In my opinion, the technique of balancing is generally preferable to that of categorization. Balancing reflects the relativity of the clashing values. It is an expression of the outlook that the law is not "all or nothing" and that conflicting values need to confront each other. I turn now to the way balancing is performed.

THE NATURE OF BALANCING

Balancing and Weight: Metaphors

The process of balancing is based on the identification of values and rights relevant to resolving a question before the judge.[12] Each of these values is given a certain weight, and placed on the scale. The result of the weighing determines the answer to the question.

---

[11] *Id.*
[12] For more on the process of balancing see Alexy, *supra* p. 165, note 5.

There is, of course, no physical scale. Physical weights and balances are not to be found. The values do not appear before the judge with a label displaying their weight. Nor is there a list of values organized according to their importance and weight. Indeed, the process is not physical but normative. The talk of "balancing," "weight," and "weighing" is metaphorical speech. Such speech cannot provide a solution to the conflict between the values. It can only present it in a descriptive way. Indeed, like other metaphorical expressions, such as the reasonable person, the metaphors do not grant normative content to the ideas brought across by them. Nor do they grant logical basis to the ideas. They merely present them in an understandable way.

Relative Societal Importance

What hides, then, behind the metaphors regarding assessing weight and balancing? The answer is that the meaning of the balancing and the weight is in the assessment of the relative societal importance of the conflicting values. The act of weighing is not a physical act but a normative one that is intended to grant the various considerations their proper place in the legal system and their societal worth in the totality of societal values. Indeed, as I wrote in *Laor*,

> these expressions—balancing, weight—are merely metaphors. Behind them stand the belief that not all principles are of identical importance in the eyes of society, and [the belief] that without statutory direction, the court must assess the relative societal importance of the various principles. Just as there is no person without a shadow, there is no principle without weight. The determination of a balance on the basis of weight means the granting of a societal assessment regarding the relative importance of the various principles.[13]

It is not that balancing and weighing determine the relative societal importance of the conflicting values. These values—with

---

[13] *Laor*, 41(1) P.D. 421, 434 (Barak, J.).

their relative societal importance—determine the weighing and the balancing.

How is the relative social importance of the conflicting values determined? The answer is that the determination is not scientific and is not precise. Balancing between conflicting values and interests is not done by scientific "tools," The "weight" that must be given to the different values and interests is inherently imprecise. Therefore, there are situations in which given conflicting values and interests can be balanced in different fashions. The judge looks out upon the legal system as a whole. The judge collects data regarding the constitutional status of the conflicting values. The relative importance of values located in the constitution is, *prima facie*, greater than that of values located outside the constitution. The judge examines the importance of the values in the eyes of statutes. The judge examines the case law of the court and attempts to learn from it about the societal importance of the different values in the past. On the basis of all these factors, the judge determines the relative importance of the competing values on the national "scale" of values. The judge attempts to thus express the view, regarding the relative societal importance of the conflicting values, of the society in which he lives.

Balancing and Discretion

Balancing is not a magic word. The use of balancing does not always lead to a single and exclusive solution. The principle of "weighing of interests", noted Kelsen,[14] "is merely a formulation of the problem, not a solution." The solution to a problem sometimes requires the use of judicial discretion. True, the assignment of weight to competing values is not arbitrary. However, it is not always dictated by the legal system, and it is related to the use of judicial discretion. This is not a call for judicial subjectivism. The discretion is not absolute. It is always limited discretion. However, the choice

[14] Hans Kelsen, *Pure Theory of Law* 352 (Max Knight trans., 1967).

between a number of legitimate options belongs to the judge, without the legal system determining the solution. Balancing is a technique; it is a way of thought; sometimes its use does not involve judicial discretion. Sometimes its use requires the use of judicial discretion.

TYPES OF BALANCING

Balancing Formulas

The social status of a fundamental principle is determined according to its relationship to all the principles of the legal system. We must compare different values of varying weights. As I wrote in one of my opinions:

> A social principle (such as freedom of expression) does not have "absolute" weight. The weight of a social principle is always relative. The status of a fundamental principle is always determined relative to other principles, with which it may conflict. The weight of the freedom of speech relative to the freedom of movement is different from its weight relative to judicial integrity, both of these are different from the weight of the freedom of speech relative to reputation or privacy, and all of these are different from the weight of the freedom of speech relative to the public interest in security and safety.[15]

The "balancing formula" reflects this relative value. The number of balancing formulas will always exceed the number of conflicting values, since within the limits of a given value (such as freedom of expression) there may be different levels of weight (political expression, commercial expression, and so on). We should not search for only one balancing formula to balance all of the conflicting principles.

---

[15] C.A. 105/92, *Re'em Eng'g Contractors Ltd. v. Municipality of Upper Nazareth*, 47(5) P.D. 189, 211.

Principled Balancing and Ad Hoc Balancing

Balancing between fundamental principles may be principled or ad hoc. Principled balancing determines a weight that is normative, leading to a legal criterion or formula that can be applied in future cases. Thus, for example, the principled balance between freedom of speech and public safety in Israeli case law is that the state may restrict the freedom of speech to protect public peace only if there is a near certainty that unrestricted speech would severely compromise public safety.[16] Ad hoc balancing, by contrast, is not based on a general formula that can be applied in similar cases other than the baseline determination that one should balance the competing principles according to what the circumstances of the case require. Principled balancing is usually preferable to ad hoc balancing. Judges should formulate a rational principle that can guide future cases.

Vertical Balancing and Horizontal Balancing

There are two main types of principled balancing: horizontal and vertical. Horizontal balancing occurs between values and principles of equal standing. This balancing will happen, for example, when two constitutional human rights conflict with one another. Thus, the freedom of speech may conflict with the rights of privacy, reputation, or movement. Horizontal balancing expresses the degree of reciprocal compromise that each of the fundamental principles must make, instructing judges to preserve the essence of the conflicting principles by crafting reciprocal compromises at the margins. This balancing attempts to ensure that the various compromises are proportionate and to give breathing space to each competing principle. One must avoid giving full expression to one fundamental principle at the expense of another. Restrictions must consider time, place,

[16] *See* Aharon Barak, "Freedom of Expression and Its Limitations," in *Challenges to Democracy: Essays in Honour and Memory of Isaiah Berlin* 167, 179–80 (Raphael Cohen-Almagor ed., 2000).

and manner, so that each of the competing principles enjoys a substantive and real existence. Therefore, traffic considerations should
not necessarily preclude a demonstration in a city's main streets, but
the city may nevertheless reasonably restrict a demonstration's time
and manner.

Vertical balancing is different. The vertical balancing formula
determines the conditions under which certain fundamental principles take precedence over others. This balancing occurs, for example, when a human right is not fully protected because of the need
to balance it with a state interest, such as public peace or public
order. Thus, for example, an Israeli court has held that national
security or public peace needs may restrict the freedom of speech
or the freedom of religion if there is a near certainty that actualizing these freedoms will cause serious damage to national security or
public safety. Similarly, considerations of national security allow
restriction of the freedom of movement outside Israel if there is a
genuine and serious fear that granting this freedom will harm
national security. Vertical balancing does not determine the boundaries of the right that is being infringed; rather, it determines the
degree of protection that the legal system affords a given right.[17]
Of course, the distinction between vertical and horizontal balance
is not absolute. In complex situations, both types of balancing are
required.

THE ADVANTAGES OF BALANCING

The technique of balancing is an important tool in realizing the
role of the judge. There are three reasons for the centrality of balancing in realizing the judicial role. First, it expresses the complexity of the human being and the complexity of human relations. Law
is not everything or nothing. Law is a complex system of values that
in certain situations are in harmony with each other and lead to

[17] For the distinction between the scope of the right and the degree of protection
afforded it, see Frederick Schauer, *Free Speech: A Philosophical Enquiry* 89 (1982).

a single conclusion, whereas in other situations, they clash with each other, making adjudication necessary. The balancing technique expresses this complexity. It nicely reflects the eclectic philosophy that takes the entirety of values into consideration and seeks to balance them according to life's changing needs. Second, balancing is particularly well-suited for realizing the judicial role. Bridging law and life and protecting the constitution and its values can best be attained through the technique of balancing, which takes modern constitutional values into consideration. This balancing, if conducted properly, bridges the gap between the old law and life's new reality, protecting the constitution and its values. Third, balancing introduces order into legal thought. It requires the judge to identify the relevant values; it requires the judge to address the problem of the relative social importance; it requires judges to reveal their way of thinking to themselves, as well as to others. It facilitates self-criticism and criticism from the outside. As Judge Coffin wrote:

> Open balancing restrains the judge and minimizes hidden or improper personal preference by revealing every step in the thought process; it maximizes the possibility of attaining collegial consensus by responding to every relevant concern of disagreeing colleagues; and it offers a full account of the decision-making process for subsequent professional assessment and public appraisal.[18]

Indeed, balancing is a way of thinking; it is a conceptual mentality; it is a process that leads to decision. It requires dealing with how genuinely problematic is the situation created by conflicting values.[19] These are the reasons that the art of balancing has blossomed in many countries. It is difficult to imagine constitutional law without it. Nevertheless, the technique of balancing has been subject to criticism, which I will now address.

[18] *See* Frank M. Coffin, "Judicial Balancing: The Protean Scales of Justice," 63 *N.Y.U. L. Rev.* 16, 25 (1988).
[19] *See* Frank Michelman, "The Supreme Court 1985 Term—Foreword: Traces of Self Government," 100 *Harv. L. Rev.* 4, 34 (1986).

CRITIQUE OF BALANCING AND RESPONSE

Critics raise a number of different claims against balancing. There are two primary claims: first, balance is nothing but a type of cost-benefit analysis that should be conducted by the legislature and that diminishes the status of the values competing for supremacy; second, whereas balancing creates a façade of scientific objectivity, in reality it is the product of judicial subjectivity. I reject both these claims.

The critique of a cost-benefit analysis is purely a terminological issue. We are not dealing with values that can be assessed financially, and that economic formula is ill-suited for the field in which we are operating.[20] On a deeper level, the balance is indeed based on comparing the relative social importance of different values. Those who wish to refer to that as cost-benefit analysis are welcome to do so. The critique of the façade and the internal content breaks down an open door. I have not claimed that balancing is scientific and that it obviates judicial discretion.

Richard Pildes has emphasized, in a number of articles, that judges who use the terminology of balancing are not balancing but rather interpreting.[21] In my opinion, Pildes is creating an artificial conflict between balancing and interpreting. The primary role of balancing is in the realm of interpretation. In determining the objective purpose of a text, the interpreter balances competing values.

Critics also contend that not all the relevant values are taken into account and that their classification is inappropriate. It is also argued that it is hard to know why the court struck one balance and not another, and it is sometimes hard to understand why balancing similar values leads to different balance points. These claims are important, but they do not negate balancing. Rather, they should motivate judges to engage in balancing in the best professional manner.

---

[20] *See* Richard Posner, *Law, Pragmatism and Democracy* 362 (2003).
[21] Richard Pildes, "Against Balancing: The Role of Exclusionary Reasons in Constitutional Law," 45 *Hastings L.J.* 711 (1994); Richard Pildes, "The Structural Conception of Rights and Judicial Balancing," 6 *Rev. Const. Stud.* 179 (2000).

Indeed, the goal of balancing is to uncover all the relevant values. It is also important to explain how the balancing takes place. That explanation, however, will not obviate judicial discretion. It will explain how such discretion is employed.

THE SCOPE OF THE BALANCING

The applicability of balancing is very broad. We balance the formal and substantive aspects of democracy, we balance the fundamental values of democracy (such as the public interest) against human rights, we balance the various fundamental values, we balance the conflict between different kinds of human rights. We also use balancing in the context of purposive interpretation.[22]

This approach is based on the broader view that law is based on values; that these values are not always in harmony, that values sometimes conflict, that every legal system establishes the proper balances between the different values, that these balances constitute the infrastructure of every legal system. Indeed, the entirety of public law is a balance of clashing values. This is the case of the internal conflicts between the various components of formal democracy. This is the case of the internal conflicts within substantive democracy. Indeed, constitutional, administrative, and criminal law are the product of these conflicts. Similarly, the entirety of private law is a balance between various human rights. For example, tort law is a balance between the individual's freedom of activity and the constitutional rights of others and the public interest.

In constitutional and statutory interpretation, the preliminary balance is sometimes conducted by the creator of the text. The judicial balance, in these instances, is secondary, and it is intended to carry out into practice the balance conducted by the creator of the text. In every instance in which legislation gives an authorized body discretion without providing guidance about the considerations that should be weighed, there is no choice, in interpreting the

[22] *See* Barak, *supra* p. 123, note 2 at 176.

authority, than for the judge to conduct the preliminary balance. Such a preliminary balance is conducted in all situations in which judges develop the common law, because then there is no legislative intent and almost no interpretive problem.

A separate question is whether it is desirable for the court to conduct the preliminary balance in constitutional and legislative interpretation, or whether the preliminary balancing should always be done by the creator of the text, so that the judge need only conduct the secondary balance. In my opinion, there is no one right answer to this question that suits every case. There will certainly be situations in which the preliminary balancing should be done through legislation. That is an outgrowth of the view that primary arrangements should be determined by the statute itself. In some cases, the legislature will seek to attain maximal flexibility. It may, for example, use open-ended phrases like "negligence," "reasonability, " or "good faith." In these and other cases, the court will conduct the preliminary balance. The legislature, of course, decides which approach to take. In the context of the common law, which is entirely judge-made, the (preliminary and secondary) balancing is conducted by the judge. Of course, not every legal problem is resolved by (preliminary or secondary) balancing. The legislature and the judge must assess every problem and evaluate whether it is suited for a solution based on balancing conflicting values or whether another approach, such as categorization, is appropriate.

CHAPTER EIGHT

Non-Justiciability, or "Political Questions"

THE ROLE AND LIMITS OF JUSTICIABILITY

An important tool that judges use to fulfill their role in a democracy is determining justiciability.[1] That is, judges identify those issues about which they ought not make a decision, leaving that decision to other branches of the state.[2] The more non-justiciability is expanded, the less opportunity judges have for bridging the gap between law and society and for protecting the constitution and democracy. Given these consequences, I regard the doctrine of non-justiciability or "political questions" with considerable wariness. Insofar as is possible, I prefer to examine an argument on its merits, or to consider abstaining from a decision for lack of a cause of action rather than because of non-justiciability.[3] In many cases where my colleagues have dismissed claims on the grounds of non-justiciability, I dismissed on the grounds that the disputed executive action was legal and therefore that the claim should be dismissed on the merits. My approach does not assume that the court is always the best institution to resolve disputes; indeed, I accept that certain disputes are best decided elsewhere. However, the court should not abdicate its role in a democracy merely because it is uncomfortable or fears

[1] On justiciability and the political question doctrine, see generally 1 Tribe, supra p. 35, note 57, § 3-13, at 365–85; Yaacov S. Zemach, Political Questions in the Courts (1976); Koopmans, supra p. xii, note 10 at 98.

[2] See Geoffrey Marshall, "Justiciability," in Oxford Essays in Jurisprudence 265, 269–70 (A.G. Guest ed., 1961); Lorne Sossin, Boundaries of Judicial Review: The Law of Justiciability in Canada (1999).

[3] See Louis Henkin, "Is There a 'Political Question' Doctrine?" 85 Yale L.J. 597, 621–22 (1976); Martin H. Redish, "Judicial Review and the 'Political Question,'" 79 Nw. U. L. Rev. 1031, 1055 (1984).

tension with the other branches of the state. This tension not only fails to justify dismissing claims, it is even desirable on occasion.[4] It is because of this tension that the freedom of the individual is guaranteed. True, the "passive virtues" that Professor Alexander Bickel advocates so persuasively do have great force.[5] Like everything, though, their power is relative and must be balanced with their significant shortcomings.[6] Overall, the benefit gained from a broad doctrine of non-justiciability is significantly smaller than the benefit gained from a narrow one. Nonetheless, I know that many judges in the Anglo-American and other legal systems think otherwise and regard the barrier of justiciability as a proper protection of the court's effectiveness in other areas. Under either view, the argument over this question goes to the heart of the judicial role, and for this reason is of fundamental importance. Below, I discuss the nature of non-justiciability and the considerations motivating my aversion to it. I begin by making a distinction that seems to me essential: between normative justiciability and institutional justiciability.[7]

TYPES OF JUSTICIABILITY

Normative Justiciability

Normative justiciability aims to answer the question whether there are legal criteria for determining a given dispute. This type of justiciability was discussed by Justice Brennan, who said that a dispute

---

[4] *See infra* p. 216.

[5] *See* Bickel, *supra* p. 96, note 184 at 111; Alexander M. Bickel, "The Supreme Court, 1966 Term—Foreword: The Passive Virtues," 75 *Harv. L. Rev.* 40, 42–58 (1961).

[6] *See generally* Gerald Gunther, "The Subtle Vices of the 'Passive Virtues'—A Comment on Principle and Expediency in Judicial Review," 64 *Colum. L. Rev.* 1 (1964).

[7] *See* H.C. 910/86, *Ressler v. Minister of Def.*, 42(2) P.D. 441 (English translation available at www.court.gov.il). The two other justices who joined the majority, President Shamgar and Deputy President Ben-Porat, reserved judgment on various aspects of my approach. For an English translation of the judgment, see Itzhak Zamir and Allen Zysblat, *Public Law in Israel* 275 (1996).

is non-justiciable—or more correctly, raises a political question—if there is "a lack of judicially discoverable and manageable standards for resolving it."[8] I reject this approach. In my opinion, every dispute is normatively justiciable. Every legal problem has criteria for its resolution. There is no "legal vacuum." According to my outlook, law fills the whole world. There is no sphere containing no law and no legal criteria. Every human act is encompassed in the world of law. Every act can be "imprisoned" within the framework of the law. Even actions of a clearly political nature, such as waging war, can be examined with legal criteria, as evidenced by the laws of war in international law.[9] The mere fact that an issue is "political"— that is, holding political ramifications and predominant political elements—does not mean that it cannot be resolved by a court. Everything can be resolved by a court, in the sense that law can take a view as to its legality. Of course, an activity's political nature may occasionally create a legal norm that, by the content of the norm, gives broad discretion to the political authority to act as it wishes. In that case, the political authority is then free to act within, but not without, the law. Naturally, in a liberal system of law, the premise is that the individual is free to do everything except what the law prohibits, and the government may not restrict his conduct without the law's authorization. This freedom of the individual is not a freedom that operates outside the law, but rather a freedom that the law recognizes. Once again, I do not claim that legal solutions are always the most important or the best; human relationships certainly extend beyond the law. Though I claim that law is everywhere, I don't claim that law is everything. I have already said that, in my opinion, the law is a tool for regulating relationships between people, but of course this tool is not the only one. My argument is instead jurisprudential: although not everything is law, there is law in everything.

Several rulings of the Supreme Court of Israel illustrate this point. One case assessed the question of whether a transitional or

[8] *Baker v. Carr*, 369 U.S. 186, 217 (1962).
[9] *See* Yoram Dinstein, *The Conduct of Hostilities Under the Law of International Armed Conflict* (2004).

"lame duck" government—that is, a government that has resigned or that does not have the confidence of parliament and is awaiting the outcome of impending elections—is authorized to negotiate peace agreements.[10] I said that it may do so, if it is reasonable in the circumstances of the case. Several other judges dismissed the action as non-justiciable. In my opinion, in the absence of a specific relevant provision, this question was governed by the general principles of public law, one of which is the principle of reasonableness. Consequently, this principle produced the legal criteria on which my decision turned.

Another case considered whether the Oslo Accords, signed by the Israeli government and marking agreement with the Palestinians, were null and void. I dismissed the petition, but not because no relevant legal norm existed.[11] I certainly would have granted the petition had it proved, for example, that Israel's negotiators received a bribe from the Palestinian side. Instead, I dismissed the petition because the petitioners failed to show that the Israeli government secured the Accords through unlawful, unreasonable conduct. I stated that different people had different and conflicting opinions about the Oslo Accords, all of which may fall within the zone of reasonableness.

In another petition, the Court assessed whether to prevent the release of a terrorist within the framework of a political "package deal."[12] Again, I decided the petition using the concept of reasonableness, and I avoided resorting to the claim—which I think was incorrect—that there were no legal criteria for resolving the disputed legal issue. Such criteria exist, according to which the release

---

[10] See H.C. 5167/00, *Weiss v. Prime Minister*, 55(2) P.D. 455.

[11] See H.C. 6057/99, *Victims of Terrorism Ass'n v. Gov't of Israel* (unreported). *See also* H.C. 3230/99, *Elias v. Gov't of Israel* (unreported); H.C. 8840/96, *Elazra v. State of Israel* (unreported); H.C. 5934/95, *Shilansky v. Prime Minister* (unreported); H.C. 4064/95, *Porat v. Chairman of Knesset*, 49(4) P.D. 177.

[12] See H.C. 6315/97, *Federman v. Prime Minister* (unreported); H.C. 2455/94, *"BeZedek" Organization v. Gov't of Israel* (unreported); H.C. 5581/93, *Victims of Arab Terrorism v. State of Israel* (unreported); H.C. 1403/91, *Katz v. Gov't of Israel*, 45(3) P.D. 353; H.C. 659/85, *Bar Yosef-Yoskovitz v. Minister of Police*, 40(1) P.D. 785.

of terrorists falls into the sphere of the executive authority's administrative discretion. If I had been convinced that the release was, for example, motivated by personal considerations or personal gain, I would not have refrained from voiding the action.

In yet another case, the Israeli government held negotiations with the Palestinian Authority concerning the future of various persons who had holed themselves up inside the Church of the Nativity in Bethlehem while the Israeli army surrounded the church. The petitioners argued that the Israeli government was not providing sufficient food to those besieged in the church.[13] The government argued that the petition should be dismissed because it was non-justiciable. I held that customary international law regulated the provision of food, and that the government was obliged to comply with that law. I further held—after analyzing these rules and verifying the supply of food—that the government had not violated these rules.

In a number of other judgments, the Israeli Supreme Court has considered the legal scope of "political agreements" (mostly coalition agreements among the parties forming the government or local councils).[14] The normative framework exists, *inter alia*, in the general principles of administrative law dealing with the restrictions that reasonableness and proportionality impose on administrative discretion.

In a petition considered recently, we were asked to rule whether the government should erect a security fence separating the state of Israel from the areas of Palestinian autonomy. We dismissed the petition on the grounds that there could be different perspectives on the erection of a border fence, all of which fell within

---

[13] *See* H.C. 3451/02, *Almadani v. Minister of Def.*, 56(3) P.D. 30 (English translation available at www.court.gov.il).

[14] *See, e.g.*, H.C. 5364/94, *Velner v. Chairman of Israeli Labor Party*, 49(1) P.D. 758; H.C. 2285/93, *Nahum v. Mayor of Petah-Tikva*, 48(5) P.D. 630; H.C. 4248/91, *Natazon v. Mayor of Holon*, 46(2) P.D. 194; H.C. 1635/90, *Zarzevski v. Prime Minister*, 45(1) P.D. 749; H.C. 1601/90, *Shalit v. Peres*, 44(3) P.D. 353 (English translation available at www.court.gov.il). For a critical analysis of the case law, see David Kretzmer, "Political Agreements: A Critical Introduction," 26 Isr. L. Rev. 407 (1992).

the scope of reasonableness.[15] In another case, the question was whether the fence the government ultimately erected was legal. The political aspects of erecting the fence did not prevent the Supreme Court from adjudicating the dispute between the state and the Palestinian inhabitants.[16] We decided that the fence in its location imposed nonproportional injuries on the inhabitants. In *Ressler v. Minister of Defense*,[17] I summarized the doctrine of normative justiciability this way:

> My approach is that where there is a legal norm, there are also legal criteria that operate the norm. To say there are no legal criteria with which to decide an issue means only that the legal norm that the petitioner argues does not apply to the matter, but that another norm does apply to it. It follows that the argument that the matter is not normatively justiciable is merely the argument that the petitioner did not indicate a legal norm that makes the executive action forbidden. Thus the argument about normative non-justiciability is merely an argument that there is no cause of action. In accepting an argument of normative non-justiciability, the Court does not evade a consideration of the legality of the action. On the contrary, it adopts an attitude with regard to the legality of the action and determines that it is legal. . . . The question arises as to whether every executive or administrative decision is justiciable. For example, are going to war and making peace also "justiciable" decisions that may be "confined" to a legal norm and a judicial proceeding? My answer is yes. Even with regard to war and peace we must determine which branch is competent to make the decision and what is the nature of its considerations (for example, the prohibition of personal corruption). It is of course possible to determine—and this question is open and difficult—that the other restrictions governing the use of administrative discretion do not apply. In this last case, the petition will be dismissed not

---

[15] *See* H.C. 3460/02, *HaLevy v. Prime Minister* (unreported).
[16] *See* H.C. 2056/04, *Beit Sourik Village Council v. the Government of Israel* (unreported, English translation available at www.court.gov.il).
[17] H.C. 910/86, *Ressler v. Minister of Def.*, 42(2) P.D. 441 (English translation available at www.court.gov.il).

because of its non-justiciability, but because the action is legal. In summary, the doctrine of normative justiciability (or non-justiciability) seems to me to have no independent existence.[18]

Institutional Justiciability

Whereas normative justiciability focuses on whether legal criteria exist to adjudicate a dispute, institutional justiciability concerns the question whether the dispute should be adjudicated in a court of law at all. As I wrote in *Ressler*:

> A dispute is not institutionally justiciable if the dispute ought not to be decided according to legal criteria in the court. Institutional justiciability therefore deals with the question whether the law and the court are the proper frameworks for deciding the dispute. The question is not whether it is possible to decide the dispute according to the law and in court; the answer to that question is yes. The question is whether it is desirable to decide the dispute—which is normatively justiciable—according to legal criteria in court.[19]

This aspect of non-justiciability was discussed by Justice Brennan, who said:

> [A dispute is non-justiciable if there is] a textually demonstrable constitutional commitment of the issue to a coordinate political department; . . . or the impossibility of a court's undertaking independent resolution without expressing lack of the respect due coordinate branches of government; or an unusual need for unquestioning adherence to a political decision already made; or the potentiality of embarrassment from multifarious pronouncements by various departments on one question.[20]

This reasoning is unconvincing. Consider the first non-justiciable matter mentioned by Justice Brennan, namely, the determination

---

[18] *Id.* at 483–88.
[19] *Id.* at 488–89.
[20] *Baker v. Carr*, 369 U.S. 186, 217 (1962).

of a question entrusted to a political authority. This is in fact the case with regard to *all* of the issues that are considered in constitutional or administrative law. That a certain matter is entrusted exclusively to one branch of the state is not a permit for that branch to act contrary to the constitution or a statute. When a certain provision of law gives authority to a branch of government, it still requires the branch to act lawfully within the framework of that authority. The provision also gives the courts the authority to interpret it in order to determine the scope of its application and to decide if it was exercised lawfully. Entrusting a decision about a certain act to a branch of state does not mean that the question of the legality of that act is also entrusted to that branch of state. On the contrary, "the final and decisive interpretive decision about a statute that is in force at any given time rests with the court, and, regarding issues submitted for consideration within the court system, the final decision lies with the highest court."[21] It follows that determining the legality of an act whose performance is entrusted to a particular branch of the state should not be regarded as non-justiciable.

The second type of dispute Justice Brennan called non-justiciable is one that is impossible to resolve judicially without expressing disrespect for coordinate branches of the state.[22] This reasoning is unpersuasive. All constitutional and administrative laws determine criteria for the legality of the behavior of government. The court must do its job and determine whether the government acted unlawfully, without letting considerations of respect for coordinate branches of the state inhibit its decision. As I have written:

> [T]he role of the court is to interpret the statute, and sometimes the court's interpretation is different from that of another governmental branch. It is inconceivable that preferring the judicial interpretation to the interpretation of the other branch (whether executive or legislative) expresses disrespect for that branch. How can we intervene

[21] H.C. 306/81, *Flatto-Sharon v. Knesset Comm.*, 35(4) P.D. 101, 141 (Shamgar, P.)
[22] *See Baker*, 369 U.S. at 217.

in the actions of the executive if we take the attitude that we are being disrespectful to it whenever we interpret the law contrary to its opinion?. . . [T]here is no disrespect to the other branches, when each branch fulfills its constitutional role and does what the law has ordered it to do. When the court interprets the law, it carries out its role, and if its interpretation is different from the one acceptable to the other branches, it advises them of their mistake, and in doing so it expresses disrespect for them.[23]

I made a similar point in *Ressler*: "The important question is not respect for one branch or another. The important question is respect for the law. Personally, I cannot see how insisting that a branch of the state respect the law can harm that branch or undermine the relationship between it and the other branches."[24]

One could argue that institutional non-justiciability is implicit in the principle of the separation of powers. I cannot accept this argument. The separation of powers is not a permit for a branch of the state to violate the constitution or a statute.[25] Admittedly, it is natural for a political branch to take political considerations into account, but to the same degree it is also natural that the judiciary should examine whether these political considerations, no matter how prudent they are, are consistent with constitutional or statutory law. As I wrote in *Ressler*:

There is nothing in the principle of separation of powers that can justify negating judicial review of government acts, whatever their character may be, and whatever their content may be. On the contrary, the principle of separation of powers is what justifies judicial review of the acts of the government, even if they are of a political nature, since it ensures that every branch acts lawfully within its sphere, thus guaranteeing the separation of powers.[26]

Nor is recognition of institutional non-justiciability implicit in the concept of democracy itself. The formal aspect of democracy

[23] H.C. 73/85, "Kach" Faction v. Chairman of Knesset, 39(3) P.D. 141, 163.
[24] *Ressler*, 42(2) P.D. at 490.
[25] *See supra* p. 41.
[26] *Ressler*, 42(2) P.D. at 491.

does not justify negating judicial involvement where the argument is that the action is contrary to the constitution or a statute. The substantive aspect of democracy does not justify negating judicial review either. On the contrary, judicial review usually aims to protect the individual and ensure his freedom, thereby promoting democracy. As I wrote in *Ressler*:

> [T]his judicial review keeps a democratic system working properly. It aims to guarantee, on the one hand, that the opinion of the majority finds proper expression within the legal frameworks established by the regime (constitution, statute, subordinate legislation, administrative rules) and does not depart from these frameworks, and that executive action is carried out within the legal framework determined by the majority through its vote in the legislature; it aims to ensure, on the other hand, that the majority does not harm individual rights, unless the law authorizes it. Democracy is not harmed by judicial review invalidating actions by other branches of the state that do take political considerations into account, when those branches act unlawfully. Note that the court does not criticize the internal logic or practical efficiency of such political considerations. The court considers their legality. This evaluation does not undermine democracy in any way. Nothing in democracy authorizes the majority to act contrary to the statute for whose legislation it is responsible. Even the most political of decisions must anchor themselves in lawful decisions. In a democracy, law is not politics, and politics is subject to law. There is therefore nothing in the principles of democracy that justifies institutional non-justiciability.[27]

JUSTICIABILITY AND PUBLIC CONFIDENCE

All that remains is the argument that institutional non-justiciability is justified because it protects the court itself from a "politicization of the judiciary" that could undermine public confidence in

---

[27] *Id.* at 491.

judicial objectivity. The argument is that the general public is not aware of the fine distinctions I have discussed and that it may mistake a judicial ruling that a government act of a clearly political nature is lawful or unlawful for a judicial ruling on the *propriety* of the act. In one case, the Israeli Supreme Court ruled that the expropriation of land in an area under Israeli military occupation for the purpose of establishing a settlement was unlawful.[28] The Court rejected the argument that the issue of settlement construction in occupied territories was non-justiciable, since reviewing individual harm is justiciable, and the settlement construction allegedly harmed an individual's property right. On this point, Justice Landau said:

> This time we have proper sources for our decision and we do not need—indeed, we are even forbidden, when sitting on the bench—to involve our personal views as citizens of the State. But there is still serious cause for concern that the court will be seen to have abandoned its proper sphere and to have entered the arena of public debate, and that our decision will be welcomed by part of the public with cheers and be wholly and fiercely rejected by the other. In this sense, I see myself here as someone whose duty it is to rule according to the law on every matter that is lawfully brought before the court. I am compelled to do so, even though I knew from the outset that the general public will not pay attention to the legal reasoning but only the final conclusion, and that the proper status of the court, as an institution above the disputes that divide the public, is likely to be undermined. But what can we do? This is our role and our duty as judges.[29]

Indeed, the public confidence argument is, in my opinion, problematic. Public confidence may be undermined if the court decides a dispute containing a political aspect, but it also may be undermined if the court refrains from deciding it. Moreover, public confidence relates not just to the content of the judicial decision but also to its motive. It would be a great mistake—a mistake likely to

[28] H.C. 390/79, *Dawikat v. Gov't of Israel*, 34(1) P.D. 1.
[29] *Id.* at 4.

undermine public confidence—to refrain from making a decision merely because the decision may undermine public confidence. The role of the court is to adjudicate disputes, even if the public or some portion of it does not like the outcome. For these reasons, I think that the United States Supreme Court rightly decided to hear *Bush v. Gore*[30] rather than abstain on grounds of non-justiciability.[31] The issue was justiciable—both normatively and institutionally—and the Court did well to rule on it.

Thus, the doctrine of institutional non-justiciability is very problematic. A number of democratic countries reject it: the German Constitutional Court has rejected it.[32] The Supreme Court of Canada has not adopted it.[33] The Supreme Court of Israel has also rejected it in many cases loaded with political tension. In one case, for example, the Court was required to review the validity of a pretrial pardon granted by the President of the state to the head of the Israeli General Security Services and to a number of its agents for illegal acts that they committed.[34] The Israeli public was divided on this question. The Court decided that the President may grant pretrial pardons. We unanimously rejected the argument of non-justiciability. In another case, the Court held that exceptional methods of interrogation (sleep deprivation, loud music, head covering, and painful sitting positions) employed by the Israeli security services against terrorists were illegal even if used to prevent the

---

[30] 531 U.S. 79 (2000).

[31] For an opposing view, see Steven G. Calabresi, "A Political Question", in *Bush v. Gore: The Question of Legitimacy* 129 (Bruce Ackerman ed., 2002); Jeffrey Rosen, "Political Questions and the Hazards of Pragmatism," in *Bush v. Gore, Id.* at 145.

[32] *See* Currie, supra p. 22, note 9, at 170.

[33] *See Operation Dismantle v. The Queen*, [1985] 1 S.C.R. 441, 455 ("[C]abinet decisions fall under s. 32(1)a of the *Charter* and are therefore reviewable in the courts and subject to judicial scrutiny for compatibility with the Constitution"); Hogg, *supra* p. 82, note 145 at 810 ("[I]t is clear that there is no political questions doctrine in Canada"). *But see* Sossin, *supra* p. 177, note 2 at 199. ("Based on the various settings in which Canadian courts have held political disputes to be non-justiciable, the view that Canada has no 'political questions' doctrine would seem in need of reappraisal").

[34] *See* H.C. 428/86, *Barzilai v. Gov't of Israel*, 40(3) P.D. 505 (English translation available at www.court.gov.il).

explosion of a "ticking bomb."[35] This question, too, was the subject of significant public dispute, but the Court did not refrain from deciding it because of non-justiciability.

Even though I am critical of the doctrine of non-justiciability, I cannot say that it should never be used. In a number of cases, Israeli judges, myself included, have resorted to it.[36] I should point out, however, that I prefer to dismiss a petition for lack of a cause of action rather than for institutional non-justiciability. In cases where my colleagues on the bench dismissed petitions because of institutional non-justiciability, I also found that the case should be dismissed, but not due to non-justiciability; rather, I found that the challenged act fell within a broad zone of reasonableness, and was thus lawful. Focusing on the legality of the act rather than on institutional non-justiciability increases public confidence in the state and allows the court to realize its role in a democracy.[37]

---

[35] *See* H.C. 5100/94, *Pub. Comm. Against Torture in Isr. v. Gov't of Israel*, 53(4) P.D. 817; [1998–99] *Isr. L. R.* 567.

[36] *See infra* p. 229.

[37] A bill proposed by legislators in the Israeli Parliament (the Knesset) provided that "[m]ilitary matters of an operational or combat character are not justiciable, and courts may not address them." The bill did not pass. Draft bill amending the Basic Law: The Judiciary (presented to the Chairman of the Knesset, May 20, 2002).

CHAPTER NINE

Standing

STANDING AND ADJUDICATION

The Importance of Standing

The issue of standing appears to be marginal in public law. This is certainly the case if one adopts the view that only a person who has experienced an injury in fact possesses standing. But if we liberalize the tests for standing, we will usher in a new era for judicial decision making whose ramifications are far greater than the issue of standing itself.[1] This is the case because liberal rules of standing enable courts to hear matters that ordinarily would not find their way before a court. Take, for example, the case I mentioned of the pretrial pardon given by the President of the State of Israel to the head of the General Security Services and his men.[2] A private lawyer brought the petition to the Supreme Court, sitting as the High Court of Justice. If the Court had restricted standing to those who suffer an injury in fact, the pardon's legality would not have been reviewed, since only a few persons in Israel, if any, would have had standing to challenge it. However, the liberal rules of standing adopted in Israel opened the door to judicial review of the pretrial pardon and the scope of the President's discretion. Liberal rules of standing have also allowed judicial review of claims challenging the legality of civil servants' behavior even where no individual inter-

---

[1] *See* Joanna Miles, "Standing in a Multi-Layered Constitution," in *Public Law in a Multilayered Constitution* 391 (Nicholas Bamford and Peter Leyland eds., 2003).

[2] *See Barzilai*, 40(3) P.D. at 505; *see supra* p. 188.

ests were harmed. The ordinary citizen would normally have no standing in these cases. The Court can consider these questions only if it adopts a liberal approach to the rules of standing. The following are several questions the Supreme Court of Israel, reviewing public petitions in its role as the High Court of Justice, has been able to consider because of its liberal standing rules: Did the attorney general exercise his discretion properly in deciding not to indict someone?[3] Did the Prime Minister exercise his discretion properly when he decided not to dismiss a cabinet minister against whom an indictment had been issued for bribery and embezzlement of public funds?[4] Did the Minister of Justice exercise his discretion properly in deciding not to extradite someone suspected of committing a crime outside Israel?[5] Did the government act lawfully when it held political negotiations over a peace agreement at a time when it did not have the confidence of Parliament?[6] Did a parole board act lawfully when it reduced a sentence imposed by a civil[7] or military[8] court?

Another standing issue involves a person whose right has been harmed but who refrains from suing. The recognition that another party—in most cases, human rights groups operating in the country—may sue allows the court to review the legality of the harm suffered. Examples from the Israeli experience include recognition of the Israel Women's Network's standing to petition the Court to enforce the provisions of the Government Corporations Law directing that the composition of boards of directors should

---

[3] *See* H.C. 935/89, *Ganor v. Attorney Gen.*, 44(2) P.D. 485, translated in Zamir and Zysblat, *supra* p. 178, note 7 at 334.

[4] *See* H.C. 4267/93, *Amitai: Citizens for Proper Admin. & Integrity v. Prime Minister of Isr.*, 47(5) P.D. 441; H.C. 3094/93, *Movement for Quality Gov't v. Gov't of Israel*, 47(5) P.D. 404 (English translation available at www.court.gov.il).

[5] *See* H.C. 852/86, *Aloni v. Minister of Justice*, 41(2) P.D. 1.

[6] *See* H.C. 5167/00, *Weiss v. Prime Minister*, 55(2) P.D. 455.

[7] *See* H.C. 1920/00, *Galon v. Parole Bd.*, 54(2) P.D. 313; H.C. 89/01, *Pub. Comm. Against Torture v. Parole Bd.*, 55(2) P.D. 838.

[8] *See* H.C. 3959/99, *Movement for Quality Gov't v. Sentencing Review Comm.*, 53(3) P.D. 721.

include members of both sexes,[9] and recognition of a citizen
watchdog group's standing in various petitions intended to ensure
proper and honest administration of the law.[10]

Standing and the Judicial Role

How a judge applies the rules of standing is a litmus test for determining his approach to his judicial role.[11] A judge who regards his role
as deciding a dispute between persons with rights—and no more—
will tend to emphasize the need for an injury in fact. By contrast, a
judge who regards his judicial role as bridging the gap between law
and society and protecting (formal and substantive) democracy will
tend to expand the rules of standing. I wrote the following in *Ressler*,
a judgment that led to the liberalization of Israel's standing rules:

> You cannot formulate the rules of standing if you do not formulate
> for yourself an outlook on the role of these rules in public law. In
> order to formulate an outlook about the nature and role of the rules
> of standing, you must adopt a position on the role of judicial review
> in the field of public law. . . . [I]n order to formulate an outlook
> with regard to the role of judicial review, you must adopt a position
> on the judicial role in society and the status of the judiciary among
> the other branches of the state. A judge whose judicial philosophy
> is based merely on the view that the role of the judge is to decide a

[9] *See* H.C. 453/94, *Isr. Women's Network v. Gov't of Israel*, 48(5) P.D. 501
(English translation available at www.court.gov.il).
[10] *See* H.C. 6673/01, *Movement for Quality Gov't v. Minister of Transp.* (not
yet reported); H.C. 932/99, *Movement for Quality Gov't v. Chairman of
Appointments Review Comm.*, 53(3) P.D. 769; H.C. 3073/99, *Movement for
Quality Gov't v. Minister of Educ.*, 44(3) P.D. 529; H.C. 6972/96, *Movement
for Quality Gov't v. Attorney Gen.*, 51(2) P.D. 757; H.C. 2533/97, *Movement for
Quality Gov't v. Gov't of Israel*, 51(3) P.D. 46.
[11] *See, e.g., Bennett v. Spear*, 520 U.S. 154, 162 (1997) "Like their constitutional
counterparts, these 'judicially self-imposed limits [i.e., standing] on the exercise
of federal jurisdiction' are 'founded in concern about the proper—and properly
limited—role of the courts in a democratic society ' . . ." (citations omitted);
Lujan v. Defenders of Wildlife, 504 U.S. 555, 562 (1992); *Allen v. Wright*, 468
U.S. 737, 752 (1984).

dispute between persons with existing rights is very different from a judge whose judicial philosophy is enshrined in the recognition that his role is to create rights and enforce the rule of law.[12]

As can be seen from this book and from a long list of judgments, my approach is that the role of a court in a democracy is not restricted to adjudicating disputes in which parties claim that their personal rights have been violated. I believe that my role as a judge is to bridge the gap between law and society and to protect democracy. It follows that I also favor expanding the rules of standing and releasing them from the requirement of an injury in fact. The Supreme Court of Israel has adopted this approach.[13] Gradually, at first in minority opinions of justices in the 1960s and 1970s and thereafter as a majority, the Court has adopted the view that when the claim alleges a major violation of the rule of law (in its broad sense), every person in Israel has legal standing to sue. Fears that the court would be flooded with frivolous lawsuits have proved groundless. In practice, it is primarily citizen watchdog groups and human rights organizations that have exploited this provision. I think that, overall, the outcome has been positive. I was happy to learn that the Republic of South Africa adopted a similar solution in its constitution. Section 38, applicable only to the Bill of Rights, provides that:

> Anyone listed in this section has the right to approach a competent court, alleging that a right in the Bill of Rights has been infringed or threatened, and the court may grant appropriate relief, including a declaration of rights. The persons who may approach a court are:
>
> a.   anyone acting in their own interest;
> b.   anyone acting on behalf of another person who cannot act in their own name;
> c.   anyone acting as a member of, or in the interest of, a group or class of persons;

---

[12] H.C. 910/86, *Ressler v. Minister of Def.*, 42(2) P.D. 441, 458 (English translation available at www.court.gov.il).

[13] *See generally* Zeev Segal, *The Right of Standing in the High Court of Justice* (1984).

    d. anyone acting in the public interest; and

    e. an association acting in the interest of its members.[14]

Like the Israeli Supreme Court, the Supreme Court of India has reached a similar result by adopting a liberal standing doctrine.[15] Other common law systems are moving toward liberalizing their standing requirements.[16]

STANDING AND SUBSTANTIVE DEMOCRACY

Standing and the Rule of Law

The rules of standing are closely related to the principle of rule of law. Closing the doors of the court to a petitioner with no injury in fact who warns of a public body's unlawful action means giving that public body a free hand to act without fear of judicial review. The result is the creation of "black holes" in which a legal norm exists but the public body is free to violate it without the possibility of judicial review. Such a situation may lead in the end to a violation of the legal norm, undermining the rule of law and undermining democracy. As I wrote in one case, "When there is no judge, there is no law. The ability to turn to the court is the cornerstone of the rule of law."[17] Lord Diplock rightly observed that

> it would, in my view, be a grave lacuna in our system of public law if a pressure group like the federation, or even a single public-spirited taxpayer, were prevented by outdated technical rules of *locus standi*

---

[14] S. Afr. Const. § 38.

[15] *See* Jamie Cassels, "Judicial Activism and Public Interest Litigation in India: Attempting the Impossible," 37 *Am. J. Comp. L.* 495, 498–99 (1989). *See also Gupta v. Union of India*, A.I.R. 1981 S.C. 87, 218–20.

[16] *See* Michael Beloff, "Who Whom? Issues in *Locus Standi* in Public Law," *Liber Amicorum in Honour of Lord Slynn of Hadley: Judicial Review in International Perspectives* 175 (Mads Andenas ed., 2000); Ivan Hare, *The Law of Standing in Public Interest Adjudication, op. cit.* p. 22.

[17] *Ressler*, 42(2) P.D. at 462.

from bringing the matter to the attention of the court to vindicate the rule of law and get the unlawful conduct stopped.[18]

Naturally, even without judicial review the law itself exerts a strong gravitational pull that shapes the way people act. Furthermore, there are other means—for example, public opinion or legislative review—of reviewing executive actions. Where these methods of supervision are effective, they may suffice. But where there is no tradition of executive self-restraint, and where the other means of review are insufficient, judicial review is critical.

Standing and the Separation of Powers

Does giving the "public petitioner" (*actio popularis*) standing undermine the separation of powers, which in itself forms a basis for the rules of standing? Can it be said that where there is no interest, there is no dispute (*lis*), and that the existence of a dispute is an essential condition for exercising judicial power? Does allowing a public petitioner to activate the exercise of judicial power, therefore, undermine the very principle of separation of powers?[19] In my opinion, the answer to these questions is no. I accept that where there is no dispute, there can be no exercise of the judicial function. But this requirement makes no demand with regard to the nature of the dispute:[20]

> [W]hat characterizes judging is the decision between claims. . . .
> Sometimes it is not the right that creates the dispute, but the dispute
> that creates the right. If a right is a desire or interest protected by law,

[18] *R. v. Inland Revenue Commissioner, ex parte National Federation of Self-Employed and Small Business Ltd.* [1982] A.C. 617, 644. *See also R. v. Somerset County Council and ARC Southern Ltd, ex parte Dixon* [1997] C.O.D. 322.

[19] For an argument that the answer is yes, see Antonin Scalia, "The Doctrine of Standing as an Essential Element of the Separation of Powers," 17 *Suffolk U. L. Rev.* 881 (1983). *Cf.* 1 Tribe, *supra* p. 35, note 57, § 3–14, at 385.

[20] *See* Hans Klinghoffer, *Administrative Law* 8 (1957) ("The concept of the dispute between the parties (*lis inter partes*) has no *a priori* test with regard to the nature of the dispute. Legal logic does not require us to regard certain matters as matters that may serve as the subject of a dispute, while excluding other matters from the possibility of being the subject of a dispute. This depends entirely on the

then it is through the judicial decision, which provides the law's protection, that the right itself is created. It follows that the judicial nature of the function is determined not by the content of the dispute but by its very existence.[21]

I take issue with a standing doctrine under which someone who claims that a public body unlawfully took his private money can resort to the courts, but someone who claims that a public body unlawfully took public money cannot. What is the principled argument, based on jurisprudence and the doctrine of separation of powers, to justify this distinction? In my view, recognition of the standing of the public petitioner closes the "circle of standing." This circle begins with the requirement that, to have standing, a petitioner have a definable right that the government has violated. At the next level, the courts recognize the standing of a petitioner with an interest in a governmental action but no definable right. At the subsequent level, courts recognize the standing of a petitioner with no tangible interest but who complains of a substantial breach of the rule of law. Finally, the circle culminates in the realization that the petitioner's right to insist on governmental compliance with the rule of law is imputed to the petitioner by his very status as a member of society. Thus, the "circle of standing" concept is based on the recognition that standing, at its core, derives from membership in society. The constitution of South Africa nicely expresses this idea by providing that "Everyone has the right to administrative action that is lawful, reasonable and procedurally fair."[22]

---

positive legal arrangement. . . . [J]udging in the functional sense has *a priori* no objective test. Judging takes place with regard to those matters with respect to which positive law gives the procedure a form of a dispute").

[21] *Ressler*, 42(2) P.D. at 465.

[22] S. Afr. Const. art. (33)1. *See also* Paul Craig, *Administrative Law* (5th ed. 2003), 751: "The presumption is therefore that citizens simply *qua* citizens have a sufficient interest in governmental legality. All else should be seen as a qualification of this."

CHAPTER TEN

Comparative Law

THE IMPORTANCE OF COMPARATIVE LAW

I have found comparative law to be of great assistance in realizing my role as a judge. The case law of the courts of the United States, Australia, Canada, the United Kingdom, and Germany have helped me significantly in finding the right path to follow. Indeed, comparing oneself to others allows for greater self-knowledge. With comparative law, the judge expands the horizon and the interpretive field of vision. Comparative law enriches the options available to us. In different legal systems, similar legal institutions often fulfill corresponding roles, and similar legal problems (such as hate speech, privacy, and now the fight against terrorism) arise.[1] To the extent that these similarities exist, comparative law becomes an important tool with which judges fulfill their role in a democracy ("microcomparison").[2] Moreover, because many of the basic principles of democracy are common to democratic countries, there is good reason to compare them ("macrocomparison").[3] Indeed, different democratic legal systems often encounter similar problems. Examining a foreign solution may help a judge choose the best local solution. This usefulness applies both to the development of the common law and to the interpretation of legal texts.[4]

---

[1] See *The Police v. Georghiades*, (1983) 2 C.L.R. 33, 50–54, 60–65, in which Justice Pikis compared different national and international legal systems to give content to the right of privacy. It was decided by the Supreme Court of Cyprus that the right of privacy applies not only vis-à-vis the state but also to relationships between individuals.
[2] *See* 1 Konrad Zweigert and Hein Kötz, *Introduction to Comparative Law* 5 (Tony Weir trans., 2d ed. 1987).
[3] *See id.* at 4–5.
[4] *See* Koopmans *supra* p. xii, note 10 at 4.

Naturally, one must approach comparative law cautiously, remaining cognizant of its limitations. Comparative law is not merely the comparison of laws. A useful comparison can exist only if the legal systems have a common ideological basis. The judge must be sensitive to the uniqueness of each legal system. Nonetheless, when the judge is convinced that the relative social, historical, and religious circumstances create a common ideological basis, it is possible to refer to a foreign legal system for a source of comparison and inspiration. Indeed, the importance of comparative law lies in extending the judge's horizons. Comparative law awakens judges to the potential latent in their own legal systems. It informs judges about the successes and failures that may result from adopting a particular legal solution. It refers judges to the relationship between a solution to the legal problem before them and other legal problems. Thus, comparative law acts as an experienced friend. Of course, there is no obligation to refer to comparative law. Additionally, even when comparative law is consulted, the final decision must always be local. The benefit of comparative law is in expanding judicial thinking about the possible arguments, legal trends, and decision-making structures available.

THE INFLUENCE OF COMPARATIVE LAW

Comparative law is a tool that aids in constitutional and statutory interpretation. This assistance may work on three levels. The first concerns interpretive theory. Comparative law helps the judge better understand the place of interpretation and the role of the judge an interpreter. For example, consider the interpretative status of the intent of the creator in understanding constitutions and statutes. Before judges decide their own position on the issue, they would do well to consider how other legal systems treat the question. The second level at which judges rely on comparative law is connected with democracy's fundamental values. Democracies share common fundamental values. Democracy must infringe on certain fundamental values in order to maintain others. It is important for judges to know how foreign law treats this question and what techniques it uses.

Does it employ a technique of balancing or of categorization? Why is one technique preferred over another? Every legal system grapples with the issue of constitutional limitations on human rights. What are these limitations, and what technique was used to reach them? What are the remedies for violating an unlawful order, and how can they be determined? The third level of aid provided by comparative law concerns the solutions it offers to specific situations. For example, how protected is racist speech? Is affirmative action recognized? How does the foreign system deal with terrorism? Of course, the resolution of these issues is intrinsically local. However, in different legal systems, they have a common core, in that they reflect the problems of democracy and the complexity of human relations. Again, I do not advocate adopting the foreign arrangement. It is never binding. I just advocate an open approach, one that recognizes that for all our singularity, we are not alone. That recognition will enrich our own legal systems if we take the trouble to understand how others respond in situations similar to those we encounter.

COMPARATIVE LAW AND INTERPRETATION OF STATUTES

Comparative law is an important source from which the judge may learn the objective purpose[5] of a statute.[6] This is the case with regard to both the specific purpose ("microcomparison") and the general purpose ("macrocomparison") of the statute. The comparison is

[5] On the objective purpose, see *supra* p. 136.
[6] For a discussion of comparative law and the courts, *see generally The Use of Comparative Law by Courts* (Ulrich Drobnig and Sjef van Erp eds., 1999); Günter Frankenberg, "Critical Comparisons: Re-thinking Comparative Law," 26 *Harv. Int'l L.J.* 411 (1985); Peter de Cruz, *Comparative Law in a Changing World* (1995); H. Patrick Glenn, "Comparative Law and Legal Practice: On Removing the Borders," 75 *Tul. L. Rev.* 977 (2001); Methias Reimann, "The Progress and Failure of Comparative Law in the Second Half of the Twentieth Century," 50 *Am. J. Comp. Law* 671 (2002); *Comparative Legal Studies: Traditions and Transitions* (Pierre Legrand and Roderick Munday eds., 2003); Mary Ann Glendon et al., *Comparative Legal Traditions* (1999); Anne-Marie Slaughter, *A New World Order* 65 (2004).

relevant even if it is clear that the legislature was not inspired by foreign law. In looking for the specific statutory purpose, a judge may
be inspired by a similar statute in a foreign democratic legal system.
This is so when he wishes to learn of the purpose underlying legislation that regulates a legal institution, such as an agency or a lease.
The judge does not refer to the details of the foreign laws. Rather,
he examines the function that the legal institution fulfills in the two
systems. If there is a similarity in the functions, he may find interpretive ideas about the (objective) purpose of the legislation. An
example of this potential use is the principle of good faith in executing a contract. To the extent that this principle fulfills a similar
function in different legal systems, it is possible to use the law of a
foreign system to discern the purpose that underlies the principle of
good faith in local law. Moreover, it is possible to use comparative
law—from other national systems and from international law—to
determine the general (objective) purpose that reflects the basic
principles of the system. Again, however, this comparative analysis is
possible only if the two legal systems share a common ideological basis.

COMPARATIVE LAW AND INTERPRETATION
OF THE CONSTITUTION

Comparative law can help judges determine the objective purpose of
a constitution. Democratic countries have several fundamental principles in common. As such, legal institutions often fulfill similar
functions across countries. From the purpose that one given democratic legal system attributes to a constitutional arrangement, one
can learn about the purpose of that constitutional arrangement in
another legal system. Indeed, comparative constitutional law is a
good source of expanded horizons and cross-fertilization of ideas
across legal systems.[7] This is clearly the case when the constitutional

[7] See Vicki C. Jackson and Mark Tushnet, *Comparative Constitutional Law*
(1999); Norman Dorsen et al., *Comparative Constitutionalism: Cases and Materials* (2003); Sujit Choudhry, "Globalization in Search of Justification: Toward
a Theory of Comparative Constitutional Interpretation," 74 *Ind. L.J.* 819
(1999); George P. Fletcher, "Comparative Law as a Subversive Discipline,"

text of one country has been influenced by the constitutional text of another. But even in the absence of any (direct or indirect) influence of one constitutional text on another, there is still a basis for interpretive inspiration. For example, a constitution may refer expressly to democratic values or democratic societies.[8] But even without such a reference, the interpretive influence of comparative law is proper.[9] This is the case with regard to determining the scope of human rights, resolving particularly difficult issues such as abortion and the death penalty, and determining constitutional remedies.

Nonetheless, as we have seen, interpretive inspiration is only proper if there is an ideological basis common to the two legal systems and a common allegiance to basic democratic principles. A common basis of democracy, however, is a necessary but insufficient condition for comparative analysis. As judges, we must also examine whether there is anything in the historical development and social conditions that makes the local and the foreign system different enough to render interpretive inspiration impracticable.[10]

---

46 *Am. J. Comp. L.* 683, 695–96 (1998); Christopher McCrudden, "A Common Law of Human Rights? Transnational Judicial Conversations on Constitutional Rights," in *Human Rights and Legal History* 29 (Katherine O'Donovan and Gerry R. Rubin eds., 2000); Kathryn A. Perales, "It Works Fine in Europe, So Why Not Here? Comparative Law and Constitutional Federalism," 23 *Vt. L. Rev.* 885 (1999); Mark Tushnet, "The Possibilities of Comparative Constitutional Law," 108 *Yale L.J.* 1225 (1999); Lorraine Weinrib, "Constitutional Conceptions and Constitutional Comparativism," in *Defining the Field of Comparative Constitutional Law* 23 (Vicki Jackson and Mark Tushnet eds., 2002); Francois Venter, *Constitutional Comparison: Japan, Germany, Canada and South Africa as Constitutional States* (2000).

[8] *See, e.g.,* Can. Const. (Canadian Charter of Rights and Freedoms), § I; S. Afr. Const. § 36(1); *see also* David M. Beatty, "The Forms and Limits of Constitutional Interpretation," 49 *Am. J. Comp. L.* 79, 102–09 (2001).

[9] *See* Donald P. Kommers, "The Value of Comparative Constitutional Law," 9 *Marshall J. Pracs. & Procs.* 685 (1976).

[10] *See R. v. Keegstra,* [1990] 3 S.C.R. 897, 740; *Rahey v. The Queen,* [1987] 1 S.C.R. 588, 639 ("While it is natural and even desirable for Canadian courts to refer to American constitutional jurisprudence in seeking to elucidate the meaning of *Charter* guarantees that have counterparts in the United States Constitution, they should be wary of drawing too ready a parallel between constitutions born to different countries in different ages and in very different circumstances"); Hogg, *supra* p. 82, note 145 at 827.

But when there is an adequate similarity, interpretive inspiration is proper. This is the case with regard to inspiration from the law of another democratic country. It is also the case with regard to interpretive inspiration from international law, as various international conventions enshrine constitutional values.[11] These conventions influence the formation of the objective purpose of different constitutional texts.[12] The case law of international and national courts that interpret these conventions ought to serve as a basis for the interpretation of the constitutions of various nations.

USE OF COMPARATIVE LAW IN PRACTICE

The use of comparative law for the development of the common law and the interpretation of legal texts is determined by the tradition of the legal system. Israeli law, for example, makes extensive use of comparative law. When Israeli courts encounter an important legal problem, they frequently examine foreign law. Reference to United States law,[13] United Kingdom law, Canadian law, and Australian law is commonplace. Those with the linguistic ability also refer to Continental law, and sometimes we use English translations of Continental (mainly German, French, and Italian) legal literature.

In countries of the British Commonwealth, there is much cross-fertilization. Each such nation refers to United Kingdom case law.

---

[11] For the products of some of the most important international conventions, *see* International Covenant on Civil and Political Rights, Dec. 19, 1966, 999 U.N.T.S. 171 (entered into force Mar. 23, 1976); International Covenant on Economic, Social and Cultural Rights, Dec. 16, 1966, 993 U.N.T.S. 3 (entered into force Jan. 3, 1976); European Convention for the Protection of Human Rights and Fundamental Freedoms, Nov. 4, 1950, Europ. T.S. No. 5, 213 U.N.T.S. 221 (entered into force Sept. 3, 1953); American Declaration of the Rights and Duties of Man, O.A.S. Official Rec., OEA/Ser. L./V./II.23, doc. 21 rev. 6 (1948); Universal Declaration of Human Rights, G.A. Res. 217A, U.N. GAOR, pt. 1, at 71, U.N. Doc. A/810 (1948).

[12] *See, e.g., Newcrest Mining (WA) Ltd. v. Commonwealth*, (1998) 195 C.L.R. 513, 655.

[13] *See* Pnina Lahav, "American Influence on Israel's Jurisprudence of Free Speech," 9 *Hastings Const. L.Q.* 23 (1981).

United Kingdom judges refer to Commonwealth case law, and Commonwealth judges in turn refer to each other's case law. The Supreme Court of Canada is particularly noteworthy for its frequent and fruitful use of comparative law.[14] As such, Canadian law serves as a source of inspiration for many countries around the world. The generous use of comparative law can be found in the opinions of the South African Constitutional Court. In South Africa's Constitution, it is explicitly determined that:

When interpreting the Bill of Rights, a court, tribunal, or forum—

a.   must promote the values that underline an open and democratic society based on human dignity, equality and freedom;

b.   must consider international law; and

c.   may consider foreign law.[15]

Regrettably, until very recently, the United States Supreme Court has made little use of comparative law.[16] Many democratic countries draw inspiration from the United States Supreme Court, particularly in its interpretation of the United States Constitution.[17] By contrast, some Justices of the United States Supreme Court do not

---

[14] *See* Anne Bayefsky, "International Human Rights Law in Canadian Courts," in *Enforcing International Human Rights in Domestic Courts* 295, 310 (Benedetto Conforti and Francesco Francioni eds., 1997).

[15] S. Afr. Const. art. 39(1).

[16] *See Printz v. United States*, 521 U.S. 898, 921 note 11 (1997) ("Justice Breyer's dissent would have us consider the benefits that other countries, and the European Union, believe they have derived from federal systems that are different from ours. We think such comparative analysis inappropriate to the task of interpreting a constitution"); *Stanford v. Kentucky*, 492 U.S. 361, 369 note 1 (1989) ("We emphasize that it is *American* conceptions of decency that are dispositive, rejecting the contention of petitioners and their various *amici* . . . that the sentencing practices of other countries are relevant"); *Thompson v. Oklahoma*, 487 U.S. 815, 868 n.4 (1988) (Scalia, J., dissenting) ("The plurality's reliance upon Amnesty International's account of what it pronounces to be civilized standards of decency in other countries. . . . is totally inappropriate as a means of establishing the fundamental beliefs of this Nation").

[17] *See* Gerald V. La Forest, "The Use of American Precedents in Canadian Courts," 46 *Me. L. Rev.* 211 (1994); Anthony Lester, "The Overseas Trade in the American Bill of Rights", 88 *Colum. L. Rev.* 537 (1988).

cite foreign case law in their judgments. They fail to make use of an important source of inspiration, one that enriches legal thinking, makes law more creative, and strengthens the democratic ties and foundations of different legal systems. Justice Claire L'Heureux-Dubé of the Canadian Supreme Court has rightly observed that "[i]f we continue to learn from each other, we as judges, lawyers, and scholars will contribute in the best possible way not only to the advancement of human rights but to the pursuit of justice itself, wherever we are."[18] Of course, American law in general, and its constitutional law in particular, is rich and developed. American law is comprised of not one but fifty-one legal systems. Nonetheless, I think that it is always possible to learn new things even from other democratic legal systems that, in their turn, have learned from American law. As Judge Guido Calabresi rightly said, "Wise parents do not hesitate to learn from their children."[19] There appears to be the beginning of change in the United States Supreme Court's attitude toward comparative law. In some recent cases, Supreme Court justices have cited case law from other jurisdictions.[20] Is the Court moving toward wider use of comparative law?

[18] *See* L'Heureux-Dubé, *supra* p. 133 note 29.
[19] *United States v. Then*, 56 F.3d 464, 469 (2d Cir. 1995).
[20] *See , e.g., Lawrence v. Texas*, 123 S. Ct. 2472 (2003).

CHAPTER ELEVEN

The Judgment

FORMULATING THE JUDGMENT AND REALIZING THE JUDICIAL ROLE

The Judgment Is the Voice of the Judge

The means for realizing the judicial role are carried out in practice via the reasoned judgment of the court.[1] The judgment is the voice of the judge, through which the judge realizes his role in a democracy. True, judges may write books and articles and sometimes give lectures and teach students. In doing so, the judge acts as an individual. Only through the judgment does the individual act as a judge. The judgment is the judge's means of expression, the exclusive means through which the judicial voice is actualized in practice. That judgment is sometimes criticized. The judge generally cannot respond to such criticism; what the judge has to say is said in the judgment. The role of the judge ends there. Of course, judges can express their positions—accepting or rejecting the criticism—in additional judgments, which will raise the issue anew.

Writing a judgment is complicated. There is a whole theory behind it, which must be studied. At the heart of this theory is the clear and concise formulation of the facts, winnowing out those that are irrelevant.[2] Care should be taken to preserve the dignity of the parties and the witnesses. In addition to the facts, the judge must explain the legal conclusion. This explanation is critical. The decision

---

[1] *See* Karl N. Llewellyn, *The Common Law Tradition: Deciding Appeals* (1960); Robert Keeton, *Judging in the American Legal System* (1999).
[2] *See* Tom Bingham, "The Judge as Juror: The Judicial Determination of Factual Issues," 38 *Current Legal Problems* 1(1985).

must explain to the parties why they won or lost; it must explain to the lawyers why a certain result was reached; it must establish case law for society as a whole. A judicial decision is written for various audiences. It fulfills different roles. Writing it properly is an art that requires study. A full examination of that question is beyond the scope of this book.

Minimalism or Maximalism?

A key question the judge faces is the judgment's level of abstraction. The question is whether to adopt a minimizing approach, at a low level of abstraction, establishing the narrowest principle necessary to justify the result, or to adopt a maximizing approach, at a high level of abstraction, establishing a general principle that should apply to a broad variety of cases. On this issue there are no rules that bind the judge. It is an issue of discretion. How should such discretion be exercised?

Sunstein claims that as a matter of principle, a judge who interprets a constitution should adopt a minimalist approach.[3] There are exceptions to this rule, for which a maximizing approach is appropriate. I prefer not to adopt a general, principled position on the issue. A judgment's level of abstraction must vary from case to case, issue to issue, period to period, legal system to legal system. Minimizing or maximizing are not *a priori* approaches. A new legal issue differs from a legal issue about which much has been written; an issue involving numerous social changes differs from an issue involving few changes; an old, established democracy (such as the United States) differs from a young democracy (such as Israel). Indeed, just as we cannot establish an advance presumption that a constitutional text should be interpreted expansively or narrowly, so

---

[3] Cass Sunstein, *One Case at a Time: Judicial Minimalism on the Supreme Court* (1999); Neil S. Siegel, "A Theory in Search of a Court, and Itself: Judicial Minimalism at the Supreme Court Bar," 103 *Mich. L. Rev.* 1951 (2005); Cass R. Sunstein, "Testing Minimalism: A Reply," 104 *Mich. L. Rev.* 123 (2005).

we cannot establish an advance presumption that a judgment interpreting the constitution should minimize or maximize. All I can say is that the judge should be sensitive to how the judgment is formulated and at what level of abstraction; in some cases the right formulation will be minimalist, in others it will be maximizing.

Rhetoric

The rhetoric of a decision is important, too. Strong rhetoric echoes loudly. The judgment's words reach the public via strong amplifiers. Is strong rhetoric desirable? It depends on the circumstances. For issues already addressed by the court, for which the case law is stable and only continuity is required, we can avoid strong rhetoric. It does not help advance the judicial role. For issues for which, in order to realize the judicial role, it is necessary to increase public awareness, strong rhetoric is sometimes appropriate. For example, in the *Zarzevski* case,[4] the Israeli Supreme Court addressed the problem of a government coalition agreement that included financial commitments between political parties. In that case, I emphasized that "power cannot be purchased with money."[5] That is strong rhetoric. I think it was appropriate. It called attention to flaws in Israeli public affairs.

Dicta

The principle of binding precedent means that something established in a ruling by the Supreme Court binds lower courts. That "thing" establishes the rule of the case. What is the rule of the case, however, and how is it determined? That question has yet to be sufficiently clarified. All agree that not every declaration in a judicial decision constitutes the rule of the case. There is a distinction between the *ratio decidendi*, which establishes the binding legal norm, and *obiter dicta*, which are not binding precedent. Deciding

[4] H.C. 1635/90, *Zarzevsky v. Prime Minister*, 45(1) P.D. 749.
[5] *Id.* at 851.

about what is *ratio* and what is *dictum* is not up to the judge who writes the decision. That decision is made in subsequent case law. Indeed, as a general matter, the very determination by a judge that a particular rule that he decided is either *ratio* or *dictum* is itself dictum. Having said that, judges, who know the distinction between *ratio* and *dicta*, often know that something they wish to write will be nothing but *dicta*. Should *dicta* be written in the knowledge that they are *dicta*? It should be noted that although *dictum* is not binding, it may have influence. Today's *dictum* may be tomorrow's *ratio*. Although it is not binding, it is often highly persuasive. Is the technique of *dicta* appropriate?

There seems to be agreement that in principle, it is appropriate for judges to employ the tool of *dicta*, on the condition that they do so in moderation. The key question is when and how to use *dicta*. My view is that *dictum* is an important tool for realizing the judicial role and should be used when it advances that role. Therefore, where a new rule is necessary or an old rule requires clarification in order to bridge the gap between law and life or to protect the constitution and its values, a judicial decision should address that issue, even if it does so not through binding case law but rather in *dicta*. The judge then expresses his opinion about the new precedent or clarification of the old. In doing so, the judge is likely to motivate the legislature to initiate action; he influences the reasonable expectations of members of the public, providing them with a kind of "warning notice" regarding what is likely happen in the future; he delineates the route that the public in general, and public agencies in particular, are likely to take.

THE JUDGE AS PART OF THE PANEL

The Individual Judge and the Panel of Judges

Most legal literature examining the role of the judge shines the spotlight on the individual judge. It examines how the judge should have exercised discretion in achieving his role. Scholars do not sufficiently consider the fact that the judge often acts as part of a panel. That is true of most of the cases brought before supreme courts and of cases brought before appellate courts or even trial courts, depending on the type of case and jurisdiction. When the judge sits as a panel of one, he must search within himself and convince himself. When the judge sits on a panel of multiple judges, the judge must consult with his colleagues. The judge must convince them. A good court is a pluralistic court, containing different and diverse views. That is certainly the case in a multicultural society. There are always mutual persuasion and exchange of ideas. Of course, there is a limit to the power that one judge has to persuade another—limits of good taste, beyond which judges should not try to insist on trying to change their colleagues' opinions. The interaction between judges sets the appropriate boundaries between a single judge and the other panel members. These limits influence the way in which the judicial role is realized. A full discussion of these limits and their significance is beyond the scope of this book.[6] I will limit myself to a few prominent issues that are important to the realization of the judicial role.

Dissent

Appellate courts generally sit in panels of judges. Obviously, the judges on the panel discuss the decision, both the result as well as the reasoning. They discuss the level of abstraction of the decision. Sometimes a judge finds himself in the dissent. The judge tries, within the limits of good taste, to convince his colleagues, to no avail.[7] At the end of the day, what should the judge do?[8]

---

[6] See Ruth Bader Ginsburg, "Speaking in a Judicial Voice," 67 N.Y.U. L. Rev. 1185 (1992); Harry Edwards, "The Effects of Collegiality on Judicial Decision Making," 151 U. Pa. L. Rev. 1639 (2003); Forrest Maltzman et al., Crafting Law on the Supreme Court: The Collegial Game (2000); Walter Murphy, Elements of Judicial Strategy (1964).

[7] See Ruth Bader Ginsburg, "Communicating and Commenting on the Court's Work," 83 Geo. L. J. 2119 (1995).

[8] There is extensive literature on dissenting opinions. See Stanley Fuld, "The Voices of Dissent," 62 Colum. L. Rev. 923 (1962); William Brennan, "In Defense

The judge may change his mind. Every judge accords substantial weight to the opinion of his colleagues. Judges analyze those opinions, willing to change their minds if they believe their colleagues are right. Every position within the discussion is a starting point for thinking, and the mind must be open to persuasion. If I have learned one thing in my many years of judging on the Israeli Supreme Court, it is the need to approach every issue with an open mind and the willingness to learn, to be persuaded, and to admit mistakes.

What should a judge do if, after all the discussions and debates, he remains un-persuaded? If the judge thinks that the legal problem has just one legal solution, and it is the one he advocates, the judge has no choice but to say so in the decision, stating his opinion about the solution. The judge will write a dissenting opinion. Perhaps, however, the judge believes that the legal problem has a number of possible solutions. In that case, the judge has discretion to choose among a few legal solutions, including the one he thinks is best. In that kind of situation, should the judge always write a dissent? My answer is no. The judge should balance the advantage of insisting on his opinion with the disadvantage created by the very expression of dissent; take into account considerations of the legal system generally and the subject he is dealing with in particular; balance the advantage of expressing a dissent that may in the future become the majority opinion with the disadvantage of the uncertainty that dissent may create within the legal system. The judge should reflect on his role as a judge in the society in which he operates. In this situation, each judge will make his own choice.[9] On more than one occasion I have abstained from expressing a dissenting opinion because I thought that the majority opinion was

---

of Dissents," 37 *Hastings L.J.* 427 (1986); Antonin Scalia, "The Dissenting Opinion," 33 *J. Sup. Ct. Hist.* (1994); Claire L'Heureux-Dubè, "The Dissenting Opinion: Voice of the Future?" 38 *Osgoode Hall L.J.* 495 (2000).

[9] See the dissent of Lord Steyn in *Fisher vs. Minister of Public Safety and Immigration*, [1998] A.C. 673, 686 ("A dissenting judgment anchored in the circumstances of today sometimes appeals to the judges of tomorrow. In that way a dissenting judgment sometimes contributes to the continuing development of the law. But the innate capacity of different areas of law to develop varies").

legitimate and that the advantage of expressing a consistent opinion, with no dissent, outweighed the disadvantages of that consistency. I have always viewed my own dissenting opinions as a necessary evil, not a source of pride.

Here is a special case: In a previous case, I wrote a dissenting opinion. Now the issue arises again, and I remain in the dissent. How should I behave? Should I accept the majority opinion or reiterate my dissent until it becomes the majority opinion? Each judge will act as he sees fit. Throughout the years my view has been that, as a rule, I accept the majority opinion and do not repeat my dissent. The law is as the majority decides, and I accept the yoke of that law. That is the rule, and I have created an important exception. I will reiterate my dissenting opinion in the cases that cut to the heart of the matter of realizing the judicial role. In such cases I will use every attempt to bring about a change in the majority opinion. I will not hesitate to repeat my dissenting opinion.[10]

Concurrence

A dissenting opinion disagrees with the result of the decision, and naturally with the reasoning, as well. A concurring opinion accepts the result but seeks to base it on different reasoning. The difference in reasoning may be based in rhetoric, level of abstraction, or the legal foundation on which the decision rests. Is it appropriate to write a concurring opinion?[11]

The answer to that question is in no way simple. We are dealing with a set of considerations that must be weighed. Of course, if the concurring opinion challenges the legitimacy of the legal basis on which the opinion rests, arguing that it should be based on an entirely different foundation, the holder of that opinion should behave as though he were in the dissent. However, what should be done when

---

[10] A good example may be found in Justice Brennan's dissents in capital punishment cases: *see* Brennan, *supra* p. 209, note 8.
[11] *See* Ruth Bader Ginsburg, "Remarks on Writing Separately," 65 *Wash. L. Rev.* 133 (199).

there is consensus over the legal basis but disagreement over rhetoric or level of abstraction? Is that sufficient to justify a concurring opinion? The answer depends on the circumstances. Sometimes, in order to realize the judicial role, the court must speak with one voice. Every concurring opinion weakens the force of the judgment. The persuasive power of the judgment, its force, and its ability to withstand criticism depend on consistency of the opinions. In these cases, the judge should give up on the rhetoric or level of abstraction that he thinks is appropriate and should add his voice to the single voice of the court.[12] Not every case falls into that category. Sometimes the problem is new. The court is taking the first step of a long journey. The direction is not yet clear. It is appropriate and desirable to express different and diverse opinions that will help shape the future law. In these cases, concurring opinions are an appropriate and desirable means by which the judge realizes his role.

---

[12] *Cooper v. Aaron*, 358 U.S. 1 (1958), is a good example.

Part Three

THE RELATIONSHIP BETWEEN THE

COURT AND THE OTHER BRANCHES

OF THE STATE

CHAPTER TWELVE

Tension among the Branches

CONSTANT TENSION

There is constant tension in the relationships between the courts and the other branches of the state,[1] a tension that stems from the different roles of the branches. The role of the judiciary is to review the actions of other branches and evaluate whether they are acting lawfully. This role naturally meets with opposition from the other branches, particularly when the judiciary, through its rulings, frustrates political goals the other branches pursue. In such circumstances many argue that a body that is not accountable to the people should not be able to frustrate the will of the people. The more cherished the voided act is to the hearts of the political authorities, the greater the criticism, amplified across all forms of media. The court has limited access to such media. As a result, the tension between it and the other branches increases. It reaches its peak when the other branches try to use their powers to change the composition or jurisdiction of the court.[2] In these situations, an impartial court examines the use of these powers by the other branches with the same objectivity that it usually exercises, for the court does not seek to protect its own composition or jurisdiction but rather to protect the values of democracy.[3]

[1] See Harry Woolf, "Judicial Review—The Tensions Between the Executive and the Judiciary," 114, *L.Q. Rev.* 579 (1998); Guarnieri, et al., *supra* p. xii, note 10 at 150.
[2] See William E. Leuchtenburg, "The Origins of Franklin D. Roosevelt's 'Court-Packing' Plan" 1966, *S. Ct. Rev.* 347 (describing President Roosevelt's desire "to pack the court").
[3] This exercise of judicial authority created a tension between the Appellate Division and the Parliament in South Africa with regard to the implementation of apartheid. *See* C.F. Forsyth, *In Danger for Their Talents* 58–128 (1985).

The court may determine, therefore, that some of these means are lawful. In the event that the court makes such a determination, the composition or jurisdiction of the court may be preserved only with the help of social forces that seek to protect democracy and the court. In this instance, public confidence in the court plays a central role.

THE TENSION IS NATURAL AND DESIRABLE

Tension between the courts and the other branches is natural and, in my opinion, also desirable. If the court's rulings were always satisfactory to the other branches, it would raise suspicion that the court was not properly fulfilling its role in the democracy. Thus, criticism of the court's rulings is proper and benefits the court itself, for this criticism helps to guard the guardians. Indeed, the constant tension between the judicial branch and the other branches stems from their distinct roles. Their different functions are based on different points of view, which in turn lead to a different perception of reality. It is much like the different perspectives different viewers have of a statue, based on their own viewing angle. The legislative viewpoint is political; the judicial viewpoint is a legal one. Other branches seek to attain efficiency; the courts seek to attain legality. The different viewpoints, the need to give explanations to the court, and the existing danger—which at times is realized—that an executive action is not proper, and the courts will determine it as such, create a constant tension between the courts and the other branches. Matters begin to deteriorate, however, when the criticism is transformed into an unbridled attack. Public confidence in the courts may be harmed, and the checks and balances that characterize the separation of powers may be undermined. When such attacks affect the composition or jurisdiction of the court, the crisis point is reached. This condition may signal the beginning of the end of democracy.

What should judges do when they find themselves in this tension? Not much. They must remain faithful to their judicial approach; they should realize their outlook on the judicial role. They must be aware of this tension but not give in to it. Indeed, every judge learns, over the years, to live with this tension. Experience strengthens the judge. Many factors affect the intensity of the tension between the court and the other branches of the state. In the following pages I consider one of these factors: the attitude toward the state and toward public officials.

THE ATTITUDE TOWARD THE STATE

The intensity of the tension between the judiciary and the other branches derives in part from the attitudes of society and the judiciary toward the state itself. This attitude in turn reflects that polity's history and the way the polity formulates its national identity. Naturally, this attitude is always complex, and I am far from an expert. Nonetheless, I think that we can distinguish roughly among three primary societal models.

The first model is that of societies that regard the state with great suspicion. In these societies, the state is perceived as a force that threatens the individual and his freedom rather than as a sovereign power that protects the individual and his freedom. The purpose of this particular constitutional arrangement is to restrict the power of the state—embodied mainly in the legislature and the executive— and thereby to protect the individual. In American society—in view of its history, particularly its revolution against British rule—this attitude seems prevalent. The Bill of Rights and other constitutional amendments are mainly composed of restrictions on the power of the branches of state ("No State shall,"[4] "Congress shall make no law"[5]). The main rights recognized in the Bill of Rights are the freedoms that the state is forbidden from harming. These freedoms thus constitute "negative" rights (*status negativus*) that are concerned with limiting state action.[6] Under these limitations,

---

[4] U.S. Const. amend. XIV. § 1.
[5] U.S. Const. amend. I.
[6] *See DeShaney v. Winnebago County Dep't of Soc. Servs.*, 489 U.S. 189, 196 (1989) ("[T]he Due Process Clauses generally confer no affirmative right to governmental

the tension between the court and the other branches of government may reach a crisis point. A longstanding political tradition and significant government restraint in exercising power—including judicial restraint based on the view that the judiciary is itself a branch of the state—are all that can prevent a crisis. Both of these safeguards, of course, exist in the United States.

Under the second model of society, the state, represented by the executive and legislative branches, is viewed as a realization of national aspirations. The attitude toward the state is one of respect and admiration rather than suspicion. I think that this was the approach in several Continental countries before the Second World War. In this model, there is minimal tension between the judiciary and other branches: the judiciary acts as a public institution representing the state and sees its purpose as allowing the state to achieve national goals and aspirations.

In the third model of society, the state is perceived as both a source of good and a source of evil. The state is feared as a source of harm to the individual, but it is also supported as a source of protection for the individual. In this model the rights of the individual include not just the negative right against state intervention but also the positive right (*status positivus*) to protect the essential

---

aid, even where such aid may be necessary to secure life, liberty, or property interests of which the government itself may not deprive the individual"); *Jackson v. City of Joliet*, 715 F.2d 1200, 1203 (7th Cir. 1983) ("[T]he Constitution is a charter of negative rather than positive liberties"); Ruth Bader Ginsburg, "An Overview of Court Review for Constitutionality in the United States," 57 *La. L. Rev.* 1019, 1026 (1997) ("Our courts, through judicial review, are accustomed to telling government what it may not do; they are not, by tradition or staffing, well-equipped to map out elaborate programs detailing what the government must do"). *But see* Steven J. Heyman, "The First Duty of Government: Protection, Liberty and the Fourteenth Amendment," 41 *Duke L.J.* 507 (1991). Professor Owen Fiss argues that the state should be responsible not just for refraining from violating an individual's right to freedom of speech, but also for protecting it. *See* Owen M. Fiss, *The Irony of Free Speech* 27–49 (1996); Owen M. Fiss, *Liberalism Divided: Freedom of Speech and the Many Uses of State Power* 32–46 (1996). *See also* Frank Michelman, "The Protective Function of the State in the United States and Europe: The Constitutional Question," in Georg Nolte (ed.), *European and U.S. Constitutionalism*, 156 (2005).

freedoms and provision of vital services.[7] I think that Australia[8] and Canada[9] can be included in this group. These countries obtained independence from England through a democratic process rather than through revolution, and so experienced continued and extensive absorption of traditional English principles.[10] These principles underlie the Canadian Charter's recognition not merely of the duty of the state not to harm the freedom of the individual, but also of the duty of the state to protect the individual.[11] Another example of this model may be Israel. For many, the establishment of the state was the realization of a longstanding dream; hence the attitude of respect and admiration for the state. But the state is also seen as the source of power and restriction of freedom; hence the suspicion of it. This tension is reflected in the fact that people trust the state somewhat, but not fully. The Israeli Bill of Rights provides, in part, that "[t]here shall be no violation of the life, body or dignity of any person as such."[12] This provision, which limits state action, reflects a conception of the state as a threat to the individual. However, another provision states that "[e]very person is entitled to protection of his life, person and dignity."[13] Here, the state

[7] *See* William W. Black, "The Charter of Rights and Freedoms and Positive Obligations," in *Law, Policy, and International Justice* 298 (William Kaplan and Donald McRae eds., 1993) (arguing that the Canadian Charter of Rights and Freedoms imposes not only negative restrictions on government but positive duties as well); David P. Currie, "Positive and Negative Constitutional Rights," 53 *U. Chi. L. Rev.* 864 (1986); Dieter Grim, "The Protective Function of the State," in Nolte, *supra* p. 218, note 6 at 137.

[8] *See* Melissa Castan and Sarah Joseph, *Federal Constitutional Law: A Contemporary View* 24 (2001).

[9] *See* Brian Dickson, "The Canadian Charter of Rights and Freedoms: Dawn of a New Era?" 2 *Rev. Const. Stud.* 1, 2–3 (1994); McLachlin, "The Role of the Court," *supra* p. ix, note 1 at 52.

[10] *See* Dickson, *supra* p. 219, note 9 at 15–16.

[11] *See McKinney v. Bd. of Governors of the Univ. of Guelph*, [1990] 76 D.L.R. 545, 624 (expressing skepticism of the proposition that "the government could not be found to be in breach of the Charter for failing to act").

[12] Basic Law: Human Dignity and Liberty § 2 (1992).

[13] *Id.* § 3.

is conceived as a force that protects the individual. Thus, for example, in one opinion I derived from this provision the right to minimum goods and services necessary to maintain human existence.[14] In societies reflecting this third model, the intensity of the tension between the judiciary and the other branches depends on the balance between acts of the state that are viewed as harming the individual and those that are viewed as protecting him.

PUBLIC OFFICIALS AS TRUSTEES

Public Trustees

This attitude of "respect and suspicion" toward the state also applies to government officeholders, based on the principle that they are the trustees of the public and owe the public a duty of loyalty. This attitude also reflects the proper view of democracy. Indeed, the fundamental perspective is that the public official is the trustee of the public. Public officials do not act for their own sake but rather for the sake of the public interest. In this view, the role of the public official in a democracy, like the role of the state itself, is to serve the interest of the public and its members. In one of my judgments I wrote:

> The government in itself has no "private" interest of its own. The government exists for the sake of individuals. The government does not exist for its "own" sake. Those who represent the government have no "self" interest that must be protected. They must act to achieve the collective interest. Indeed, there is a serious concern—a concern that history has repeatedly validated—that representatives of the government will develop their own interests and use the tremendous power granted them for purposes that do not reflect the collective good. The duty of loyalty seeks to prevent that. The duty of

---

[14] *See* C.A. 4905/98, *Gamzu v. Yeshiahu*, 55(3) P.D. 360, 375–76. *See supra* p. 87.

loyalty seeks to guarantee that the government takes care of the public and not itself; the general duty of loyalty seeks to guarantee that the government takes care of the public and not itself.[15]

General Duty of Fairness

This view, of public officials as public trustees, is not just judicial rhetoric. In practice, it is the basis for case law, establishing modes of behavior by public officials. Trusteeship demands fairness. Indeed, we derive a general duty of fairness from the view that public officials act as trustees. The general duty of fairness seeks to guarantee that governmental authority is exercised in a way that serves the collective, and not the government itself. In the past, the duty was seen as deriving from the power and authority granted to the public official by statute. According to that view, acting in the absence of administrative fairness was a deviation from the authority of the public agency (*ultra vires*). Today, we need not cling only to that view. Public officials owe a duty of fairness, derived also from their role as public trustees. It is not just a question of authority but also of the public trustee exercising discretion. The state owes a duty of administrative fairness in its activities,[16] and the same is true of the public servant who acts on its behalf.

The Content of the Duty of Trusteeship

The duty of trusteeship imposes derivative duties upon the state:

> Trusteeship requires fairness, and fairness requires integrity, relevance, equality, and reasonableness. This list of principles derived from the position of trusteeship is not closed, and the list of values derived from the duty of fairness is not fixed. Values and principles, by nature, are on the one hand stable and on the other hand evolving. They are

[15] H.C. 164/97, *Conterm Ltd. v. Finance Ministry*, 52(1) P.D. 289, 347; [1998–9] IsrLR 1, 71–72.
[16] S. Afr. Const. art. 33(1). *See supra* p. 196, note 22.

sown in the soul of the nation and are not subject to passing trends. They are full of vitality, and they evolve to provide fitting solutions to new problems.[17]

Case law recognizes a long line of secondary principles derived from the trusteeship of public officials and their duty to act with fairness. Here is a partial list: the duty to act reasonably, the duty not to discriminate among persons, the duty to refrain from acting arbitrarily, the duty to act in accordance with the rules of natural justice, the prohibition against being subject to a conflict of interests, the duty to respect promises and agreements, the duty to refrain from making political appointments, the duty to disclose political agreements, the duty to disclose public information to the individual, the duty to act with professional ethics, the duty to take distributive justice into account.

DUTIES OF THE INDIVIDUAL TOWARD THE STATE

Rights and Duties in a Democracy

We tend to emphasize that democracy is about human rights. We thus express a view that in democracy, rights are natural to the individual and the state is the creation of the individuals. The point of departure is liberty vis-à-vis the state, whereas the state's rights and the individual's duties toward it require an explicit arrangement. However, it seems that we do not sufficiently emphasize the duties of the individual.[18] Indeed, democracy is not just a regime of rights. Democracy is also a regime of duties. This is obvious regarding relations between individuals. The right of A is a duty owed by B. But it is also true regarding the relations between the individual and the state. These relations are made up not only of the rights granted to the individual toward the state, they are also made up of the individual's duties toward the state. I noted in one case

---

[17] H.C. 1635/90, *Zarzevsky v. Prime Minister*, 45(1) P.D. 749, 841 (Barak, J.).
[18] *See* Hodgson, *supra* p. 75, note 126.

that "beside human rights there are also human duties; that the normative world is not only one of rights, but also one of duties; that beside the right of an individual stands his duty towards a fellow individual, and his duty toward society."[19] In another case I noted:

Democracy is not only human rights. Democracy is also human duties—duties toward the other individuals and duties toward the government. Indeed, democracy is based on living together, and on national interest. The government acts for the good of the public. For that purpose, it must be granted rights (in the wide sense of the term), otherwise it will not be able to fulfill the interest of society. Granting of rights to the government means imposing duties toward the government upon the individual. These duties are intended to enable the government to achieve the goals expected of it in a democracy. They are derived from the circumstances of living together and from the need to advance the liberty of each and every individual. They are based on the view of the modern welfare state and on social solidarity. They are derived from a view that sees the individual as part of society, and therefore, necessarily, within his personality, there is a "social aspect" from which the internal need to be considerate of society is drawn. Moreover, they are derived from society's demands of the individual as part of society, to act for the good of society. They are the result of a balance between the needs of society and the rights of the individual.[20]

Varied and numerous are the duties of the individual toward the state, from duties owed to the state *qua* state—including the most important, the duty to give one's life in defense of the state, to be loyal to it, and not to betray it—to the duties that the individual owes the state when, as in the case of a contractual relationship, the state behaves as an "individual."

---

[19] C.A. 6821/93, *United Mizrahi Bank Ltd. v. Migdal Cooperative Village*, 49(4) P.D. 221, 443.
[20] H.C. 164/97, *Conterm Ltd. v. Ministry of Finance, Customs and V.A.T. Branch*, 52(1) P.D. 289, 349; [1998–9] IsrLR 1.

Does the Individual Have a General Duty
of Fairness toward the State?

The state and the public officials are the trustees of the public. This trusteeship obligates them with a general duty of fairness toward each and every individual in society. Does the individual have a general duty of fairness toward the state? The question arose in the *Conterm* case.[21] In my concurring opinion, I expressed the view that, in a democracy, the individual owes no general duty of fairness to the state but rather specific duties that depend on the circumstances:

> The duties of the individual are duties based upon the view of the individual in a democratic society and upon the role of the government in a democratic society. Their point of departure is the liberty of the individual, on the one hand, and the role of the government on the other. Tension exists between these poles, since the government must act for the good of society, and the good of society is likely to conflict with the right of the individual. This tension is released through various duties that the individual owes to the government. These duties are not based on a general duty imposed on every individual. Such a general duty is not proper. Naturally, the individual's duties toward the government are the result of a balance between conflicting values. They are a compromise between the human right of the individual and the interest of the public. In this balance, the stronger the infringement on the right of the individual and the weaker the interest of the people, the milder the individual's obligation will be. However, the weaker the infringement on the individual's right and the stronger the public interest, the stronger the individual's obligation will be. In the middle stand the hard cases, in which the infringement on the individual's right is strong and the public interest is strong. In these situations, the balance point—from which the individual's duty is derived—is determined according to that society's beliefs regarding the proper relations between the

---

[21] *Id.*

individual and society, between the individual and the public. The complex relations between individual and government are not based on one general duty of the individual toward the government. Individuals' duties are sporadic duties with common characteristics, as called for in the specific circumstances. The individual has no general duty toward the government—beyond the duty to obey the law—and most certainly not a general duty of fairness. The individual's duties are "pinpoint" ones . . . true, the relations between the government and the individual are a two-way street, but they are neither reciprocal nor equal.[22]

Justice M. Cheshin expressed a similar view. In his opinion, "the individual may and is entitled to do anything (or to omit doing anything) that he or she is not prohibited from doing (or required to do), unless he or she bears a duty to do it (or not to do it)."[23] The individual is born free and owes nothing to the government except duties that are explicitly or implicitly established.

I note, however, that the third justice on the panel took a different view. According to Justice I. Zamir, the individual owes the government a general duty of fairness. He wrote:

In my opinion, the citizen should therefore owe a duty of fairness to the agency, as the agency owes a duty of fairness to the citizen. This requirement is deeply rooted: it springs from the social contract at the foundation of the state . . . In a well-ordered society, the duty of fairness must express the appropriate relationship between the public administration, which acts as the trustee of the public, and citizens, who are the public. This relationship is a reciprocal relationship between partners in a goal-oriented activity, based on respect, trust, and reliability.[24]

---

[22] *Id.* at 350–51.
[23] *Id.* at 366.
[24] *Id.* at 320.

CHAPTER THIRTEEN

The Relationship between the Judiciary and the Legislature

THE UNIQUENESS OF THE LEGISLATURE

The Importance of the Legislature

The foundation of democracy is a legislature elected freely and periodically by the people. Without majority rule, as reflected in the power of the legislature, there is no democracy. As judges and legal scholars, we often forget this fundamental principle. Common law legal thought focuses mainly on the judiciary and neglects the legislature. Jeremy Waldron has rightly said that "legislation and legislatures have a bad name in legal and political philosophy, a name sufficiently disreputable to cast doubt on their credentials as respectable sources of law."[1] In contrast, my concept of the role of a judge in a democracy recognizes the central role of the legislature. Undermining the legislature undermines democracy. My concept of the rule of law and of the separation of powers do not undermine the legislature. Rather, they ensure that all branches of state act within the framework of the constitution and statutes. Only thus can we maintain public confidence in the legislature; only thus can we preserve the dignity of legislation. Purposive interpretation is also intended to protect the status of the legislature. Indeed, in interpreting legislation, purposive interpretation considers the legislature's subjective intent. I regard it as an internal inconsistency in Waldron's approach that he wishes to guarantee the status and importance of the legislature[2] but is not prepared to interpret

[1] Jeremy Waldron, *The Dignity of Legislation* 1 (1999).
[2] *See id.* at 2.

its legislation according to its own intent.[3] My concept of the partnership between the judge and the legislature is intended to emphasize the importance of the legislature and its senior position with regard to legislation. Justice McLachlin rightly said that in democracies, "the elected legislators, the executive and the courts all have their role to play. Each must play that role in a spirit of profound respect for the other. We are not adversaries. We are all in the justice business, together."[4]

The "Nondelegation" Doctrine

Because of the democratic importance of the legislature, I regard with concern the growing tendency of legislatures to delegate their legislative powers to the executive. I am aware of the practical considerations that underlie this tendency. Nonetheless, it seems to me that the status of the legislature should be preserved at all costs. Thus, we must ensure that the legislature prescribes all fundamental legal arrangements by statute, and that the administrative agency has only the power to implement the legislative will. The principle of separation of powers requires this relationship. It implies that the legislature "lay[s] down the general policy and standards that animate the law, leaving the agency to refine those standards, 'fill in the blanks,' or apply the standards to particular cases."[5] The German Constitutional Court has discussed this requirement of the separation of powers principle, stating that "[i]f [a statute] does not adequately define executive powers, then the executive branch will no longer implement the law and act within legislative guidelines but will substitute its own decisions for those of the legislature. This violates the principle of the separation of powers."[6]

[3] See id. at 26–28.
[4] McLachlin, "Charter Myths," supra p. 94, note 177 at 36.
[5] Indus. Union Dep't v. Am. Petroleum Inst., 448 U.S. 607, 675 (1980) (Rehnquist, J., concurring). See Tribe, supra p. 35, note 57, § 5–19, at 977–78.
[6] 8 BVerfGE 274, 325 (1958), translated in Kommers, supra p. 22, note 9 at 138. See also Currie, supra p. 22, note 9 at 132–33; Kommers, supra p. 22, note 9 at 145.

The rule of law "requires the legislature to establish the primary arrangements and principled standards, whereas the administration has authority to actualize these primary arrangements by establishing secondary arrangements and modes of implementation."[7] As the German Constitutional Court has explained:

> The basic tenets of the rule of law require that an empowering statute adequately limit and define executive authorization to issue burdensome administrative orders according to content, subject matter, purpose, and scope . . . so that official action [will] be comprehensible and to a certain extent predictable for the citizen.[8]

Indeed, the principle of democracy demands that

> the substantive decisions regarding the policy of the State and the needs of society must be made by its popularly elected representatives. [The legislature] is elected by the people to enact its laws, and it therefore enjoys social legitimacy in this activity. . . . The legislature may not refer the critical and difficult decisions to the executive without giving it guidance.[9]

In legislative decisions that restrict human rights, the legislature must determine the primary arrangements of the restrictions. Only in this way will it be possible, in a democracy, to protect human rights properly. Even a regime whose constitution protects human rights may restrict them under certain conditions, one of which is that when the restriction is made by statute, the statute must set out the principled, basic criteria for the restriction.

Naturally, the dividing line between primary arrangements, which must be established by the legislature, and secondary arrangements, which may be established in secondary legislation, is not clearly defined. The realities of life sometimes necessitate a compromise in this respect. It is difficult, in a modern democracy, to maintain fully this principled approach to primary arrangements. The legislature

---

[7] H.C. 3267/97, *Rubinstein v. Minister of Def.*, 52(5) P.D. 481, 507; [1998–9] IsrLR 139.
[8] 8 BverfGE, at 325.
[9] *Rubinstein*, 52(5) P.D. at 508–10.

can be given some space to maneuver. Although a reasonably high level of abstraction may be acceptable for criteria and policy guidelines, the essential distinction between the roles of primary and secondary legislation must remain. Primary legislation must determine the general plan and the criteria for making decisions that are critically important to the life of the individual. From the statute itself—according to its accepted interpretation—it must be possible to deduce the zone in which the executive may act, and the primary directions that should guide the executive in its actions.

Other countries have adopted this principled approach. The United States Supreme Court accepts the doctrine of nondelegation, although this doctrine has been clouded and infrequently applied.[10] The German Constitutional Court more actively applies the doctrine in limiting the legislature's ability to delegate power to executive officers or other institutional actors.[11] In Israel, use of the doctrine began only recently.[12] If we wish to preserve the proper status of the legislature in a democracy, we must ensure that the legislature makes critical lawmaking decisions and establishes criteria for other important decisions in its legislation.

JUDICIAL REVIEW OF LEGISLATION

Most courts in democracies—ordinary courts and constitutional courts—exercise judicial review of the constitutionality of statutes.[13] Since the end of World War II most new constitutions have included

---

[10] *See* 1 Tribe, *supra* p. 35, note 57, § 5–19, at 977–78 *See also* Cass R. Sunstein, *Designing Democracy: What Constitutions Do* 137 (2001).

[11] *See* Currie, *supra* p. 22, note 9 at 132–33; Kommers, *supra* p. 22, note 9 at 145.

[12] *See Rubinstein*, 52(5) P.D. at 502.

[13] *See Comparative Judicial Review and Public Policy* (Donald W. Jackson and C. Neal Tate eds., 1992); *Human Rights and Judicial Review: A Comparative Perspective* (David M. Beatty ed., 1994); C. Neal Tate and Torbjörn Vallinder, "The Global Expansion of Judicial Power: The Judicialization of Politics," in *The Global Expansion of Judicial Power* 1, 1–10 (C. Neal Tate and Torbjörn Vallinder eds., 1995); Bruce Ackerman, "The Rise of World Constitutionalism," 83 *Va. L. Rev.* 771, 772 (1997).

express provisions about judicial review, thereby ending the legal debate over its legitimacy. Naturally, the debate about the wisdom of implementing this review continues, although "the worldwide debate does not usually occur within the same terms as it does in the United States."[14] A number of countries have constitutional provisions stating that there is no judicial review of the constitutionality of statutes.[15] Even in these countries, there is no room for argument as to the legitimacy of the absence of judicial review. What remains is debate over the wisdom of the constitutional provision. In several countries, including the United States and Israel, there is no express provision in the constitution for judicial review of legislation. Nonetheless, the courts in these two countries have held that judicial review of legislation is implied by interpretation of the constitution. In the United States, this ruling was made in 1803.[16] In Israel, it was made in 1995.[17] In both countries, there are still those who argue against the legitimacy of these rulings. I think that in the United States, this argument is on the wane. But in Israel it is still alive and vibrant, particularly because some of the founders of the Israeli Constitution are alive, and they do not hesitate to state their opinions on the rulings of the Supreme Court. Imagine the lively debate that would take place in the United States today over judicial review of the constitutionality of statutes if Madison, Jefferson, and Hamilton were active participants!

The position of Israeli judges is therefore not easy, and they are subject to tremendous tension. But they must fulfill their role. If our legislature—which is also the constitutive authority that is competent to change our Constitution—is not pleased with the existence of judicial review, it may amend the Constitution. I hope that such amendment will not occur. The likelihood that it will is small, since judicial review enjoys the confidence of the public.

[14] L'Heureux-Dubé, *supra* p. 133, note 29 at 242; Koopman, *supra* p. xii, note 29 at 108.
[15] *See, e.g.*, Grw. Ned. art. 120 ("The constitutionality of Acts of Parliament and treaties shall not be reviewed by the courts").
[16] *See Marbury v. Madison*, 5 U.S. (1 Cranch) 137 (1803).
[17] *See* C.A. 6821/93, *United Mizrahi Bank Ltd. v. Migdal Coop. Vill.*, 49(4) P.D. 221.

JUDICIAL REVIEW OF NONLEGISLATIVE
DECISIONS OF THE LEGISLATURE

Jurisdiction to Review

Is a court authorized to practice judicial review of legislative decisions that are not statutes in the formal sense? For example, the legislature or one of its organs may make determinations of a quasi-judicial nature, such as decisions regarding the impeachment of the President and federal judges in the United States or revoking some kinds of immunity of a member of Parliament in Israel. Similarly, the legislature, or one of its organs, may make internal administrative decisions. This practice occurs when the speaker of the legislature or the chairman of a parliamentary committee makes decisions, subject to the rules of parliament, about the agenda of the plenum or committee, or about the composition of the various committees. Is a decision of the legislature (or of one of its organs) that does not have the formal guise of a statute subject to judicial review? In the absence of an express provision in the constitution—which most constitutions do not have—the answer is derived from the view of the legal system and its judges toward the principle of separation of powers. The American position is narrow in support-ing a rigid separation of powers.[18] The approach of English law is also narrow.[19] The approaches of the constitutional courts in Germany[20] and Spain[21] are different. These courts regard them-selves as competent to exercise judicial review of all decisions of the legislature. Thus, for example, the German Constitutional Court has exercised judicial review on the following questions: Do parliamentary rules requiring two readings for statutes that

[18] *See supra* p. 49.
[19] *See Rediffusion (H.K.) Ltd. v. Attorney Gen.*, [1970] A.C. 1136 (P.C.) (appeal taken from H.K.); *Harper v. Home Sec'y*, 1 Ch. 238 (C.A. 1954); *Bilston Corp. v. Wolverhampton Corp.*, 1 Ch. 391 (1942); *Bradlaugh v. Gossett*, 12 Q.B.D. 271 (1884).
[20] *See* Kommers, *supra* p. 22, note 9.
[21] *See* E.A. Álvarez, *Los Actos Parlamentarios No Normativos y Su Control Jurisdiccional* (1998).

address certain issues violate the constitution?[22] Was the amount of time set for deliberations of the plenum over a matter of great public importance sufficient?[23] Is the exclusion of members of a certain party from one of the parliamentary committees unconstitutional?[24] Are parliamentary rules limiting the rights of an independent member of parliament who left his party—such as restrictions on his right to address the plenum and the time allotted to him and limitations on his right to submit private bills—consistent with constitutional guarantees concerning the rights of a member of parliament?[25] The Supreme Court of Israel has adopted a similar attitude,[26] based on the principle of separation of powers.[27]

Discretion in Review

Jurisdiction and discretion are distinct. This distinction raises the question of whether the scope of judicial review of nonstatutory legislative decisions is the same as the scope of judicial review of the decisions of the executive branch. The answer of the German Constitutional Court is yes,[28] but this is not the answer of the Supreme Court of Israel. We distinguished between two types of actions by the Knesset. One is quasi-judicial decisions; the other is administrative—or intermanagement—decisions. The Court decided that when the Knesset carries out a quasi-judicial action, full judicial review is appropriate. Therefore we have on several occasions voided a decision of the Knesset to revoke or not to

---

[22] *See* BVerfGE 1, 144 (1952).
[23] *See* BVerfGE 104 (1959).
[24] *See* BVerfGE 70, 324 (1986).
[25] *See* BVerfGE 80, 188 (1989).
[26] *See* David Kretzmer, "Judicial Review of Knesset Decisions," 8 *Tel Aviv U. Stud. L.* 95 (1988); Meir Shamgar, "Judicial Review of Knesset Decisions by the High Court of Justice," 28 *Isr. L. Rev.* 43 (1994).
[27] *See infra* p. 233.
[28] *See* Kommers, *supra* p. 22, note 9.

revoke the immunity of a member of the Knesset.[29] In those cases, we interpreted statutory provisions dealing with the scope of legislative immunity, determining the parameters that the members of the Knesset must consider and evaluating whether those parameters were met in practice. Naturally, in light of the broad scope of considerations the legislature may take into account, only in a few cases will the court determine that the Knesset exercised its discretion unlawfully. The number of cases is small, however, not because decisions of the Knesset are institutionally nonjusticiable but because they are usually lawful. As I wrote in one of my opinions:

> The special status of the Knesset is taken into account in formulating the substantive law that applies to its quasi-judicial activity. This special status does not need to come into play once again, to curtail the scope of judicial review. Judicial review is intended to ensure a minimal threshold required to preserve the validity of a quasi-judicial decision. Self-restraint in exercising judicial discretion in the course of judicial review of quasi-judicial decisions means undermining the elementary fairness of the parliamentary process. There is no justification for this.[30]

The Supreme Court has adopted a different approach with regard to Knesset decisions of an administrative nature.[31] On one hand, the court considered the rule of law in the legislature. The rule of law implies that every organ of the Knesset must observe the rules that apply to the Knesset's internal operations. As long as the Knesset does not change them, its rules bind it as does any other legal norm. On the other hand, the court considered the Knesset's need to decide its internal management on its own, and decided that the Knesset is best equipped to resolve these matters. In balancing these two considerations, the Supreme Court held

---

[29] See *Pinhasi*, 49(1) P.D. at 492; H.C. 761/86, *Miari v. Chairman of Knesset*, 42(4) P.D. 868.

[30] *Pinhasi*, 49(1) P.D. at 702.

[31] See H.C. 652/81, *Sarid v. Chairman of Knesset*, 36(2) P.D. 197, translated in Zamir and Zysblat, *supra* p. 178, note 7 at 318.

that it will exercise discretion, and will review the legality of an act of the Knesset or one of its organs in matters of internal management only if the Court decides that intervention is necessary to prevent substantial harm to the fabric of democratic life and the foundations of the regime's structure. I said in this case:

> The proper balance between the need to ensure the "rule of law in the legislature" and the need to respect the exclusivity of the Knesset in its decisions on internal matters will be ensured if we adopt a criterion that takes into account the degree of alleged harm to the texture of parliamentary life, as well as the degree to which that harm affects the structural foundations of our constitutional regime. . . . In adopting the aforementioned criterion, which considers the extent of harm and the interest harmed, we wish to establish a flexible test inherently amenable to precise definition, whose content and scope will be determined by the court according to the needs of time and place.[32]

Critics on both sides have attacked the Israeli Supreme Court's approach to this issue. One side argues that self-restraint is insufficient. According to this view, all intraparliamentary decisions should be (institutionally) nonjusticiable.[33] The other side argues that self-restraint is inappropriate, claiming that an intraparliamentary decision is the same as any other unlawful decision by a state institution. This clash of opinions was presented to us in one case. We rejected the conflicting viewpoints. This is what I wrote in the judgment:

> [S]elf-restraint . . . is proper. It should not be made too broad and it should not be made too narrow. It expresses a proper balance between the principle of the "rule of law in the legislature" . . . and the uniqueness and status of the Knesset. This balance gives proper weight to the fact that at the end of the day, at issue are the internal affairs of the Knesset and not actions with legislative effect (statutes, secondary legislation). It reflects a recognition that the Knesset—like

---

[32] *Id.* at 204.
[33] *See* Kretzmer, *supra* p. 232, note 26 at 97–99.

every institution—requires basic rules that regularize its various activities, and, by extension, recognition of the importance of autonomy in implementing these rules. This self-restraint properly expresses "the great caution obligatory in every judicial decision that has implications for the interrelationship between the main branches of the state and that determines their form. . . . ." It aptly expresses the "relationship of mutual respect between the legislature and the judiciary." This self-restraint constitutes a "kind of golden path . . . between full judicial activism and full self-restraint. . . ." On one hand self-restraint ensures a situation in which "the court will not turn itself into part of the political struggle, for which the Knesset is the central and national arena," by means of the court's distancing itself from "the everyday affairs of internal management. . . ." On the other hand, the restrictions on self-restraint protect the principle of the rule of law and the supremacy of the constitution.[34]

Using this framework, we considered and invalidated decisions by the Speaker of the Knesset preventing the tabling of a racist draft bill in the plenum[35] and establishing a rule that only a multimember party could propose a vote of no confidence in the government.[36] We thought that both of these decisions materially undermined the fabric of our democratic life. In contrast, we have dismissed many petitions challenging decisions by the Speaker of the Knesset and of committee chairpersons setting the time for deliberations on various draft bills.[37] We thought that these decisions related merely to the day-to-day internal management of Parliament and that it was therefore not proper to exercise judicial review of them.

Is the balance we have struck proper? Viewed in terms of theoretical consistency, the German approach is the proper one. All branches of state are subject to judicial review in *all* of their acts, even decisions

---

[34] H.C. 9070/00, *Livnat v. Chairman of Constitution, Law & Justice Comm.*, 55(4) P.D. 800, 813.

[35] *See* H.C. 742/84, *Kahana v. Chairman of Knesset*, 39(4) P.D. 85.

[36] *See* H.C. 73/85, *Kach Faction v. Chairman of Knesset*, 39(3) P.D. 141.

[37] For a list of the judgments, see *Livnat*, 55(4) P.D. at 814.

of internal management. The propriety of the self-restraint displayed by the court in Israel is not self-evident:

> It allows an illegal act of the Knesset to stand, without its validity being undermined by reason of its illegality. This self-restraint there-fore allows the Knesset to violate its own law. It is not easy to see what justifies the court's self-restraint, which effectively allows an illegal act to stand.[38]

Despite this difficulty, the Supreme Court has chosen to main-tain the delicate balance that I have discussed. Only time will tell whether we are justified in doing so.

THE DIALOGUE BETWEEN THE JUDICIARY
AND THE LEGISLATURE

The Concept of Dialogue

In addition to the constant tension, there is also a constant dialogue between the judiciary and the legislature. This dialogue does not take place at meetings between judges and legislators; it takes place when each branch carries out its constitutional role. The main role of the legislature is to enact statutes. These statutes are subject to judicial review of their constitutionality and judicial inter-pretation of their meaning. If the judiciary determines that a statute is unconstitutional, the matter returns to the legislature. In many such cases, the legislature may enact a new statute that achieves the same fundamental purpose as the voided statute while adopting more proportionate means. If the legislature does not want to do this, it can, in legal systems that permit this (such as Canada and Israel), enact a conflicting ordinary statute by using an override.[39]

---

[38] *Id.* at 810.

[39] For a discussion of the legislature's override power under Section 33 of Canada's Charter of Rights and Freedoms, see Peter W. Hogg and Allison A. Bushell, "The Charter Dialogue Between Courts and Legislatures (or Perhaps the Charter of Rights Isn't a Bad Thing After All)," 35 *Osgoode Hall L.J.* 75, 83–84 (1997).

It can also—again, if this is feasible in the relevant legal system—amend the constitution and then reenact the statute.[40] This new statute is also subject to judicial review, and the process can continue. This process is a proper dialogue between the branches.[41] In this dialogue, the legislature usually enjoys considerable latitude.

A similar dialogue occurs when the judiciary interprets a statute in a way that is unacceptable to the legislature. The legislature may enact a new statute or amend the original one to better achieve its aim. The cycle of interpretation and amendment can then repeat. Such amendment does not constitute a forbidden intervention of the legislature into the judicial sphere, provided that the new legislation does not retroactively apply to the original case decided by the court. The new statute does not "interpret" the older statute. The new statute creates a fresh normative reality reflecting the wish of the legislature. Enacting a new statute is the right and the power of the legislature.[42] It does not constitute disrespect of

[40] India's Supreme Court developed an approach that basic or fundamental features of the constitution cannot be amended. See *Golak Nath v. State of Punjab AIR* 1967 SC 1643; *Kesavananda Bharati v. State of Kerala AIR* 1973 SC 1461; *Indira Nehru Gandi v. Raj Narjain* 1975 S.C. 2299; *Minerva Mills Ltd v. Union of India AIR* 1980 S.C. 1789; *Waman Rao v. Union of India* 1981 S.C. 271.

[41] On the concept of dialogue, *see* Jeremy Waldron, "Some Models of Dialogue Between Judges and Legislators," 23 *S.C.L.R.* (2d) 7 (2004); For various discussions of how this "dialogue" works in the Canadian system, see *Vriend v. Alberta*, [1998] 1 S.C.R. 493, 565–67; Hogg and Bushell, *supra* p. 236, note 39 at 79–81; Manfredi and Kelly, "Six Degrees of Dialogue: A Response to Hogg and Bushell," 37 *Osgood Hall L.J.* 513 (1999); Peter Hogg and Thornton, "Reply to Six Degrees of Dialogue," 37 *Osgood Hall L.J.* 529 (1999); Kent Roach, *The Supreme Court on Trial: Judicial Activism or Democratic Dialogue* (2001); Mathan, "Constitutional Dialogue in Canada and the United States," 14 *N.J.C.L.* 403 (2003); Peter Hogg, "Discovering Dialogue," 23 *S.C.L.R.* (2d) 3 (2004); Kent Roach, "Dialogic Judicial Review and Its Critics," 23 *S.C.L.R.* (2d) 49 (2004); Christopher Manfredi, "The Life of a Metaphor: Dialogue in the Supreme Court," 23 *S.C.L.R.* (2d) 105 (2004).

[42] For a discussion of this legislative prerogative in the American system, see *James v. United States*, 366 U.S. 213 (1961) (Black, J., concurring in part and dissenting in part), which notes that Congress may change statutory interpretations "when it believes that this Court's interpretation of a statute embodies a policy that Congress is against." *Id.* at 233–34. *See also Regina v. Mills*, [1999] 3 S.C.R. 668 (Can.).

the judiciary.[43] On the contrary, it is a "healthy practice"[44] that properly expresses the dialogue between the branches that are partners in the legislative enterprise. Thus, the Supreme Court of Israel has written:

> [I]n enacting a statute that aims to change the court's ruling, the legislature reveals understanding of judicial interpretive activity, considers it on the merits, and responds to it on the basis of its advantages and drawbacks. This is the unending "dialogue" between a legislature and a judge, between one branch of the State and another.[45]

The Importance of the Concept

This dialogue provides several benefits for democracy. First, the dialogue—particularly the fact that the legislature has the power to respond to and effectively modify judicial rulings[46]—expresses the complex democratic accountability of the judiciary. Second, judicial-legislative dialogue enriches public debate by placing issues on the public and legislative agenda that would otherwise remain within the confines of the executive branch in the absence of judicial adjudication.

---

[43] *See* Richard A. Paschal, "The Continuing Colloquy: Congress and the Finality of the Supreme Court," 8 *J.L. & Pol.* 143, 198 n.198 (1991) ("Congress understands that it is not constitutional blasphemy to criticize the Court or to seek to overturn a decision by subsequent legislation"). *Cf.* William N. Eskridge, Jr., "Overriding Supreme Court Statutory Interpretation Decisions," 101 *Yale L.J.* 331, 387–89 (1991) (suggesting that congressional overrides can occur when congressional preferences change, when the Court misinterprets congressional preferences, or when the Court has signaled that congressional action is needed). *But see* Abner J. Mikva and Jeff Bleich, "When Congress Overrules the Court," 79 *Cal. L. Rev.* 729, 731 (1991) (noting that "[u]nfortunately, the overruling dialogue between Congress and the Court is not always based on such a healthy relationship").

[44] William O. Douglas, "Legal Institutions in America," in *Legal Institutions Today and Tomorrow* 274, 292 (Monrad G. Paulsen ed., 1959).

[45] H.C. 5364/94, *Velner v. Chairman of Israeli Labor Party*, 49(1) P.D. 758, 791 (Barak, J., dissenting).

[46] *See Vriend*, [1998] 1 S.C.R. at 566.

Naturally, judges should examine the content of a new statute. Sometimes the statute may undermine the principles of (substantive) democracy. In such a case, review of a new statute should focus not on the fact that it changes the previous ruling of the court but on the fact that it undermines democracy. Moreover, everything is a question of degree. If the interpretation of a statute is met with an immediate and hasty response from the legislature in the form of new legislation, uncertainty about the law will result, and the public will lose confidence in the legislative branch. This is not the case, however, when the change in legislation after a judicial ruling reflects a thorough and deliberate examination of the ruling and an objective expression of the will of the legislature.

Dialogue and Monologue

At times, the tension between the branches leads to a deterioration in their relations. The dialogue between the branches ceases. In its place comes monologue. Power replaces discretion. The rules of the game are broken. There are various reasons for this. Some are personal: this or that official feels personally hurt by this or that court decision. Some reasons are local: this or that judgment detracts from the realization of a political agenda, and the response is a loss of temper, which breaks down communication. Some reasons are institutional: misunderstandings regarding the judicial role and regarding appropriate dialogue between the judicial and other branches. In all these situations, the court may indeed make a wrong decision at times, but the response to an incorrect judgment is not to abandon communication and break the rules of the game but to use the existing relationship to create a situation in which the result of the mistake will be corrected.

Breaking the rules of the game crosses the red line, and is likely to take on many forms: wild and unrestrained criticism of the judgment, attacks on the very legitimacy of the judicial decision, recommendations (which are sometimes enacted) to narrow the scope of the courts' jurisdiction, threats to create new courts in order to overcome undesirable judgments, attempts to increase the political influence on judicial appointments and promotions, calling for prosecution of judges merely because of the content of the judgments they wrote, demands to terminate judicial appointments or to impeach judges due to the views expressed in judgments. All these lead, in the end, to the breakdown of the relationship. This is the beginning of the end of democracy.

What should the judge do when the red line is crossed? Not much. He should remain loyal to the democratic system and to society, continue to honor the legislative branch, and work toward the realization of his understanding of the judicial role. The judge must guard the part of the relationship that remains. The judge must be aware of what is going on around him. The judge must not surrender to the ill winds. The judge should of course examine whether or not a mistake has been made. At the foundation of this approach is the basic view that the court does not fight for its own power. The efforts of the court should be directed toward protecting the constitution and its values.

CHAPTER FOURTEEN

The Relationship between the Judiciary and the Executive

THE SCOPE OF REVIEW

Judicial Review and Democracy

The executive derives its powers from the constitution and statutes. Therefore, it must act within the framework of the constitution and statutes. If it exceeds the authority given to it, or if it exercises that authority unlawfully, the judiciary must exercise the power of review given to it by the constitution and statutes.[1] The judiciary should use this power to determine the consequences of the executive's actions. In this activity, the judiciary does not confront the countermajoritarian argument, because in such cases, as long as no constitutional problem arises, the legislature has the power, if it so wishes, to change the outcome reached by the judiciary by amending the statute. Indeed, when the judiciary reviews executive acts, it operates within the framework of its classic role in the separation of powers and in accordance with its role of maintaining the rule of law. In this respect, there is no difference between the chief executive and any one of its many public officials. Every person who has authority must exercise it lawfully, and if authority has been exercised unlawfully, it must be subject to judicial review. Therefore, if the president of the state grants a pardon, his action is subject to judicial review. There is nothing in the nature of this act or in the status of the person committing it to prevent this review. The court must examine the criteria used by the president and evaluate

---

[1] See *Judicial Review and Bureaucratic Impact: International and Interdisciplinary Perspectives* (Marc Hetogh and Simon Halliday eds., 2004).

whether he acted lawfully. This is how the Supreme Court of Israel acted with regard to a petition in which the legality of the President's pretrial pardon of the head of the General Security Service and several members of the service was considered.[2] With regard to the claim that there should be no judicial interference with the President's pardons, I responded:

> We are one branch of the state, and our role is to ensure that the other branches act within the framework of the law, in order to preserve the rule of law in the state. The branches of the state are lofty, but the law is higher than all of us. We would not fulfill our judicial role if, in the context of lawfully submitted petitions, we did not review the actions of the other branches as they appear from the petitions before us.[3]

With regard to the merits of the case, the court decided, by a majority opinion from which I dissented, that the President had the power to give a pardon before trial and that this power had been lawfully exercised.

The Supreme Court of Israel adopted a similar approach when it considered the cases of a cabinet minister indicted for bribery[4] and a deputy minister indicted for making false entries in corporate documents and for fraud,[5] who both refused to resign their positions despite these serious charges. The petition before us challenged the Prime Minister's decision not to dismiss the cabinet minister and deputy minister. We decided in both cases that the Prime Minister unlawfully failed to exercise his power of dismissal and ordered him to dismiss them. They resigned before the power of dismissal was exercised. In the petition referring to the deputy minister, I said:

> [T]he Government, the Prime Minister, and all other ministers are public trustees. They have nothing of their own. All that they have, they have for the good of the public. . . . From this fiduciary duty

[2] H.C. 428/86, *Barzilai v. Gov't of Israel*, 40(3) P.D. 505 (English translation available at www.court.gov.il).
[3] *Id.* at 585–86.
[4] H.C. 2533/97, *Movement for Quality Gov't v. Gov't of Israel*, 51(3) P.D. 46.
[5] H.C. 4267/93, *Amitai—Citizens for Proper Admin. & Integrity v. Prime Minister of Isr.*, 47(5) P.D. 441.

derives the law—a general law that applies to every governmental authority, including a Government, a Prime Minister, and other ministers—that discretion granted to a public authority must be exercised fairly and honestly, making reasonable use of relevant considerations alone. . . . The fiduciary duty of the Prime Minister, the Government and each of the ministers imposes a duty to consider whether to terminate the tenure of a deputy minister who has been indicted. . . . Neither the Prime Minister, nor the Government, nor any of its ministries may say: "the law has given us power to terminate the tenure of a deputy minister; if we wish, we may terminate it, and if we wish, we may refrain from doing so. The discretion is ours, and we will exercise it as we see fit." Every power given to a branch of state must be exercised fairly and reasonably. Every power has limits. We do not recognize "absolute" discretion, bereft of any limits or restrictions.[6]

In that case, it was argued that we should distinguish between an "ordinary" civil servant and an elected public official, on the ground that an elected public official holds office because of the public's confidence in him, as expressed through a democratic electoral process, and that this same process empowers the public to remove him from office. I replied to this argument by saying:

The judgment of the voter is no substitute for the judgment of the law. Indeed, the very fact that a person is an elected public official requires him to adhere to a stricter, more ethical standard of behavior than an "ordinary" civil servant. Whoever is elected by the people must set an example for the people, be faithful to the people, and deserve the trust that the people have shown him. Therefore, when the executive holds the power to terminate [a public official's tenure], it must exercise it when the official undermines the confidence of the public in the government, whether the official is elected (such as a member of Knesset serving as a deputy minister) or is a civil servant (such as an employee of the State whom a minister has the power to dismiss).[7]

[6] *Id.* at 461–62.
[7] *Id.* at 470.

Similarly, in another case, we invalidated the appointment of the director-general of a government ministry because he had admitted to very serious offenses for which he had been pardoned (as part of a pretrial pardon that the President gave to the members of the General Security Service).[8] We balanced the accomplishments of the candidate and the pardon that he had received (ten years before the appointment) against the offenses to which he had confessed. We determined that in this case, his criminal past was decisive. In particular, we emphasized that the director-general of a ministry exercises disciplinary powers over the employees of his ministry. Giving such an important public office to this man would undermine public confidence in the civil service.[9] His defenders argued that once the government decided upon the appointment, there was no basis for judicial intervention. The government, it was argued, had balanced the various considerations, and after it had decided to make the appointment, the Court should not have intervened and supplanted the government's discretion with its own discretion. We rejected this argument by concluding that the appointment amounted to an unreasonable action in the extreme. We said that "the lofty status of the Government, as the State's executive authority . . . cannot give it powers that the law does not give. Every state authority that makes an unreasonable decision is subject to the court's intervention, and the Government is no exception to this rule."[10] At the end of the opinion I added:

> [T]his is the strength of a democracy that respects the rule of law. This is the formal rule of law, under which all state authorities, including the Government itself, are subject to the law. No authority is above the law; no authority may act unreasonably. This is also the substantive rule of law, under which a balance must be struck among the values, principles, and interests of the democratic society, while empowering the State to exercise discretion that appropriately balances the proper considerations.[11]

[8] H.C. 6163/92, *Eisenberg v. Minister of Housing*, 47(2) P.D. 229 (English translation available at www.court.gov.il).
[9] *Id*. at 266.
[10] *Id*. at 274 (citation omitted).
[11] *Id*.

The Sources of Judicial Review

What is the source of judicial review?[12] There are those argue that the source of judicial review of administrative action comes from the interpretation of the legislation granting powers to the administration (the *ultra vires* doctrine).[13] Others argue that the main source for judicial review is from common law.[14] In my view, the source of judicial review is the constitution itself.[15] This assumes a rich understanding of democracy as both formal and substantive; it assumes viewing the rule of law both in its formal and in its substantive meanings; it assumes purposive interpretation of the constitution and of statutes; it assumes a rich understanding of separation of powers. Under those assumptions, the constitution is the source of judicial review of administrative action.

If there is a formal constitution, it is above both statutes and the common law. The power of the executive branch, its limitations, and the power of the judicial branch to review it derive from the constitution itself. If there is no formal constitution, as is the case in the United Kingdom, then the (material) constitution and the common law are merged, and they are the source of judicial review.

---

[12] *See generally Judicial Review and the Constitution* (Christopher Forsyth ed., 2000); Craig, *supra* p. 196, note 22 at 4.

[13] *See* T.R.S. Allan, *Law, Liberty, and Justice: The Legal Foundations of British Constitutionalism* (1993); William Wade and Christopher Forsyth, *Administrative Law* (8th ed. 2000); Christopher Forsyth, "Of Fig Leaves and Fairy Tales: The *Ultra Vires* Doctrine, the Sovereignty of Parliament and Judicial Review," [1996] *Camb. L.J.* 122; T.R.S. Allan, "The Constitutional Foundations of Judicial Review: Conceptual Conundrum or Interpretive Inquiry?" 61 *Camb. L. J.* 87 (2002); T.R.S. Allan, "Constitutional Dialogue and Justification of Judicial Review," 32 *Oxford J.L. Stud.* 563 (2003); Christopher Forsyth and Mark Elliot, "The Legitimacy of Judicial Review," *Pub. Law* 286 (2003).

[14] *See* Craig, *supra* p. 196, note 22 at 4; Dawn Oliver, "Is the *Ultra Vires* Rule the Basis of Judicial Review," *Pub. Law* 543 (1987); Paul Craig, "The Common Law, Shared Power and Judicial Review," 24 *Oxford J.L. Stud.* 237 (2004).

[15] *See* David Dyzenhaus, "Reuniting the Brain: The Democratic Basis of Judicial Review," 9 *Pub. L. Rev.* 98 (1998); Jeffrey Jowell, "Of *Vires* and Vacuums: The Constitutional Context of Judicial Review," in *Judicial Review and the Constitution* 327 (Christopher Forsyth ed., 2000); Paul Craig, "Constitutional Foundations, the Rule of Law and Supremacy," [2003] *Pub. Law* 92.

JUDICIAL INTERPRETATION AND EXECUTIVE INTERPRETATION

Since the *Chevron*[16] decision, United States case law has provided that when certain conditions exist, such as when the intention of the legislature regarding the jurisdiction of the executive is unclear and its language is ambiguous, the court must defer to the executive's interpretation, provided that this interpretation is reasonable.[17] I accept that, in interpreting a statute dealing with the powers of a government authority that has expertise in a field pertaining to the statute, some weight should be attached to this authority's understanding of the statute. This weight increases as the statute becomes more technical or professional. I do not, however, accept that the judiciary should defer to the executive's interpretation simply because this interpretation is reasonable. In my view, the constitutional role of interpreting every legal text, whether it is the constitution itself or a statute, belongs to the court: "The question that the court must ask itself is not whether the executive's interpretation is reasonable. The question that the court must ask itself is what is the correct interpretation of the state power."[18] The responsibility of the judge, within the framework of the separation of powers, is to give the proper interpretation to the constitution and statutes. The judge cannot escape this responsibility.

Interpreting a statute is different from implementing or executing it. A court's interpretation of a statute gives it a meaning that establishes the scope of executive authority. In implementing a statute, the executive branch uses this authority. Using interpretation to determine the scope of authority is the job of the court. In contrast, when there is more than one way to implement a statute, the executive branch has the constitutional authority to choose how to implement it. The court will not interfere with a lawful and reasonable implementation by the executive, even if it would not have

---

[16] *Chevron U.S.A. Inc. v. Natural Res. Def. Council, Inc.*, 467 U.S. 837 (1984).
[17] *See* 1 Tribe, *supra* p. 35, note 57, § 5–19, at 993–94.
[18] H.C. 693/91, *Efrat v. Dir. of Population Register*, 47(1) P.D. 749, 761–62.

implemented the statute in the same way. For this very reason, though, the court must intervene in a lawful and reasonable interpretation by the executive if the court's own interpretation differs. The "professional" implementer of the statute is the executive; the "professional" interpreter of the statute is the judiciary. In the constitutional structure of a democratic state, the responsibility for interpreting statutes lies with the judiciary, and it must ensure that its interpretation—and not merely a reasonable interpretation of the executive—be given to the statute: "A court will not be allowed to abandon its duty—and its authority—in favor of the statutory interpretation of experts or the competent public body. The court is the 'expert' in statutory interpretation. . . ."[19] I expressed this idea in one of my opinions:

[W]hen a judge faces two lawful interpretive solutions, he need not suppress his view of the proper interpretation because of the public authority. The court must form its own opinion regarding which of the lawful interpretations is proper. In doing so, it must take into consideration all the circumstances of the matter. One of the "circumstances" in this regard is the viewpoint of the public authority with regard to the proper interpretation. This approach is vital to an orderly regime. It does not ignore the professionalism and responsibility of the other branch. At the same time, it does not ignore the professionalism and responsibility of the judiciary. Indeed, the court's interpretation of any given statute integrates, in this way, into the court's interpretation of the entire body of legislation. A statute does not stand alone. Nor is it interpreted only by the public authority that implements it. All of the statutes constitute one system, in which they mesh together in legislative harmony. When one interprets one statute, one interprets all statutes. The overall responsibility for uniting the systems lies with the court, and within the court system, the responsibility is with the Supreme Court. The Supreme Court may not escape this responsibility.[20]

[19] H.C. 3648/97, *Stameka v. Minister of Interior*, 53(2) P.D. 728, 744.
[20] H.C. 399/85, *Kahana v. Broad. Auth. Mgmt. Bd.*, 41(3) P.D. 255, 305–06.

This approach is also accepted by the courts of other nations, including those of the United Kingdom[21] and Canada.[22]

EXECUTIVE REASONABLENESS

On Reasonableness

When the executive authority exercises its power reasonably, it operates within its authority and the judge will not intervene. This is true even if the judge, had the executive authority been granted to him, would have used the power in a different reasonable way. There is no room for judicial intervention if the exercise of executive authority lies within the "zone of reasonableness." The court must refrain from imposing its own preferences regarding implementation onto the society in which it operates.

The key test here is reasonableness.[23] Put simply, the executive must act reasonably, for an unreasonable act is an unlawful act. In many cases the test of reasonableness allows for only one possibility, which the executive *must* choose. Sometimes, however, the reasonableness test allows for several possibilities, thereby creating a "zone of reasonableness." The executive has freedom of choice within this range. The principle of separation of powers requires the executive, rather than the judiciary, to choose one possibility within this zone. But the principle of separation of powers requires the court, rather than the executive, to determine the limits of the zone of reasonableness.[24]

---

[21] *See Black-Clawson Int'l Ltd. v. Papierwerke Waldhof-Aschaffenburg AG*, [1975] All E.R. 810, 828 ("[I]t is the function of the courts to say what the application of the words [of a piece of legislation] used for particular cases or individuals is to be. . . . [I]t would be a degradation of that process if the courts were to be merely a reflecting mirror of what some other interpretation agency might say").

[22] *See Southam Inc. v. Dir. of Investigation & Research*, [1997] 1 S.C.R. 748, 751–52.

[23] On reasonableness, *see supra* p. 67.

[24] *See supra* p. 42.

The zone of reasonableness sets the boundaries for determining the scope of judicial review of the executive's implementation. Nonetheless, the concept of reasonableness is notoriously vague. It is a "category of illusory reference."[25] The only way to further the discussion about the substance of reasonableness is to recognize that reasonableness is neither a physical nor a metaphysical concept but a normative one. Reasonableness means that one identifies the relevant considerations and then balances them according to their weight.[26] Indeed, reasonableness is an evaluative process, not a descriptive process. It is not a concept that is defined by deductive logic. It is not merely rationality. A decision is reasonable if it was made by weighing the necessary considerations, including fundamental values in general and human rights in particular.[27] Nothing is reasonable "in itself."

How does one determine the weight of the considerations which determine the zone of reasonableness? Justice I. Zamir answered that question in the following way:

> The question of whether an administrative decision is extremely unreasonable depends on the bounds of the zone of reasonableness. This is the zone within which the administrative agency may use its discretion to make a decision. The bounds of any zone of reasonableness depend on the characteristics of the authority being exercised: the language and purpose of the authorizing statute; the identity of the administrative agency; the issue being regulated by the authority; whether the authority is exercised primarily based on factual findings, policy considerations, or professional evaluations such as

---

[25] Julius Stone developed the concept of categories of illusory reference. *See* Julius Stone, *The Province and Function of Law* 171 (1950); Julius Stone, *Legal System and Lawyers' Reasonings* 235 (1968).

[26] *See* Manuel Atienza, "On the Reasonable in Law," 3 *Ratio Juris* 148 (1990); MacCormick, *supra* p. 68, note 119 at 131.

[27] *See* Jeffrey Jowell, "Courts and the Administration in Britain: Standards, Principles and Rights," 22 *Isr. L. Rev.* 409, 419 (1988); Jeffrey Jowell and Anthony Lester, "Beyond *Wednesbury*: Substantive Principles of Administrative Law," 1987 *Pub. L.* 368, 370–71.

medical or engineering decisions. The zone of reasonableness varies with these characteristics: sometimes it is narrow, and sometimes it is wide.[28]

Above these considerations are the fundamental values of the legal system, and the proper balance between them affects the delineation of the zone of reasonableness. Reference to these fundamental values guarantees the connection between public law and other branches of law. It establishes law as a general normative framework governing the way government agencies treat individuals and the way individuals treat each other.[29]

When I engage in judicial review of executive activity, the criterion of reasonableness and the zone of reasonableness play a central role. These factors are particularly important when the relevant balance is between the needs of the public and the rights of the individual[30] or in matters dealing with government ethics and proper administration. For example, our Court used the principle of reasonableness to hold that a minister and deputy minister indicted for serious offenses were obliged to resign;[31] indeed, it would have been unreasonable not to dismiss them. Similarly, we held that a person with a significant criminal past cannot be appointed as director-general of a government ministry.[32] The principle of reasonableness has also guided us in deciding to review the legality of the attorney general's use of prosecutorial discretion[33] in holding that the army should not promote officers who had committed sexual harassment[34] and in restricting a transitional or "lame duck" government's scope of power to negotiate a peace agreement.[35]

---

[28] H.C. 2533/97, *Movement for Quality Gov't v. Gov't of Israel*, 51(3) P.D. 46, 57.

[29] *See The Unity of Public Law* (David Dyzenhaus ed., 2004).

[30] *See* Jowell and Lester, *supra* p. 249, note 27 at 373.

[31] *See supra* p. 242.

[32] *See supra* p. 244.

[33] *See infra* p. 252.

[34] *See* H.C. 1284/99, *Anonymous v. Army Chief of Staff*, 52(2) P.D. 57.

[35] *See* H.C. 5167/00, *Weiss v. Prime Minister*, 55(2) P.D. 55.

Criticism

This last ruling met with criticism in Israel. Those same individuals who supported the use of the reasonableness test in the context of human rights strongly criticized its use in the government ethics context. I understand this criticism, but I disagree. It is appropriate to use the reasonableness test in reviewing executive actions, including issues of government ethics. Naturally, in countries where there is self-restraint in government, there may be no need to develop the principle of reasonableness in government ethics. But in countries where this self-restraint is lacking—and the concept of "it is not done" is insufficiently developed—it is proper to extend the principle of reasonableness to all government actions. I do not see any possibility of restricting reasonableness to one field. If the principle of reasonableness should be applied in protecting the freedom of the individual, it should also be applied to other kinds of protections involving government activity. Consistent application of this principle can strengthen public confidence in the government, which is fundamental to government's operation.

I should reemphasize that the reasonableness test requires the evaluator not to consider how he himself would act in the role of the civil servant but how the "reasonable civil servant" would act. Acting as the reasonable civil servant, I do not impose my subjective perspective on the government but instead recognize that there can be multiple reasonable ways to achieve a given goal. As with all of my judicial activity, when applying the reasonableness test, I give weight to the various considerations and balance them.

Judges sometimes say that they are "deferring" to the decision of the executive branch. I don't think the term deference is justified in this context, for the following reason: if the administrative authority's decision is within the zone of reasonableness, the court refrains from invalidating it not out of deference but because the decision is legal. If the administrative authority's decision exceeds the zone of reasonableness, it must be invalidated, and there is no room for deference. In determining the zone of reasonableness, there is no room for deference of any kind. The zone is determined by interpreting the scope of the administrative authority's power. This interpretive activity, at the end of the day, is the responsibility of the judicial branch, and it does not implicate any deference.

This view of mine has a rhetorical aspect as well. Judges often ask themselves whether or not there is room to "intervene" in the decision of the executive branch. In my opinion, that is not the right question to ask. The right question is whether the administrative agency acted legally. If it acted legally, there is no room to intervene. If it acted illegally, there is room to intervene. Indeed, the legality or illegality of the action decides the question of intervention; the intervention does not decide the legality or illegality of the action. Of course, sometimes the illegality is established in the judgment itself, such that it—the illegality—is what has created the law. That eventuality should not, however, influence the proper rhetoric, which should not be the rhetoric of intervention but rather the rhetoric of the rule of law. This is the case in the field of private law, where we do not use the rhetoric of intervention but rather the rhetoric of rights and remedies, even when these are created by the court. There is no reason to adopt a different approach in public law.

Example: Judicial Review of the Attorney General's Decisions

A good example of the role of reasonableness in Israel can be found in the judicial review of the attorney general's decision regarding criminal prosecutions. The attorney general in Israel—who is a civil servant and not a political appointee—has extensive powers to issue indictments. Are these powers subject to judicial review?[36] The Supreme Court of Israel has said that they are.[37] The attorney general does not have a special status; he is not immune from

---

[36] See generally Abraham S. Goldstein, *The Passive Judiciary: Prosecutorial Discretion and the Guilty Plea* (1981).

[37] The main judgment is in H.C. 935/89, *Ganor v. Attorney General*, 44(2) P.D. 485, translated in Zamir and Zysblat, *supra* p. 233, note 7 at 334.

judicial review. He, like every other civil servant, must exercise his discretion lawfully. He must act according to relevant considerations, without discrimination, fairly, and reasonably. If he deviates from this mandate, the Court will exercise judicial review over the legality of his actions. But the Court will not consider the wisdom of those actions or set itself up as a super–attorney general. The Court will treat the attorney general like every other civil servant whose actions are subject to judicial review. It follows that:

> the key question is not the extent of the court's intervention, but the validity of the Attorney General's decision. The real question is not the grounds for the court's intervention, but the grounds that invalidate the decision. . . . The question is not the court's discretion, but the discretion of the Attorney General. Indeed, the extent of the court's intervention maps onto the extent of the illegality of the Attorney General's decision. . . . In a country ruled by law, where the rule of law governs, there is no justification for using special criteria to assess the validity of the discretion of the person who heads the public prosecution service. Note that this conclusion does not mean replacing the discretion of the Attorney General with the discretion of the court. This conclusion does not mean invalidating a "wrong" decision of the Attorney General—that is, one in which he chooses an undesirable but lawful decision. This conclusion means only that all governmental actors are equal in the eyes of the law.[38]

The Court has acted in accordance with this principle. We have invalidated the attorney general's exercise of discretion when he declined, for lack of public interest, to indict bankers in charge of several of Israel's banks. According to the findings of a State Commission of Inquiry—findings that the attorney general accepted—these bankers acted contrary to the law, caused serious damage to many investors, and caused serious pecuniary loss to the state.[39] In a similar vein, we held that the attorney general exercised his discretion unlawfully when he decided not to file a disciplinary

[38] *Ganor*, 44(2) P.D. at 527–28 (citation omitted), translated in Zamir and Zysblat, *supra* p. 233, note 7 at 365.
[39] *See id.*

claim against the chief police commissioner, who unlawfully received gifts of small monetary value, not for acts related to his position, but from persons who came into contact with him as a result of his position as a policeman.[40] In a much greater number of cases, though, we dismissed petitions against the attorney general after holding that he had acted reasonably.[41]

In these rulings, we determined a proper legal regime for the behavior of the attorney general. The head of the prosecution has significant power. Power without responsibility becomes arbitrariness. We prevented this arbitrariness. By doing so we also protected the office of the attorney general against all those who wished to reduce its powers. One of the defenses against critics of these powers is that they are not absolute because they are subject to judicial review. It is no surprise that Israel has had no Watergate, since an attorney general who participates in illegal activity would very quickly have to explain his actions and justify his decisions before the Supreme Court. Every attorney general, including myself during my tenure in that position, knows this, and it helps him protect the constitution and democracy.

PROPORTIONALITY

The Central Test for the Activity of the Executive Branch

In recent years a new concept has developed for determining the scope of protection of the constitution and its values. This concept is proportionality. It was born in the European law countries.[42]

---

[40] *See* H.C. 7074/93, *Suissa v. Attorney Gen.*, 48(2) P.D. 749.

[41] *See* H.C. 2534/97, *Yahav v. State Attorney*, 51(3) P.D. 1; H.C. 6781/96, *Olmert v. Attorney Gen.*, 50(4) P.D. 793; H.C. 4162/93, *Federman v. Attorney Gen.*, 47(5) P.D. 309; H.C. 223/88, *Sheftel v. Attorney Gen.*, 43(4) P.D. 356.

[42] *See* Jurgen Schwarz, *European Administrative Law* (1992); N. Emiliou, *The Principle of Proportionality in European Law* (1996); *The Principle of Proportionality in Laws of Europe* (Evelyn Ellis ed., 1999); Marc-Andre Eissen, "The Principle of Proportionality in the Case-Law of the European Court of Human Rights," 125 in *The European System for the Protection of Human Rights* (R. Macdonald et al. eds., 1993); Takis Tridjmas, *The General Principles of EC Law* 89 (2000).

From there it crossed over to most of the common law countries.[43] Indeed, alongside reasonableness, proportionality is today a central standard directing the actions of the executive branch. The point of departure is that a disproportionate act that infringes upon a human right is an illegal act. The court, which guards the legality of the acts of the executive branch, performs judicial review over these acts and examines whether they fulfill the tests of proportionality.

The Characteristics of Proportionality

Proportionality is a standard that examines the relationship between the objective the executive branch wishes to achieve, which has the potential of infringing upon a human right, and the means it has chosen in order to achieve that infringing objective. It is derived— if not by explicit provision—from the fiduciary duty of the executive branch and of each of its officials. The fiduciary duty—from which the administrative duty of fairness and administrative reasonableness are derived—demands administrative proportionality as well.

A Worthy Objective

The point of departure of proportionality is a worthy objective. An objective is worthy "if it serves an important social goal which is sensitive to human rights . . . if it is intended to fulfill social goals important to the existence of a social framework which recognizes the constitutional importance of human rights and the need to protect them."[44] "Human rights" means all human rights. The term covers the rights anchored in the constitution, as well as the human

---

[43] See Michael Fordham and Thomas de la Mare, "Identifying the Principle of Proportionality," 27 in Understanding Human Rights Principles (Jeffrey Jowell and Jonathan Cooper eds., 2001); Jeremy Kirk, "Constitutional Guarantees, Characterisation and the Concept of Proportionality," 21 Melbourne U.L. Rev. 1(1997); Robert Thomas, Legitimate Expectations and Proportionality in Administrative Law (2000); David Beaty, The Ultimate Rule of Law (2004).

[44] C.A. 6821/93, United Mizrahi Bank Ltd. v. Migdal Coop. Vill., 49(4) P.D. 221, 434–35 (Barak, P.).

rights that are part of the common law. At times the component of objective is removed from the tests of proportionality. This view is regrettable. One cannot separate the goal from the means. Proportionality is about the relationship between the means and the goal. Both the means and the goal must be worthy, and together they are the two components of the test of proportionality.

A Worthy Means: Fit

The means that public administration uses must be proportionate. Courts have developed three subtests, or three cumulative elements, which express this aspect of proportionality. The first element is that a link of fit is needed between the objective and the means. The means that public administration employs must be derived from the achievement of the objective that the administration seeks. The means must rationally lead to the achievement of the objective. That is the fitting means or rational means test. Here is an example from German law:[45] "[L]et us assume, for example, that the administrative agency is authorized, pursuant to a statute, to take steps necessary to remove a danger to the public caused by a car parked in an illegal parking place. If the agency gives a private person an order to break into the car and distance it from the place it is parked, that is an unfitting means, since it is illegal; and if it decides to cancel the driver's license of the owner of the car, that is an unfitting means, seeing as it does nothing to remove the danger caused by the parked car."

A Worthy Means: Necessity

The second element of administrative proportionality is that the means chosen by the administration must injure the individual to the smallest extent possible. The administrative tailor must sew the administrative suit so that it will be cut to fit the objective directing

---

[45] Itzhak Zamir, 1 *Administrative Authority* 131 (1996).

it, while choosing the means least injurious to the individual. Here is an example:[46] Let us assume that a band plays loudly in a coffee shop until the late hours, disturbing the neighbors' rest. The administrative authority that gave the license to the coffee house is permitted to take steps to remove the noise nuisance. For this purpose, it may revoke the coffee house's license, so that it will close completely, or change the conditions of the license. In such a situation there is no need to revoke the coffee house's license, even though that would be a fitting means, since it has the potential of causing the proprietor more damage than necessary; therefore, the agency must make due with changing the conditions of the license. The agency can impose various conditions: prohibition of band playing in coffee houses, a determination that a band shall not be permitted to play after a certain hour of the night, or a condition that the coffee house be acoustically sealed so that the noise nuisance is prevented. Each of these means is a fitting means, but the agency must choose, from among the various conditions, the condition that, on the one hand, will fulfill the objective, but on the other hand, has the potential to cause less damage to the license holder than the other conditions. However, if in the circumstances of the case the mildest condition that causes the least damage does not suffice to achieve the objective, the agency may determine a more burdensome condition, to the extent necessary to achieve the objective. The metaphor of the rungs of a ladder is helpful: the court examines whether the administrative agency has chosen, out of rungs all of which lead to the objective yet with increasing injury to human rights as one climbs to the top of the ladder, the lowest rung.

A Worthy Means: A Proper Proportion

The third element is that the human rights-infringing means chosen by the administration are worthy, that there is a proper proportion between the means and the goal. This is the "narrow"

[46] *Id.*

proportionality test. The means chosen by the administration are not worthy if the injury to the individual is disproportionate to the utility that it brings by attaining the goal. This is a balancing test.

The Administration's Margin of Appreciation

In employing the proportionality test, the governmental agency's maneuvering space should be recognized.[47] There are often many ways in which the duty of proportionality can be fulfilled. Not infrequently, the case is a borderline one. In these and other situations, a zone of consideration toward the governmental agency should be recognized. This zone is similar to the zone of reasonableness of the executive branch. This recognition of space for governmental discretion is based on the institutional advantage of the governmental agency in examining possible alternatives, and on its national responsibility—a responsibility imposed upon it in the framework of the principle of separation of powers—for the achievement of the worthy objective. Therefore, if there are different ways in which one can fulfill the duty of proportionality, the choice will be made by the administrative agency. The question that the judge must ask himself is not which proportionate action he would choose if he were an administrative agency. The question the judge must ask is whether the act that the administration performed was proportionate. If the answer is positive, the judge should affirm the choice of the administration, even if it is not the judge's choice.

Assessing Proportionality

Proportionality is an important standard for assessing the legality of administrative action. It has a concretization that is lacking in the standard of reasonableness. It does not replace reasonableness; it

---

[47] *See* R. Macdonald, "The Margin of Appreciation," 83 in *The European System for the Protection of Human Rights* (R. Macdonald et al. eds., 1993).

supplements it. However, one must be aware of its limitations. First, it is used when the problem that has arisen is that of a proper proportion between the ends and the means. It is unclear whether one can use proportionality when the needed balancing is not between a goal and a means but between two different goals. Second, the fit test and the necessity test are of a mainly technical character. Their essence is not one of a standard of values. That is inherent in the "narrow" proportionality test, which is a balancing test, to which much weight should be given. However, the focus on the "narrow" proportionality test blurs the boundaries between proportionality and reasonableness and weakens the concretization advantage that characterizes proportionality. Finally, the administration's margin of appreciation, recognized by case law in the context of proportionality, like the zone of reasonableness in the context of reasonableness, shrinks the amount of protection which the proportionality test grants to human rights. That is certainly the case if different levels of examination are determined, which are lenient with the administration more often than not, except in the case of those few human rights considered most important. Thus, proportionality should not be seen as a magical equation. The search must continue for new devices that will assist in achieving the role of the judge as guardian of the constitution and its values. We must not be satisfied with the existing tools. We must search constantly for additional ways to fulfill our role.

Part Four

EVALUATION OF THE ROLE

OF A JUDGE IN A DEMOCRACY

CHAPTER FIFTEEN

Activism and Self-Restraint

DEFINITION OF THE TERMS

The Need for a Definition

Judicial decisions are commonly characterized along the continuum of activism and self-restraint. Those who make these classifications seldom define their terms. The result is chaos and misunderstanding conducive neither to debate nor to evaluation. For many, these terms have become code words for criticism or praise: X is a good judge because he is activist; Y is a good judge because she exercises self-restraint. But what do we mean by activism and self-restraint? Is one good and the other bad? The answer to this question seems to vary depending on the period in which it is asked. At some points in time, judicial activism is viewed as a good thing, and at other times it is viewed negatively. The same is true of self-restraint. What accounts for variation in the way judicial activity is viewed? Unless we agree on what we mean by activism and self-restraint, our use of the terms is an exercise in empty slogans. These terms are unlikely to go away. Jurists, politicians, and the public continue to use them, and we should therefore try to define and understand them, so that we may evaluate and critique them.[1]

---

[1] J. Daley, "Defining Judicial Restraint," in *Judicial Power, Democracy and Legal Positivism* 279 (T. Campbell and J. Goldsworthy eds., 2000); McWhinney, "The Great Debate: Activism and Self-Restrain and Current Dilemmas in Judicial Policy-Making," 33 *N.Y.U. L. Rev.* 775 (1958); Mason, "Judicial Activism: Old and New," 55 *V. L. Rev.* 385 (1969); John Agresto, *The Supreme Court and Constitutional Democracy* (1988); Wright, "The Judicial Right and the Rhetoric of Restraint: A Defense of Judicial Activism in an Age of Conservative Judges," 14 *Hastings Const. L.Q.* 487 (1987); Mahoney, "Judicial Activism and Judicial

Relevant Only When There Is Judicial Discretion

Activism and self-restraint are relevant only when judicial discretion exists. A judge who declares what the law is, without creating new law, exercises neither activism nor self-restraint. A judge who issues an opinion holding that the speed limit on a particular road is as provided in the traffic statute acts as the "mouth" of the legislature. His declaration is neither activist nor restrained; he does no more than declare what exists. Activism or self-restraint exists only when judges make law.

Consider an example at the other extreme: A judge holds that the speed limit on a highway is such that it contradicts the provisions of the statute. A decision like that cannot be characterized as activist or restrained. It is illegitimate. Neither activism nor self-restraint justify or permit a decision that violates the law. The concept of activism or self-restraint operates only when the judicial ruling is according to law, within the zone of judicial reasonableness. Even those who agree with and advocate for judicial activism do not attempt to justify it when the judicial ruling violates the law. We would not classify a judge who tosses a coin to decide a dispute as either activist or self-restrained; he is a judge who acts illegitimately. The terms activist or self-restrained do not apply.

I therefore decline to classify a judge who decides cases according to his personal view of the world as an activist, just as I do not categorize a judge who suppresses his personal view of the world in

Self-Restraint in the European Court of Human Rights: Two Sides of the Same Coin," 11 *H.R.L.J.* 57 (1990); Luban, "Justice Holmes and the Metaphysics of Judicial Restraint," 44 *Duke L.J.* 449 (1994); Kirby, "Judicial Activism," 27 *W. Aust. L. Rev.* 1 (1997); Christopher Wolfe, *Judicial Activism: Bulwark of Freedom or Precarious Security?* (1997); F.P. Lewis, *The Context of Judicial Activism: The Endurance of the Warren Court Legacy in a Conservative Age* (1999); Ernest Young, "Judicial Activism and Conservative Politics," 73 *U. Colo. L. Rev.* 1139 (2002; William Marshall, "Conservatives and the Seven Sins of Judicial Activism," 73 *U. Colo. L. Rev.* 1217 (2002); Rebecca Brown, "Activism is Not a Four-Letter Word," 73 *U. Colo. L. Rev.* 1257 (2002); Michael Gerhardt, "The Rhetoric of Judicial Critique: From Judicial Restraint to the Virtual Bill of Rights," 10 *Wlm. and Mary Bill Rts. J.* 585 (2002).

favor of the law as self-restrained. As I have tried to show, judicial objectivity is a condition of judicial decision making.[2] No judge may impose his personal opinions on society. We can discuss activism and self-restraint only in the zones in which a judge has discretion to choose different courses of action. This discretion does not include the judge's personal beliefs which are not shared by society at large.

Of course, sometimes the line between legal and illegal, legitimate and illegitimate, are so fine as to appear invisible. What seems to one person to be illegal or illegitimate may appear to another as an appropriate exercise of activism or self-restraint, and there will be disagreement over the use of the terms. Once an activity has exceeded the bounds of legality, however, it has also exceeded the bounds of activism or self-restraint.

Liberal versus Conservative

It would be a mistake to define an activist judge as a liberal judge and a restrained judge as a conservative judge. Liberal and conservative are appropriate terms to evaluate the result of the judicial activity. For example, from the turn of the twentieth century until the end of the 1930s, the United States Supreme Court was an activist conservative court that invalidated a number of statutes that sought to recognize individual rights. The Warren Court of the 1970s was an activist liberal court. And today's United States Supreme Court, whose majority is conservative, behaves as an activist court in many areas of law.[3] A liberal judge like Brandeis was viewed as a judge who exercised self-restraint; a conservative judge like Scalia is seen as an activist judge. Definitions of activism and self-restraint should therefore address the way judicial discretion is exercised, irrespective of the evaluation of the outcome.

[2] *See supra* p. 101.
[3] *See* Thomas M. Keck, *The Most Activist Supreme Court in History: The Road to Modern Judicial Conservatism* (2000).

Activism and Self-Restraint Are Two Ends of a Continuum

Activism and self-restraint are two extremes of a continuum. We can speak of degrees of activism and degrees of self-restraint. There is no one criterion for defining activism and self-restraint. A judicial decision, a judge, or a court may embody different aspects of activism or self-restraint, measured along different axes. Indeed, we should not assume that judges can be divided according to those who are always activist and those who always exercise self-restraint. This absolute approach is inconsistent with a judge's need to act within the framework of his zone of discretion, which at various times will demand more or less activism and more or less self-restraint.

The Terms Depend on the Social Context and the Legal Culture

The definitions of activism and self-restraint are closely linked to the particular society and the legal culture in which they operate. There is no point in seeking a definition that suits every society and legal system, and in any case one is not to be found. Consider, for example, English law, which does not authorize judges to review the constitutionality of statutes. A definition of activism or self-restraint that focuses on judicial review of the constitutionality of statutes, as is the case in the United States and Canada, has no meaning or relevance to English law. Likewise, the United States legal system is engaged in a vigorous debate over the weight to give the intention of the founders of the Constitution and to the "original understanding" of the Constitution by the generation that founded it. It is natural that the terms activism and self-restraint play a role in this dispute. In other legal systems, in contrast, such as those of Canada and Germany, there is agreement that little weight should be accorded to the intent of the founders and the original understanding of the constitution. In those systems, there is no point in classifying a judge according to his stance on the question. The terms become significant in cases in which there is dispute over the exercise of judicial discretion.

SOME DEFINITIONS AND THEIR CRITIQUES

Bork

Robert H. Bork defines activist judges as those who "enact their own beliefs."[4] He adds that:

> Activist judges are those who decide cases in ways that have no plausible connection to the law they purport to be applying, or who stretch or even contradict the meaning of that law. They arrive at results by announcing principles that were never contemplated by those who wrote and voted for the law.[5]

The first part of Bork's description is not of an activist judge but rather of a judge who is not worthy of the position he occupies. None of us may turn our personal beliefs into the law of the land. The second part of his description refers to a system of interpretation that is legitimate but, as I have tried to show, is not the proper system. I do accept, however, that the choice between legitimate systems of interpretation may indicate a judge's degree of activism or self-restraint.

Posner

Judge Robert Posner views judicial activism in terms of the separation of powers, or what he calls "structural restraint."[6] In his view, a judge exercises self-restraint when he is "trying to limit his court's power over other government institutions."[7] An activist judge, on the other hand, tries to expand the power of the judiciary at the expense of the other branches of government. For Posner, structural restraint is neither liberal nor conservative; it does not vary according to the policies of the other branches; it does not apply to private law;

---

[4] Robert Bork, *Coercing Virtue: The Worldwide Rule of Judges* 9 (2003).
[5] *Ibid*, p. 8.
[6] Robert Posner, *The Federal Courts: Challenge and Reform* 304 (1996). *See also* Robert Posner, *Law, Pragmatism and Democracy* 211(2003).
[7] Posner, *The Federal Courts*, at 318.

it does not assume a "modest, deferential, timid" judge; it is not an absolute value, and there are cases in which it is not desirable; it does not reflect an entire judicial philosophy; it has nothing to do with the decision whether or not to deviate from precedent; it is not related to the distinction between substance and formalism.

The benefit of Posner's definition is the way in which it weeds out irrelevant considerations that have grown around the terms activism and self-restraint. His definition fails, however, because there need not be a connection between activism and expanding the power of the judiciary, on the one hand, and between restraint and restricting the power of the judiciary, on the other hand. Many judicial decisions implicating activism and self-restraint have nothing to do with the power of the court but rather deal with the powers of the other branches. A decision on the relationship between the executive and the legislature falls outside Posner's framework, but it certainly implicates questions of activism and self-restraint. It may not affect the authority of the judiciary, but it is an exercise of the court's power on the other branches. I see no difference between invalidating a statute that infringes on executive authority (which, according to Posner, would not implicate activism or self-restraint) and invalidating a statute because it violates human rights. In both instances the court determines the consequence of the legislation, and we must be able to analyze both cases in terms of activism and self-restraint. In addition, Posner's discussion of activism and self-restraint is limited to public law, ignoring their effects on private law. A thousand years of common law history are a thousand years of judging that can and should be analyzed in terms of activism or self-restraint. For these reasons, I think Posner's definition is too narrow to encompass all aspects of activism and self-restraint.

Canon

Writing in 1982, Bradley C. Canon assembles various definitions of activism and self-restraint to create six dimensions for understanding judicial activism, each of which may find expression at varying levels of intensity (high activist, somewhat activist, nonactivist).[8] The six dimensions are (1) majoritarianism—the degree to which policies adopted through democratic processes are judicially negated, as when a court invalidates an unconstitutional statute passed by the legislature; (2) interpretive stability—the degree to which earlier court decisions, doctrines, or interpretations are changed; (3) interpretive fidelity—the degree to which constitutional provisions are interpreted contrary to the clear intentions of their drafters or the clear implications of the language used; (4) determining substance rather than democratic procedure—the degree to which judicial decisions make substantive policy rather than affect the preservation of the democratic process; (5) specificity of policy—the degree to which a judicial decision establishes policy itself, as opposed to leaving it to the discretion of other agencies or individuals; and (6) the availability of an alternative policy maker—the degree to which a judicial decision supercedes serious consideration of the same problem by other governmental agencies. Canon acknowledges that he does not create a new way of measuring activism but rather pulls together existing definitions from American legal literature. There is some overlap among his dimensions, and some of them contradict each other. The first dimension (majoritarianism) overlaps substantially with the fourth (creating substance rather than preserving procedures), the fifth (creating policy), and the sixth (the availability of an alternative policy maker). On the other hand, when a court deviates from a precedent that invalidated a statute, it exercises high self-restraint as measured by the first dimension (majoritarianism) but engages in high activism as measured by the second definition (deviation from precedent). I find Canon's definition better than those of his predecessors. He correctly stresses that activism and self-restraint are expressed in degrees of intensity and that judges or courts may be activist on one dimension but restrained along another. However, his definition seems to me to be overly complicated and burdened. It lacks conceptual coherence. It is particular to American law.

[8] Bradley C. Canon, "A Framework for the Analysis of Judicial Activism," in *Supreme Court Activism and Restraint* 385 (Stephen C. and Charles M. eds., 1982).

Roach

Kent Roach examines activism and self-restraint according to the model of dialogue that he developed.[9] This model addresses the relationship between the legislature and the courts in the context of invalidating statutes that violate human rights protected by the Canadian Charter of Rights and Freedoms. He identifies four components necessary to evaluate activism: (1) "the degree to which judges are free to read their own preferences into law when interpreting the constitution," (2) "the degree to which judges are eager to make constitutional judgments not necessary to decide a live dispute," (3) "the extent to which courts recognize rights as trumping interests and the extent to which they defer to other social interests," and (4) "the extent to which court decisions displace those of the legislature and the executive and the extent to which courts have the final words in their interactions with those institutions."[10] This definition is restricted to addressing the dialogue between the judiciary and the executive. It cannot contribute to a comprehensive understanding of activism and self-restraint.

DEFINITION OF ACTIVISM AND SELF-RESTRAINT

Defining the Terms according to their Objectives

My definition of activism and self-restraint must derive from the objective that these terms are to achieve. For me, that objective is to evaluate the role of a judge in a democratic society. Activism and self-restraint must therefore relate to how well they realize the judicial role of bridging the gap between law and society's changing reality and the role of protecting the constitution and its values.

---

[9] Kent Roach, *The Supreme Court on Trial: Judicial Activism or Democratic Dialogue* (2001).
[10] *Id.* at p. 106.

Does this framework mean that judicial activism is always preferred, because it allows for more aggressive action to exhaust all aspects of the judicial role, while self-restraint is to be avoided, because it requires a judge to avoid realizing his judicial role? My answer is no. Realizing these twin aspects of the judicial role requires a ceaseless and appropriate balance between conflicting values. This balance cannot always be attained through activism, and it is not always frustrated by self-restraint.

The Definition of Activism and Self-Restraint

Against the background of the essence of this definition, I hereby define activism and self-restraint as follows: judicial activism is the judicial tendency—conscious or unconscious—to achieve the proper balance between conflicting social values (such as individual rights against the needs of the collective, the liberty of one person against that of another the authority of one branch of government against another) through change in the existing law (invalidating an unconstitutional statute invalidating secondary legislation that conflicts with a statute, reversing a judicial precedent) or through creating new law that did not previously exist (through interpreting the constitution or legislation, through developing the common law). In changing an existing law or creating a new law, the activist judge does not hesitate to invalidate a legal policy created by other branches of government in the past, by judges who preceded him, or by individuals. To achieve his goals, the activist judge is willing to develop new judicial measures and means (including systems of interpretation, ways of overruling precedent, rules that open the court's doors to litigants) that will allow him to change the existing law or create new law.

Self-restraint encompasses the opposite qualities. I define self-restraint as follows: it is the judicial tendency—conscious or unconscious—to achieve the proper balance between conflicting social values by preserving existing law rather than creating new law.

It finds expression in a judge's reluctance to invalidate a legal policy that was determined in the past. The self-restrained judge generally achieves his goals using existing judicial means.

Comprehensiveness

My definition of activism and self-restraint is comprehensive. It extends to all branches of law. I characterize as activist or restrained not just decisions in public law (addressing relations between the state and individual rights) but also decisions in private law.

The Problem of Judicial Legitimacy

Activism and self-restraint operate within the bounds of judicial legitimacy. I therefore do not define judicial activism as changing the law or creating new law in every case and in all circumstances (whether legitimate or not). In some circumstances, changing the law is illegal, and no judge has the power to do so. Similarly, self-restraint does not mean preserving existing law in all circumstances (whether legitimate or not), because sometimes doing so will be illegal. The distinction between activism and self-restraint is one of degree, not kind. No judge is always activist, just as no judge always exercises self-restraint. If such a judge did exist, he would sometimes act against the law. My definition of activism and restraint applies only to legal activity. One should notice, of course, that activist judges are less influenced by considerations of security, certainty, preserving the status quo, and the institutional constraints. On the other hand, self-restrained judges accord significant weight to security, certainty, and preserving the status quo. They respect the institutional constraints that preserve existing law and prevent changes.

Because judicial legitimacy determines the bounds of activism and self-restraint, activist judges are likely to try to change the bounds of legitimacy. They may develop new means to be used by judges, including new systems of interpretation, in order to play an activist role. Any development of new judicial means must be legitimate. On this issue, a self-restrained judge faces a dilemma: by developing new means in order to preserve the status quo, the self-restrained judge engages in judicial activism. The same is true if he invalidates existing judicial means that permit judicial activism. If, however, a self-restrained judge avoids any development of new means, the existing means are likely to be used to further judicial activism.

Activism, Self-Restraint, and a Judge's Personal Views

A judge may not impose his personal views on the society in which he judges. A judge who does so acts outside the bounds of law. Every exercise of judicial discretion must take place within the values recognized by society, reflecting its basic perspectives. There is no connection between activism and personal views, just as there is no connection between activism and tossing a coin. Neither is a case of judicial activism but rather of illegitimate judicial activity.

Having said that, where there is judicial discretion—and we are concerned only with those cases—there comes a point at which the decision is not dictated by the legal system. The decision is the product of judicial subjectivity. This subjectivity does not express the personal views of a judge. It is a much narrower subjectivity; it is a subjectivity that chooses among a system of objective components and balances them; it is a subjectivity governed by objective principles. Within that narrow and important area in which a judge may express his subjectivity, there is a difference between a judge who accords greater significance to the need for change and the judge who accords greater significance to the need for security and certainty in legal relationships. This zone highlights the difference between judges who accord more or less significance to policies that others created (whether governmental institutions or individuals).

Relationship to Legal Policies Determined in the Past

An activist judge seeking to realize his role will not always seek to change legal policies that others created. Similarly, a self-restrained judge seeking to realize his role will not always preserve the existing legal policies, determined by others. However, an activist judge will accord relatively little significance to the fact that he is creating a new policy that differs from that created by others, including by officials in one of the three branches of government. On the other hand, a self-restrained judge accords significant weight to these existing legal policies. Both types of judges act within the zone of judicial reasonableness; neither will invalidate a decision of another branch unless it deviates from the zone of reasonableness which characterizes that branch.

Is it the case that judicial activism expands the power of a court, vis-à-vis the other branches of government, while self-restraint reduces it? As noted,[11] that is Posner's approach to these terms. These results do not define activism and self-restraint, but activism and self-restraint are likely to lead to that outcome.

Systems of Interpretation

Is there a link between judicial activism and objective systems of interpretation (the intent of the reasonable author; the fundamental values of the system)? Is there a correlation between judicial self-restraint and subjective systems of interpretation (authorial intent)? I assume, of course, that a judge acts within a legal system in which he is free to choose any of these purposes in interpreting a legal text.[12] I assume that either of these two kinds of systems is legitimate. Given that assumption, is it accurate to characterize an objective system of interpretation as being consistent with judicial activism, while a subjective system of interpretation is consistent with self-restraint? In my

[11] *See supra* p. 267.
[12] *See supra* p. 127.

opinion, there is no basis to that link. Both systems contain elements of activism and self-restraint. Of course, there is a natural link between judicial activism and objective interpretation, because the values of a society are not frozen in time, and they change as the society changes. These changes are conducive to judicial activism. However, subjective interpretation can also be conducive to judicial activism, in the absence of precise information about the historical intent of the author and given the possibility of using judicial discretion to sort through intention at various levels of abstraction. A change in the approach to the intention of the author brings about a change in the law, in accordance with the perspective of an activist judge. We can conduct a similar analysis of self-restraint and the different systems of interpretation. This restraint works well with objective systems of interpretation, to the extent that there has been no change in the fundamental values of the system and the perspective attributed to the reasonable author. This restraint is also suited to subjective interpretation, to the extent that research into authorial intent produces unequivocal information, and there is no dispute over the appropriate level of abstraction.

In general, however, there is a greater chance of finding judicial activism within objective systems of interpretation and of finding self-restraint to be the tool of subjective systems. The reason is that judges operating within objective systems of interpretation are generally, though not always, accorded greater interpretive freedom than their counterparts working in subjective systems of interpretation.

Precedent

How do activism and self-restraint relate to judicial precedents? The question arises, of course, only for judges who are authorized to diverge from precedent. This question arises most commonly for judges on supreme courts, who have the final word on establishing new precedents. Will an activist judge diverge from precedent, while a self-restrained judge avoids doing so? According to my definition, the question depends on the judge's principled approach

and tendency. Indeed, an activist judge accords relatively less significance to precedents. Of course, such a judge will not diverge
from them when they reflect the views with which he agrees. When
such a judge disagrees with a prior ruling, however—even if it is
legitimate—an activist judge will diverge from it. An activist judge
will not accord significant weight to considerations of *stare decisis*,
such as security and certainty in law and preserving reasonable
expectations.

The stance of the self-restrained judge is more complex. On the
one hand, self-restraint brings him to preserve the status quo and
respect precedents. On the other hand, those precedents may
be the outcome of an activist approach repugnant to such judges'
philosophy of restraint. Self-restrained judges face a dilemma: by
straying from precedent, they also stray from their characteristic self-
restraint; by respecting precedent, they perpetuate the activism with
which they disagree. In cases like these, self-restrained judges will
weigh the benefit of preserving existing law against the cost of preserving an inappropriate precedent resulting from activism, in order
to reach a decision. Self-restrained judges may decide that it is better
to adopt an activist stance in the short run (diverging from precedent) in order to lay the foundation for self-restraint in the long run
(the law created by the new ruling). Otherwise, it would never be
possible to diverge from precedents created by activist judges.

The Means Available to a Judge

Self-restrained judges and activist judges adopt different
approaches to the means available to realize their roles. We have
already discussed their relationship to systems of interpretation and
respecting precedent. We will now discuss other means of judging,
evaluating them along the continuum between absolute self-
restraint and absolute activism.[13]

---

[13] *See* H.J. Abraham, *The Judicial Process* 373 (4th ed, 1980).

An activist judge will take an expansive view of standing and a narrow view of non-justiciability. An activist judge will not hesitate to use dicta, will base his ruling with broad explanations ("maximization"), and will develop new measures and remedies to protect the rights he recognizes. A self-restrained judge will hesitate to employ dicta—with the exception of dicta in favor of self-restraint—and will lay a narrow foundation for his ruling ("minimalism") and will avoid developing new means or remedies.

Activist judges will seek to expand the scope of judicial review of public governance; they will narrow the zone of reasonableness, leaving room to declare the actions of a government agency to be unreasonable; in reviewing administrative action, they will not insist on exhausting other measures as a precondition for deciding the dispute; they will not object to delivering advisory opinions. Self-restrained judges, on the other hand, will narrow the scope of judicial review of administrative action; they will expand the zone of reasonableness, leaving less room to declare the actions of a government agency to be unreasonable; they will insist on exhausting other measures as a precondition for hearing a dispute; they will avoid issuing advisory opinions that are not necessary to decide an actual dispute.

How do activism and self-restraint relate to the theory of balancing?[14] Activist judges prefer balancing over categorization. They prefer principled balancing over ad hoc balancing. Restrained judges prefer categorization over balancing. The framework of balancing is likely to create a dilemma for restrained judges. On the one hand, they will prefer ad hoc balancing over principle balancing, because doing so will permit them to minimize the change in law or limit any creation of new law to the particular situation at hand, such that the ruling will not have a general effect. On the other hand, they are likely to prefer principled balancing that gives normative validity to the self-restraint in which they believe. The decision between these conflicting considerations will—as was the considerations will—as was the case in the discussion of precedent—depend on case in the discussion of precedent—depend on the relative weight of each consideration.

[14] On the theory of balancing, *see* supra p. 164.

There is a noticeable difference between activism and self-restraint concerning the scope of judicial review of the constitutionality of statutes. Both approaches operate within the rules applicable to this field. However, these two approaches will result in determining different rules—a product of judicial discretion. Activist judges believe in the indispensability and importance of judicial review of the constitutionality of statutes. They are more likely than self-restrained judges to find that the minimal conditions for exercising judicial review have been met. At the moment of decision, the activist judges is more likely to declare a statute unconstitutional. Self-restrained judges, on the other hand, may have doubts about the appropriateness of judicial review itself. They will insist that the conditions for applying judicial review have been fully met. At the moment of decision, self-restrained judges are ready to declare a statute unconstitutional only in exceptional cases.

No Complete Activism or Complete Self-Restraint

Both activist and restrained judges will sometimes find themselves in difficult dilemmas. Activist judges will face a dilemma when judicial activism creates tension between the values that they seek to realize. For example, activist judges may find tension between the desire to expand the scope of human rights and the desire to expand the defense of state security and public safety. Activist judges may also face a conflict between the values they seek to advance and public confidence in them, which may be undermined by an activist approach. I therefore think that complete activism— even for generally activist judges—does not exist. We can only talk about a tendency toward complete activism, nothing more.

Self-restrained judges will also face a dilemma in cases of tension between the values they seek to realize. For example, if they stick to their basic approach and exercise restraint, such restraint may allow activist judges to exercise their activism. In these cases, self-restrained judges must balance between their commitment to self-restraint and their opposition to activism. Most self-restrained judges will seek a balance between these competing values. Therefore, there is no such thing as judges who practice complete restraint. Such restraint would advance the agenda of activist judges, sounding the death knell for restraint, anyway. The most we can find is judges who tend toward complete self-restraint.

Among reasonable judges, we do not find complete activism or complete self-restraint, but rather only judges who tend in one direction or another. Nevertheless, it seems to me that we are more likely to find activist judges who tend toward complete activism than to find self-restrained judges who tend toward complete restraint. The question is whether this tendency toward complete activism or complete restraint is desirable. I will now address that question.

THE DESIRABILITY OF ACTIVISM OR SELF-RESTRAINT

Activism, Self-Restraint, and the Role of the Judge

Defining activism and self-restraint is difficult and complex; hence the tendency to go no further than the definition. The more important question, however, is whether activism or self-restraint is desirable. Is an activist judge or a self-restrained judge a "good" or a "bad" judge? Few address this question, despite the importance of the answer. What does it matter what activism or self-restraint is, if those terms are irrelevant to answer the question of whether activism or self-restraint is good and desirable?

Determining the desirability of activism or self-restraint is a difficult task, for five reasons. First, there are no judges who are completely activist or completely restrained. We are operating in a narrow interim zone between the two extremes. The line between more activist and more restrained is fine, too fine for our relatively coarse analytical tools to analyze seriously. To complicate matters, a judge may sometimes be activist in one area of law and restrained in another. These complications make it difficult to analyze activism or self-restraint as such, and require us to make distinctions according to the nature of the issue and the identity of the judge. Second, as we move away from the extremes of complete activism or self-restraint, we enter an area of evaluation. What to one observer appears to be an activist tendency seems to another to be a tendency toward self-restraint. Third, this evaluation is particularly difficult when a judge uses activist rhetoric but in practice—in decisions in concrete cases—exercises self-restraint. How do we categorize a judge like that? Shall we look at the actual (self-restrained) ruling made in the present, or consider the rhetoric suggesting that future decisions will be activist? How do we evaluate the likelihood of future decisions being activist? Fourth, in evaluating activism or self-restraint, should we focus on a given judicial opinion, regardless of which judges issued it? Should we focus on a particular judge, analyzing his decisions over time? Should we look at a particular court over a given period of a year, a decade, throughout the court's history? There is a noticeable difference between these points of view. In focusing on a judge, we should take into consideration the changes occurring in the way that particular judge carries out his judicial duties. In focusing on a court, we should take into consideration the personnel changes on the court. These evaluations are complicated, and they require a certain distance of time and place. Fifth, "good" and "bad" are terms that relate to a particular model of judging. Activism and self-restraint are good or bad depending on whether they help actualize that model. But what is the model? Different people have different models of judging. Their views of the benefits and drawbacks of activism and self-restraint will vary with the changes in which model they think is appropriate. In this book, I have presented a model of proper judging. How do judicial activism and judicial self-restraint relate to this model? As I noted, the role of the judge is to bridge the gap between law and society and to protect the constitution and its values. Should a judge seeking to realize those roles exercise activism or self-restraint?

Bridging the Gap between Law and Society

I view bridging the gap between law and society as a central task of a judge. Does that mean that a judge should bridge this gap wherever it exists? If that were the case, I would advocate using complete judicial activism to fulfill this role. I do not believe this is so. I favor graduated change in law, whether effected through changes in interpretation of the law or through development of the common law. I discussed the need to effect change through stability; I emphasized the importance of change in accordance with the general framework of the system, normative coherence, organic growth, natural development, continuity, and consistency. I noted that when a judge bridges the gap between law and society's changing reality, he must consider the institutional constraints, including the sporadic nature of reform, the partial information to which he may have access, and the lack of sufficient legal tools, all of which caution against change. I also noted the importance of considering the scope of change and the substantive considerations behind the legal policy. It is one thing for a judge to change the law because of human rights considerations about which he has substantial information. It is quite another to change the law for economic reasons based on polycentric considerations beyond the judge's expertise.

These considerations lead to the conclusion that a judge can best bridge the gap between law and society by exercising partial activism and partial restraint. Complete activism or complete restraint is not only impossible, it is undesirable.

Protecting the Constitution and Its Values

The balancing approach, tending neither toward activism nor toward self-restraint, is not only the best approach to bridging the gap between law and society, it also applies to protecting the constitution and its values. Protecting the constitution requires balancing the different values internal to a particular society. It requires balancing between the principle of majority rule and values that even the majority may not undermine, between the needs of the collective and individual rights, between the rights of one individual and those of another. A judge must protect and maintain this delicate balance, something that requires some measure of activism and some measure of self-restraint.

New Means

This middle ground, so appropriate for bridging the gap between law and society and protecting the constitution and its values, is also the right approach to preparing the judicial means with which a court will exercise its discretion. In this important area, tendencies toward complete activism or complete self-restraint are out of place. The use of each mean should be done with an eye toward all the means available. It may sometimes be appropriate to exercise more self-restraint in using a particular mean (such as the proper system of interpretation), while the use of other means may justify more activism (expanding access to the courts through a broad view of standing and a restrictive view of non-justiciability). Balance is required to develop a theory of balancing. This theory does not suit every situation, and it should be applied carefully. Such is the case in using comparative law: it should be done with the appropriate caution, and when the judge formulates the decision, he should do so with an awareness of the consequences of the rhetoric employed. The judge should balance the various considerations.

CHAPTER SIXTEEN

The Judicial Role and the Problem of Terrorism

TERRORISM AND DEMOCRACY

Tension between Democracy and the Fight against Terror

Terrorism plagues many countries. The United States realized its devastating power on September 11, 2001. Other countries, such as Israel, have suffered from terrorism for a long time.[1] While terrorism poses difficult questions for every country, it poses especially challenging questions for democratic countries, because not every effective means is a legal means. I discussed this in one case, in which our Court held that violent interrogation of a suspected terrorist is not lawful, even if doing so may save human life by preventing impending terrorist acts:

> We are aware that this decision does not make it easier to deal with that reality. This is the fate of democracy, as not all means are acceptable to it, and not all methods employed by its enemies are open to it. Sometimes a democracy must fight with one hand tied behind its back. Nonetheless, it has the upper hand. Preserving the rule of law and the recognition of individual liberties constitute an important component of its understanding of security. At the end of the day, they strengthen its spirit and strength and allow it to overcome its difficulties.[2]

[1] For a comparison of the American experience and the Israeli experience, see William J. Brennan, Jr., "The Quest to Develop a Jurisprudence of Civil Liberties in Time of Security Crises," 18 *Isr. Yearbook Hum. Rts.* 11 (1988).
[2] H.C. 5100/94, *Pub. Comm. Against Torture in Isr. v. Gov't of Israel*, 53(4) P.D. 817, 845; [1998–9] IsrLR 567.

In another case, dealing with the legality of a security fence built in the West Bank, I observed:

> Our task is difficult. We are members of Israeli society. Although we are sometimes in an ivory tower, that tower is in the heart of Jerusalem, which is not infrequently hit by ruthless terror. We are aware of the killing and destruction wrought by the terror against the state and its citizens. Like any other Israelis, we too recognize the need to defend the country and its citizens against the wounds inflicted by terror. We are aware that in the short term, this judgment will not make the state's struggle against those rising up against it easier. But we are judges. When we sit in judgment, we are subject to judgment. We act according to our best conscience and understanding. Regarding the state's struggle against the terror that rises up against it, we are convinced that at the end of the day, a struggle according to the law will strengthen its power and its spirit. There is no security without law. Satisfying the provisions of the law is an aspect of national security.[3]

Terrorism creates much tension between the essential components of democracy.[4] One pillar of democracy, the rule of the people through its elected representatives (formal democracy), may encourage taking all steps effective in fighting terrorism, even if they are harmful to human rights. The other pillar of democracy, human rights, may encourage protecting the rights of every individual, including the terrorists, even at the cost of undermining the fight against terrorism. Struggling with this tension is primarily the task of the legislature and the executive, which are accountable to the people.

---

[3] H.C. 2056/04, *Beit Sourik Village Council v. The Government of Israel, supra* p. 182, note 16 at para. 86 (English translation available at www.court.gov.il) .
[4] See Michael Ignatieff, *The Lesser Evil: Political Ethics in an Age of Terror* (2004); *The Security of Freedom: Essays on Canada's Anti-Terrorism Bill* (Ronald J. Daniels et al. eds., 2001); Georg P. Fletcher, *Romantics at War: Glory and Guilt in the Age of Terrorism* (2002); Alan M. Dershowitz, *Why Terrorism Works: Understanding the Threat, Responding to the Challenge* (2002); James X. Dempsey and David Cole, *Terrorism and the Constitution: Sacrificing Civil Liberties in the Name of National Security* (2d ed., 2002).

But true democratic accountability cannot be satisfied by the judgment of the people alone. The legislature must also justify its decisions to judges, who are responsible for protecting democracy and the constitution.

We, the judges in modern democracies, are responsible for protecting democracy both from terrorism and from the means the state wants to use to fight terrorism. Of course, matters of daily life constantly test judges' ability to protect democracy, but judges meet their supreme test in situations of terrorism. The protection of every individual's human rights is a much more formidable duty in times of terrorism than in times of peace and security. If we fail in our role in times of terrorism, we will be unable to fulfill our role in times of peace and security. It is a myth to think that we can maintain a sharp distinction between the status of human rights during a period of war and the status of human rights during a period of peace. It is self-deception to believe that a judicial ruling will be valid only during the battle against terrorism and that things will change in peacetime. The line between terror and peace is thin: what one person calls peace, another calls terror. In any case, it is impossible to maintain this distinction over the long term. Since its founding, Israel has faced a security threat. As a justice of the Israeli Supreme Court, how should I view my role in protecting human rights given this situation? I must take human rights seriously during times of both peace and conflict. I must not make do with the mistaken belief that, at the end of the conflict, I can turn back the clock.

The Danger of a Mistake

Furthermore, a mistake by the judiciary in times of terrorism is worse than a mistake of the legislature and the executive in times of terrorism. The reason is that the judiciary's mistakes will remain with the democracy when the threat of terrorism passes and will be entrenched in the case law of the court as a magnet for the development of new and problematic laws. This is not so with a mistake of the other branches, which can be erased through legislation or executive action and usually forgotten. In his dissent in *Korematsu v. United States*,[5] Justice Jackson expressed this distinction well:

> [A] judicial construction of the due process clause that will sustain this order is a far more subtle blow to liberty. . . . A military order, however unconstitutional, is not apt to last longer than the military emergency. . . . But once a judicial opinion rationalizes such an order to show that it conforms to the Constitution, or rather rationalizes the Constitution to show that the Constitution sanctions such an order, the Court for all time has validated the principle of racial discrimination in criminal procedure and of transplanting American citizens. The principle then lies about like a loaded weapon ready for the hand of any authority that can bring forward a plausible claim of an urgent need. . . . A military commander may overstep the bounds of constitutionality, and it is an incident. But if we review and approve, that passing incident becomes the doctrine of the Constitution. There it has a generative power of its own, and all that it creates will be in its own image.[6]

Indeed, we judges must act coherently and consistently.[7] A wrong decision in a time of terrorism plots a point that will cause the judicial graph to deviate after the crisis passes. This is not the case with the other branches of state, whose actions during a time of terrorism may amount to an episode that does not affect decisions made during times of peace and security.

The Test of Judicial Independence

Moreover, democracy ensures us, as judges, independence. Because of our unaccountability, it strengthens us against the fluctuations of public opinion. The real test of this independence comes in situations of terrorism. The significance of our unaccountability becomes clear in these situations, when public opinion is more likely to be unanimous.

---

[5] 323 U.S. 214 (1944).
[6] *Id.* at 245–46 (Jackson, J., dissenting).
[7] *See supra* p. 13.

Precisely in these times, we judges must hold fast to fundamental principles and values; we must embrace our supreme responsibility to protect democracy and the constitution. Lord Atkins's remarks on the subject of administrative detention during World War II aptly describe these duties of a judge. In a minority opinion in November 1941, he wrote:

> In England amidst the clash of arms the laws are not silent. They may be changed, but they speak the same language in war as in peace. It has always been one of the pillars of freedom, one of the principles of liberty for which . . . we are now fighting, that the judges . . . stand between the subject and any attempted encroachments on his liberty by the executive, alert to see that any coercive action is justified in law.[8]

Admittedly, the struggle against terrorism turns our democracy into a "defensive democracy" or a "militant democracy."[9] Nonetheless, this defense and this fight must not deprive our regime of its democratic character. Defensive democracy, yes; uncontrolled democracy, no. The judges in a modern democracy must act in this spirit. We have tried to do so in Israel, and I will discuss several fundamental views that have guided us in these efforts.

IN BATTLE, THE LAWS ARE NOT SILENT

There is a well-known saying that when the cannons speak, the Muses are silent. Cicero expressed a similar idea when he said, "*silent enim leges inter arma*" (in battle, indeed, the laws are silent).[10] These statements are regrettable; I hope they do not reflect our democracies today.[11] I *know* they do not reflect the way things should be. Every battle a country wages—against terrorism or any other

---

[8] *Liversidge v. Anderson*, 3 All E.R. 338, 361 (1941).
[9] On militant democracy, *see supra* p. 22, note 9.
[10] Cicero, *Pro Milone* 16 (N.H. Watts trans., Harvard Univ. Press, 5th ed. 1972).
[11] *See Re Application Under* S. 83.28 of the Criminal Code [2004], 2 S.C.R. 248, 260: "While Cicero long ago wrote '*inter arma silen legas*' we, like others, must strongly disagree" (Iacobucci and Arbour, JJ). *But cf.* William H. Rehnquist, *All the Laws But One: Civil Liberties in Wartime* 224 (1998).

enemy—is done according to rules and laws. There is always law—domestic or international—according to which the state must act. There are no "black holes."[12] And the law needs Muses, never more urgently than when the cannons speak. In one opinion I wrote:

> Israel finds itself in the middle of a difficult battle against a furious war of terrorism . . . this combat is not taking place in a normative void. It is being carried out according to the rules of international law, which provide principles and rules for combat activity. The saying, "When the cannons roar, the Muses are silent," is incorrect. Cicero's aphorism that laws are silent during war does not reflect modern reality. The foundation of this approach is not only the pragmatic consequence of a political and normative reality. Its roots lie much deeper. It is an expression of the difference between a democratic state fighting for its life and the aggression of terrorists rising up against it. The state fights in the name of the law and in the name of upholding the law. The terrorists fight against the law and exploit its violation. The war against terror is also the law's war against those who rise up against it.[13]

In another case I remarked:

> Israel is not an isolated island. She is a member of an international system. The military operations of the IDF are not conducted in a legal vacuum. There are legal norms that set out how military operations should be conducted.[14]

We need laws most in times of terror. As Harold Koh said, referring to the September 11, 2001, attacks:

> In the days since, I have been struck by how many Americans—and how many lawyers—seem to have concluded that, somehow, the destruction of four planes and three buildings has taken us back to a state of nature in which there are no laws or rules. In fact, over the years, we have

---

[12] *See* Steyn, *supra* p. xv, note 26 at 195.

[13] H.C. 3451/02, *Almadani v. Minister of Def.*, 56(3) P.D. 30 (English translation available at www.court.gov.il).

[14] H.C. 4764/04, *Physicians for Human Rights v. The Commander of IDF Forces in the Gaza Strip* (unreported, English translation available at www.court.gov.il).

developed an elaborate system of domestic and international laws, institutions, regimes, and decision-making procedures precisely so that they will be consulted and obeyed, not ignored, at a time like this.[15]

During the Gulf War, Iraq fired missiles at Israel. Israel feared chemical and biological warfare as well, so the government distributed gas masks. A suit was brought against the military commander, arguing that he distributed gas masks unequally in the West Bank. We accepted the petitioner's argument. In my opinion, I wrote:

> When the cannons speak, the Muses are silent. But even when the cannons speak, the military commander must uphold the law. The power of society to stand up against its enemies is based on its recognition that it is fighting for values that deserve protection. The rule of law is one of these values.[16]

This opinion sparked criticism; some argued that the Supreme Court had improperly interfered in Israel's struggle against Iraq. I believe that this criticism is unjustified. We did not intervene in military considerations, for which the expertise and responsibility lie with the executive. Rather, we intervened in considerations of equality, for which the expertise and responsibility rest with the judiciary. Indeed, the struggle against terrorism is not conducted *outside* the law but *within* the law, using tools that the law makes available to a democratic state. Terrorism does not justify the neglect of accepted legal norms. This is how we distinguish ourselves from the terrorists themselves. They act against the law, by violating and trampling it, while in its battle against terrorism, a democratic state acts within the framework of the law and according to the law. Justice Haim Cohen of Israel's Supreme Court expressed this idea well more than twenty years ago, when he said:

> What distinguishes the war of the state from the war of its enemies is that the State fights while upholding the law, whereas its enemies fight while violating the law. The moral strength and objective justness of

[15] Harold Hongju Koh, "The Spirit of the Laws," 43 *Harv. Int'l L.J.* 23 (2002).
[16] H.C. 168/91, *Morcos v. Minister of Def.*, 45(1) P.D. 467, 470–71.

the government's war depend entirely on upholding the laws of the state: by conceding this strength and this justness, the government serves the purposes of the enemy. Moral weapons are no less important than any other weapon, and perhaps more important. There is no weapon more moral than the rule of law. Everyone who ought to know should be aware that the rule of law in Israel will never succumb to the state's enemies.[17]

Indeed, the fight against terrorism is the fight of a law-abiding nation and its law-abiding citizens against lawbreakers. It is, therefore, not merely a battle of the state against its enemies; it is also a battle of the law against its enemies. My opinion in the case involving the alleged food shortage among the besieged Palestinians in the Church of the Nativity in Bethlehem addressed this role of the rule of law as a primary actor in matters of terrorism. We considered the petition and applied the relevant rules of international law. In doing so, I said:

> Israel is in a difficult war against rampant terrorism. It is acting on the basis of its right to self-defense. . . . This armed conflict is not undertaken in a normative vacuum. It is undertaken according to the rules of international law, which establish the principles and rules for armed conflicts. The saying that "when the cannons speak, the Muses are silent" is incorrect. . . . The reason underlying this approach is not merely pragmatic, the result of political and normative reality. The reason underlying this approach is much deeper. It is an expression of the difference between a democratic state fighting for its survival and the battle of terrorists rising up against it. The state is fighting for the law and for the law's protection. The terrorists are fighting against and in defiance of the law. The armed conflict against terrorism is an armed conflict of the law against those who seek to destroy it . . . But in addition, the State of Israel is a state whose values are Jewish and democratic. Here we have established a state that preserves law, that achieves its national goals and the vision of generations, and

---

[17] H.C. 320/80, *Kwasama v. Minister of Def.*, 5(3) P.D. 113, 132.

that does so while recognizing and realizing human rights in general and human dignity in particular. Between these two there are harmony and accord, not conflict and estrangement.[18]

Therefore, as Justice Mishael Cheshin has written, "[W]e will not falter in our efforts for the rule of law. We have sworn by our oath to dispense justice, to be the servant of the law, and we will be faithful to our oath and to ourselves. Even when the trumpets of war sound, the rule of law will make its voice heard."[19]

Discussing democracy's war on terrorism, Justice Kirby has rightly pointed out that it must be waged while "[k]eeping proportion. Adhering to the ways of democracy. Upholding constitutionalism and the rule of law. Defending, even under assault, and even for the feared and hated, the legal rights of suspects."[20]

THE BALANCE BETWEEN NATIONAL SECURITY AND HUMAN RIGHTS

The Need for Balance

Democratic nations should conduct the struggle against terrorism with a proper balance between two conflicting values and principles. On the one hand, we must consider the values and principles relating to the security of the state and its citizens. Human rights are not a stage for national destruction; they cannot justify undermining national security in every case and in all circumstances. Similarly, a constitution is not a prescription for national suicide.[21]

---

[18] H.C. 3451/02, *Almadani v. IDF Commander in Judea & Samaria*, 56(3) P.D. 30, 34–35 (English translation available at www.court.gov.il).

[19] H.C. 1730/96, *Sabiah v. IDF Commander in Judea & Samaria*, 50(1) P.D. 353, 369.

[20] Kirby, *supra* p. 22, note 11 at 32.

[21] *See* E.A. 2/84, *Neiman v. Chairman of Cent. Elections Comm. for Eleventh Knesset*, 39(2) P.D. 225, 310 (English translation available at www.court.gov.il). *Cf. Terminiello v. Chicago*, 337 U.S. 1, 37 (1949) (Jackson, J., dissenting).

But on the other hand, we must consider the values and principles relating to human dignity and freedom. National security cannot justify undermining human rights in every case and under all circumstances. National security does not grant an unlimited license to harm the individual.

Democratic nations must find a balance between these conflicting values and principles. Neither side can rule alone. Justices Iacobucci and Arbour of the Canadian Supreme Court expressed this need for balance:

> The challenge for democracies in the battle against terrorism is not whether to respond, but rather how to do so. This is because Canadians value the importance of human life and liberty, and the protection of society through respect for the rule of law. Although terrorism necessarily changes the context in which the rule of law must operate, it does not call for the abdication of law. Yet, at the same time, while respect for the rule of law must be maintained in the response to terrorism, the Constitution is not a suicide pact. . . . The challenge for a democratic state's answer to terrorism calls for a balancing of what is required for an effective response to terrorism in a way that appropriately recognizes the fundamental values of the rule of law.[22]

A similar approach was taken by the American Supreme Court in the *Hamdi* case.[23] Justice O'Conner observed in that case:

> [B]oth emphasize the tension that often exists between the autonomy that the government asserts is necessary in order to pursue effectively a particular goal and the process that a citizen contends that he is due before he is deprived of a constitutional right. The ordinary mechanism that we use for balancing such serious competing interests, and for determining the procedures that are necessary to ensure that a citizen is not "deprived of life, liberty or property" without due process of law . . . is the test . . . that the process due in any given instance is determined by weighing "the private interest that

[22] Re Application Under S.83.28 of the Criminal Code, *supra* p. 287, note 11 at 260.
[23] *Hamdi v. Rumsfeld* 124 S. CT. 2633.

will be affected by the official action" against the Government's asserted interest "including the function involved" and the burdens the Government would face in providing greater process.[24]

In a case that dealt with the legality of administrative detention, I said:

> In a democracy aspiring to freedom and security, there is no avoiding a balance between freedom and dignity, on the one hand, and security on the other. Human rights must not become a tool for denying security to the public and the state. A balance is required—a sensitive and difficult balance—between the freedom and dignity of the individual, and national security and public security.[25]

This synthesis between national security and individual freedom reflects the rich and fertile character of the principle of rule of law in particular and of democracy in general. It is within the framework of this approach that the courts in Israel have made their decisions concerning the state's armed conflict against the terrorism that plagues it. Our Supreme Court, which in Israel serves as the court of first instance for complaints against the executive branch, opens its doors to anyone with a complaint about the activities of a public authority. Even if the terrorist activities occur outside Israel or the terrorists are being detained outside Israel, we recognize our authority to hear the issue. We have not used the act of state doctrine or non-justiciability under these circumstances.[26] We consider these issues on their merits. Nor do we require injury in fact as a standing requirement; we recognize the standing of anyone to challenge the act.[27] In the context of terrorism, the Israeli Supreme Court has ruled on petitions concerning the power of the state to arrest suspected terrorists and the conditions of their confinement.[28] It has ruled on petitions concerning the rights of suspected terrorists to legal representation and

---

[24] *Id.* at 2467.

[25] Cr.A. 7048/97, *Anonymous v. Minister of Def.*, 54(1) P.D. 721, 741.

[26] *See supra* p. 179.

[27] *See supra* p. 190.

[28] *See* H.C. 3278/02, *Center for Defence of the Individual Founded by Dr. Lotta Salzberger v. Commander of IDF Forces in the West Bank*, 57(1) P.D. 385 (English translation available at www.court.gov.il):

the means by which they may be interrogated. These hearings sometimes take place just hours after the alleged incident about which the suspected terrorist complains. When necessary, the Court issues a preliminary injunction preventing the state from continuing the interrogation until the Court can determine that it is being conducted legally. In one case, the state sought to deport 400 suspected terrorists to Lebanon. Human rights organizations petitioned us. I was the justice on call at the time. Late that night, I issued an interim order enjoining the deportation. At the time, the deportees were in automobiles en route to Lebanon. The order immediately halted the deportation. Only after a hearing held in our Court throughout the night that included comprehensive argumentation, including testimony by the army's chief of staff, did we invalidate the deportation order.[29] We ruled that the state breached its obligation to grant the deportees the right to a hearing before deporting them, and we ordered a post factum right to a hearing.

In all these decisions—and there have been hundreds of this kind[30]—we have recognized the power of the state to protect its security and the security of its citizens on the one hand; on the other hand, we have emphasized that the rights of every individual must be preserved, including the rights of the individual suspected of being a terrorist. In a case dealing with detention for interrogation purposes, I observed:

> Detention for the purpose of investigation infringes upon the liberty of the detainee. Occasionally, in order to prevent the disruption of investigatory proceedings or to ensure public peace and safety, such

---

This Court has always exercised wide-ranging judicial review concerning conditions of imprisonment and detention. The Court has done so regarding Israeli prisoners and detainees. It has done so regarding prisoners and detainees from the area. In all these cases, the Court thoroughly investigated the arguments, even considering the smallest details of the conditions of detention. (Para. 29)

[29] *See* H.C. 5973/92, *Ass'n for Civil Rights in Isr. v. Minister of Def.*, 47(1) P.D. 267.
[30] For a collection of English translations of recent judgments, see *Judgments of Israel Supreme Court: Fighting Terrorism within the Law* (www.mfa.gov.il; www.court.gov.il)

detention is unavoidable. A delicate balance must be struck between the liberty of the individual, who enjoys the presumption of innocence, and public peace and safety. Such is the case with regard to the internal balance within the state—between the citizen and his state— and such is the case with regard to the external balance outside of the state—between the state that is engaged in war and persons detained during the war. Such is the case with regard to this balance in times of peace, and such is the case with regard to this balance in time of war.[31]

The balancing point between the conflicting values and principles is not constant, but rather differs from case to case and from issue to issue. The damage to national security caused by a given terrorist act and the nation's response to that act affect the way the freedom and dignity of the individual are protected. Thus, for example, when the response to terrorism was the destruction of the terrorists' homes, we discussed the need to act proportionately. We concluded that only when human life has been lost is it permissible to destroy the buildings where the terrorists lived, and even then the goal of the destruction may not be collective punishment (which is forbidden in an area under military occupation).[32] Such destruction may be used only for preventive purposes, and even then the owner of the building to be destroyed has a right to a prior hearing unless such a hearing would interfere with current military activity.[33] Obviously, there is no right to a hearing in the middle of a military operation. But when the time and place permit—and there is no danger of interference with security forces that are fighting terrorism— this right should be honored as much as possible.[34]

---

[31] H.C. 3239/02, *Maraab v. The Commander of IDF Forces in the West Bank*, 57(2) P.D. 349 (English translation available at www.court.gov.il).

[32] *See* H.C. 5510/92, *Turkeman v. Minister of Def.*, 48(1) P.D. 217. Harsh criticism has been leveled at this opinion and others like it. *See* David Kretzmer, *The Occupation of Justice: The Supreme Court of Israel and the Occupied Territories* 160–61 (2002).

[33] *See* H.C. 6696/02, *Adal Sado Amar v. IDF Commander in the W. Bank*, (www.court.gov.il).

[34] *See id.*

When it was necessary to use administrative detention against terrorists, we interpreted the relevant legislation to determine that the purpose of administrative detention laws is twofold: on the one hand, protecting national security; on the other hand, protecting the dignity and freedom of every person. We added that "protection of national security is a social interest that every state strives to satisfy. Within this framework, democratic freedom-loving countries recognize the 'institution' of administrative detention."[35] We also concluded that "defending and protecting . . . freedom and dignity extend even to the freedom and dignity of someone whom the state wishes to confine in administrative detention."[36] Against this background, we held:

> [I]t is possible to allow—in a democratic state that aspires to freedom and security—the administrative detention of a person who is regarded personally as a danger to national security. But this possibility should not be extended to the detention of a person who is not regarded personally as any danger to national security and who is merely a "bargaining chip."[37]

The battle against terrorism also requires the interrogation of terrorists, which must be conducted according to the ordinary rules of interrogation. Physical force must not be used in these interrogations; specifically, the persons being interrogated must not be tortured.[38]

Balance and the Need for Limitation

Any balance that is struck between security and freedom will impose certain limitations on both. A proper balance will not be achieved when human rights are fully protected as if there were no terrorism.

---

[35] *Anonymous v. Minister of Defence*, 54 (1) P.D. 72, 740.
[36] *Id.*
[37] *Id.* at 741.
[38] H.C. 5100/94, *Pub. Comm. Against Torture in Isr. v. Gov't of Israel*, 53(4) P.D. 817, 835; [1998–9] IsrLR 567.

Similarly, a proper balance will not be achieved when national security is afforded full protection, as if there were no human rights. The balance and compromise are the price of democracy. Only a strong, safe, and stable democracy may afford and protect human rights, and only a democracy built on the foundations of human rights can have security. It follows that the balance between security and freedom does not reflect the lack of a clear position. On the contrary, the proper balance is the result of a clear position that recognizes both the need for security and the need for human rights. I discussed this in a difficult case addressing whether the state may forcibly relocate residents of an occupied territory who pose a threat to state security: "A delicate and sensitive balance is necessary. That is the price of democracy. It is expensive but worthwhile. It strengthens the state. It gives it a reason to its fight."[39]

When I speak about balance, I do not mean an external normative process that changes the scope of rights and the protection accorded them because of terror. I mean the ordinary process that takes place every day, when we address the relationship between individual rights and the needs of society. In this latter process, rights are not absolute. They may be limited to serve the needs of society. I do not have the right to shout "fire" in a crowded theater. The threat of terrorism increases the probability that serious damage may occur, which allows the right to be limited. But note that we do not conduct two systems of balancing, one for regular times and an additional one under threat of terrorism. There is one balancing process, and terrorism determines the physical conditions under which the balance takes place.

When a court rules on the balance between security and freedom during times of terrorist threats, it often encounters complaints from all sides. The supporters of human rights argue that the court gives too much protection to security and too little to human rights. The supporters of security argue the converse. Frequently, those making these arguments only read the judicial conclusions without considering the judicial reasoning that seeks to reach a

---

[39] H.C. 7015/02, *Ajuri v. IDF Commander in the W. Bank*, 56(6) P.D. 352, 383 (English translation available at http://www.court.gov.il).

proper balance among the conflicting values and principles. None of this should intimidate the judge; he must rule according to his best understanding and conscience.

SCOPE OF JUDICIAL REVIEW

Open Door

Our point of departure in Israel has been that the doors of the Supreme Court—which in Israel serves as a court of first instance for complaints against the executive branch—are open to anyone wishing to complain about the activities of a public authority. There are no black holes where there is judicial review.

The open door approach is expressed in a number of ways. First, it is very rare that the court would close its doors on the ground of non-justiciability.[40] At times the state may argue that most of its counterterrorism activities are beyond the reach of the judiciary because they take place outside the country, because they constitute an act of state, or because they are political in nature. All these arguments were made before us in the Israeli Supreme Court, and most of them were rejected when human rights are directly affected. Thus, we have ruled on petitions concerning the power of the state to arrest suspected terrorists, and the conditions of their confinement.[41] We have ruled on petitions concerning the rights of suspected terrorists to legal representation and the means by which they may be interrogated.[42]

[40] *See supra* p. 179.
[41] *See* H.C. 3239/02, *Maraab v. Commander in Judea and Samaria,* 57(2) P.D. 349 (English translation available at www.court.gov.il); H.C. 3278/02, *Center for Defence of the Individual Founded by Dr. Lotta Salzberger v. IDF Commander in the W. Bank,* 57(1) P.D. 385 (English translation available at www.court.gov.il); H.C. 5591/02, *Yassin v. Commander of Kziot Military Camp,* 57(1) P.D. 403 (English translation available at www.court.gov.il); H.C. 253/88, *Sajadia v. Minister of Def.,* 42(3) P.D. 801.
[42] *Maarab,* 57(2) P.D. at 377 (the right to legal representation). *See* H.C. 5100/94, *Public Comm. Against Torture v. State of Israel,* 53(4) P.D. 817; [1998–9] IsrLR 567 (means of interrogation).

Second, the court opens its doors to anyone claiming that civil rights have been violated. Everyone has standing. This is the general approach of the court in time of peace.[43] We apply it also in times of terror. Thus, civil rights associations often come to us in defense of human rights of those sectors of society that most people do not wish to protect—including, of course, suspected terrorists.

Real Time

Judicial review of the battle against terrorism by its nature raises questions regarding the timing and scope of judicial intervention. There is no theoretical difference between applying judicial review before or after the fights on terrorism. In practice, however, as Chief Justice Rehnquist has correctly noted, the timing of judicial intervention affects its content. As he stated, "courts are more prone to uphold wartime claims of civil liberties after the war is over."[44] In light of this recognition, Chief Justice Rehnquist goes on to ask whether it would be better to abstain from judicial adjudication during warfare.[45] The answer, from my point of view—and, I am sure, that of Chief Justice Rehnquist—is clear: I will adjudicate a question when it is presented to me. I will not defer it until the fight against terror is over, because the fate of a human being may hang in the balance. The protection of human rights would be bankrupt if, during armed conflict, courts, consciously or unconsciously, decided to review the executive branch's behavior only after the period of emergency has ended. Furthermore, the decision should not rest on issuing general declarations about the balance of human rights and the need for security. Rather, the judicial ruling must impart guidance and direction in the specific case before it. As Justice Brennan correctly noted, "abstract principles announcing the applicability of civil liberties during times of war

---

[43] *Supra* p. 190.
[44] Rehnquist, *supra* p. 287, note 11 at 222.
[45] *Id.*

and crisis are ineffectual when a war or other crisis comes along unless the principles are fleshed out by a detailed jurisprudence explaining how those civil liberties will be sustained against particularized national security concerns."[46]

From a judicial review perspective, the situation in Israel is unique. Petitions from suspected terrorists reach the Supreme Court—which has exclusive jurisdiction over such matters—in real time. The judicial adjudication may take place not only during combat, but also often while the events being reviewed are still taking place. For example, the question whether the General Security Service may use extraordinary methods of interrogation (including what has been classified as torture) did not come before us in the context of a criminal case in which we had to rule, *ex post*, on the admissibility of a suspected terrorist's confession.[47] Rather, the question arose at the beginning of his interrogation. The suspect's lawyer came before us at the start of the interrogation and claimed, on the basis of past experience, that the General Security Service would torture his client. When we summoned the state's representative hours later, he confirmed the lawyer's allegation but nonetheless argued that the interrogation was legal. We had to make a decision in real time. Another example is the case of *Physicians for Human Rights*.[48] The petition was brought before us while IDF soldiers were in the middle of a military operation in one of the neighborhoods of the city of Rafa in the Gaza Strip. We were asked to review the supply of water, electricity, medical equipment, medicines, and food to the population while the military operation was in progress. How must we, as judges in a democracy, approach such an issue?

---

[46] Brennan, *supra* p. 283, note 1 at 19.

[47] *See* H.C. 4054/95, *Pub. Committee Against Torture in Isr. v. Gov't of Israel*, 43(4) P.D. 817; [1998–9] IsrLR 567.

[48] *See* H.C. 4764/04, *Physicians for Human Rights v. The Commander of IDF Forces in the Gaza Strip* (*unreported*, English translation available at www. court.gov.il).

"Security" Is No Magic Word

I believe that the court should not adopt a position on the efficient security measures for fighting against terrorism: "this court will not take any stance on the manner of conducting the combat."[49] For example, in a petition filed by citizens who were in the precincts of the Church of the Nativity when it was besieged by the army—a petition that was filed while negotiations were being held between the government of Israel and the Palestinian Authority regarding a solution to the problem—I wrote that "this court is not conducting the negotiations and is not taking part in them. The national responsibility in this affair lies with the executive and those acting on its behalf."[50] Indeed, the efficiency of security measures is within the power of the other branches of government. As long as these branches are acting within the framework of the zone of reasonableness,[51] there is no basis for judicial intervention. On the other hand, the executive often will argue that "security considerations" led to a government action, and request that the court be satisfied with this argument. Such a request should not be granted. "Security considerations" are not magic words. The court must insist on learning the specific security considerations that prompted the government's actions. The court must also be persuaded that these considerations actually motivated the government's actions and were not merely pretextual. Finally, the court must be convinced that the security measures adopted were the available measures least damaging to human rights. Indeed, in several of the many security measure cases that the Supreme Court has heard, senior army commanders and heads of the security services testified. Only if we were convinced, in the total balance, that the security consideration was the dominant one and that the

---

[49] H.C. 3114/02, *Barakeh v. Minister of Def.*, 56(3) P.D. 11, 16 (English translation available at www.court.gov.il).
[50] H.C. 3451/02, *Almadani v. IDF Commander in Judea & Samaria*, 56(3) P.D. 30, 36 (English translation available at www.court.gov.il).
[51] *See supra* p. 42.

security measure was proportionate to the terrorist act did we dismiss the challenge against the action.[52] In the case challenging the route of the West Bank separation barrier built by Israel, the question was whether the security measures were proportional, in light of the harm to individual residents. In my judgment, I wrote:

> This question raises no problems in the military field; rather it relates to the severity of the injury caused to the local inhabitants by the route decided upon by the military commander. In the framework of this question we are dealing not with military considerations but rather with humanitarian considerations. The question is not the proportionality of different military considerations. The question is the proportionality between the military consideration and the humanitarian consideration. . . . The standard for this question is not the subjective standard of the military commander. The question is not whether the military commander believed, in good faith, that the injury is proportionate. The standard is objective. The question is whether, by legal standards, the route of the separation fence passes the test of proportionality. This is a legal question, the expertise for which is held by the court.[53]

[52] In *Secretary of State for the Home Department v. Rehman*, No. UKHL47, 2001 WL 1135176 (H.L. Oct. 11, 2001) (U.K.), Lord Hoffman noted that "the judicial arm of government [needs] to respect the decisions of ministers of the Crown on the question of whether support for terrorist activities in a foreign country constitutes a threat to national security." I hope the meaning of these comments is limited to the general principle that a court determines not the means of fighting terrorism but rather the lawfulness of the means employed.

[53] H.C. 2056/04, *Beit Sourik Village Council*, *supra* p. 182, note 16. In the *Physicians for Human Rights* case, *supra* p. 300, note 48, I observed:

> Judicial review does not examine the wisdom of the decision to engage in military activity. In exercising judicial review, we examine the legality of the military activity. Therefore, we assume that the military activity that took place in Rafa was necessary from the military standpoint. The question before us is whether this military activity satisfies the national and international standards that determine the legality of that activity. The fact that the activity is necessary on the military plane does not mean that it is lawful on the legal plane. Indeed, we do not substitute our discretion for that of the military commander's, as far as it concerns military considerations. That is his expertise. We examine the results on the plane of the humanitarian law. That is our expertise. (Para. 48)

We should be neither naive nor cynical. We should analyze objectively the evidence before us. In a case dealing with review, under the Geneva Convention, of the state's decision to assign the residence of Arabs from the West Bank to the Gaza Strip, I noted that:

> In exercising judicial review . . . we do not make ourselves into security experts. We do not replace the military commander's security considerations with our own. We take no position on the way security issues are handled. Our job is to maintain boundaries, and to guarantee the existence of conditions that restrict the military commander's discretion . . . because of the important security aspects in which the commander's decision is grounded. We do not, however, replace the commander's discretion with our own. We insist upon the legality of the military commander's exercise of discretion and that it fall into the range of reasonableness, determined by the relevant legal norms applicable to the issue.[54]

Arguments against Judicial Review

Is it proper for judges to review the legality of the fight on terrorism? Many, at both extremes of the political spectrum, argue that the courts should not become involved in these matters. On one side, critics argue that judicial review undermines security; on the other side, critics argue that judicial review gives undeserved legitimacy to government actions against terrorism. Both arguments are unacceptable. Judicial review of the legality of the battle on terrorism may make this battle harder in the short term, but it also fortifies and strengthens the people in the long term. The rule of law is a central element in national security. As I wrote in the case of the pretrial pardon given to the heads of the General Security Service:

> There is no security without law. The rule of law is a component of national security. Security requires us to find proper tools for interrogation. Otherwise, the General Security Service will be unable

---

[54] H.C., 7015/02, *supra* p. 297, note 39 at 375.

to fulfill its mission. The strength of the Service lies in the public's confidence in it. Its strength lies in the court's confidence in it. If security considerations tip the scales, neither the public nor the court will have confidence in the Security Service and the lawfulness of its interrogations. Without this confidence, the branches of the state cannot function. This is true of public confidence in the courts, and it true of public confidence in the other branches of state.[55]

I concluded my opinion in that case with the following historical analogy:

> It is said that there was a dispute between King James I and Justice Coke. The question was whether the king could take matters in the province of the judiciary into his own hands and decide them himself. At first, Justice Coke tried to persuade the king that judging required expertise that the king did not have. The king was not convinced. Then Justice Coke rose and said, *"Quod rex non debet sub homine, sed sub deo et lege."* The king is not subject to man, but subject to God and the law. Let it be so.[56]

The security considerations entertained by the branches of the state are subject to "God and the law." In the final analysis, this subservience strengthens democracy. It makes the struggle against terrorism worthwhile. To the extent that the legitimacy of the court means that the acts of the state are lawful, the court fulfills an important role. Public confidence in the branches of the state is vital for democracy. Both when the state wins and when it loses, the rule of law and democracy benefit. The main effect of the judicial decision occurs not in the individual instance that comes before it but by determining the general norms according to which governmental authorities act and establishing the deterrent effect that these norms will have. The test of the rule of law arises not merely in the few cases brought before the court but also in the many potential cases that are not brought before it, since governmental authorities are aware of

---

[55] H.C. 428/86, *Barzilai v. Gov't of Israel*, 40(3) P.D. 505, 622 (English translation available at www.court.gov.il) (citation omitted).
[56] *Id.* at 623.

the court's rulings and act accordingly. The argument that judicial review necessarily validates the governmental action does not take into account the nature of judicial review. In hearing a case, the court does not examine the wisdom of the war against terrorism, but only the legality of the acts taken in furtherance of the war. The court does not ask itself if it would have adopted the same security measures if it were responsible for security. Instead, the court asks if a reasonable person responsible for security would be prudent to adopt the security measures that were adopted. Thus, the court does not express agreement or disagreement with the means adopted, but rather fulfills its role of reviewing the constitutionality and legality of the executive acts.

Naturally, one must not go from one extreme to the other. One must recognize that the court will not solve the problem of terrorism. It is a problem to be addressed by the other branches of government. The court's role is to ensure the constitutionality and legality of the fight against terrorism. It must ensure that the battle against terrorism is conducted within the framework of the law. This is the court's contribution to democracy's struggle to survive. In my opinion, it is an important contribution, one that aptly reflects the judicial role in a democracy. Realizing this rule during a fight against terrorism is difficult. We cannot and would not want to escape from this difficulty, as I noted in one case:

> The decision has been laid before us, and we must stand by it. We are obligated to preserve the legality of the regime even in difficult decisions. Even when the artillery booms and the Muses are silent, law exists and acts and decides what is permitted and what is forbidden, what is legal and what is illegal. And when law exists, courts also exist to adjudicate what is permitted and what is forbidden, what is legal and what is illegal. Some of the public will applaud our decision; others will oppose it. Perhaps neither side will have read our reasoning. We have done our part, however. That is our role and our obligations as judges.[57]

[57] H.C. 2161/96, *Rabhi Said Sharif v. Military Commander*, 50(4) P.D. 485, 491.

CHAPTER SEVENTEEN

The Role of the Judge: Theory, Practice, and the Future

THEORY

The Role of the Judge

At the opening of this book, I asked what the role of the judge in a democracy is.[1] I also asked whether there are criteria for evaluating how the judicial role is realized. I wanted to know which tests determine whether a judge is a good judge. In this book, I have tried to give an answer to these questions. My answer concerning the role of the judge is this: the role of the judge is to adjudicate the dispute brought before him. In order to do so, the judge must decide the law according to which the dispute will be decided. In making this determination, the judge often acts as the "mouth of the legislature." The judge repeats the language of the statute, as opposed to creating a new norm ("easy case"). That is generally but not always the case. In some cases ("hard cases"), determining the law requires creating the law. That is certainly the case of the development of the common law. It can also be true of interpreting a text created by others (the founding fathers of the constitution, the legislatures, the parties to a contract, a testator). In each of these cases, there is no prior law, or the prior law contains uncertainty. In these cases the judge makes new law.

In creating new law, the judge should aspire to realize two central goals. The first is to bridge the gap between social reality and law. The judge should adapt the law to life's changing needs.

[1] *Supra* p. ix.

The second is to protect the constitution and its values. In working toward both goals, the judge should behave objectively, remaining sensitive to social consensus, to the extent that it exists. The judge should maintain public confidence in his fairness.

To realize these two roles, the judge should use the tools that the law provides (such as interpretation, developing the common law, balancing, the use of comparative law). The judge may not use means that are not legitimate. It is not enough for judges to know where they are going; they must use legitimate tools to achieve their goals. Without a legitimate ladder, one cannot reach the desired rooftop. In the absence of existing tools, one should consider creating new tools. Such creation is appropriate if the judge is authorized to do so.

Realizing the judicial role using these available means will create tension between the judge and the legislative and executive branches. Such tension is natural, even desirable. The judge should respect the special status of the legislature and recognize that there is a dialogue between him and the legislature. The judge is not accountable to the legislature or the nation in the way that a member of the legislature is. A judge is not a politician. A judge is accountable to the constitution and its values. That is the (personal and institutional) independence of the judge. Within the principle of separation of powers, the judge should make sure that each of the other branches operates within the boundaries of the law. Judicial review of the constitutionality of legislation and of administrative actions realizes democracy. It protects the constitution and its values.

A Good Judge

Who is a good judge? My answer is that a good judge is a judge who, within the bounds of the legitimate possibilities at his disposal, makes the law that, more than other law he is authorized to make, best bridges the gap between law and society and best protects the constitution and its values. A good judge is aware of his role and makes use of the means at his disposal in order to achieve it. In the absence of means, he examines whether it is possible to create new means to help realize the judicial role. Regarding some issues, he will be active. On others, he exercises self-restraint. The judge never assumes that it is always worthy to be either activist or self-restrained. The good judge is always limited by the text according to which he adjudicates the dispute. The judge may not give the text a meaning that its language cannot bear. However, the text is not the end-all. Every text operates in a context, which must be understood in order to understand the text. The good judge recognizes the text and sees it as a starting point, but not an ending point. Good judges lift their eyes and see the legal system in all its nuances, values, and foundations. The good judge locates the meaning of the text within this general context. Indeed, the good judge does not make do with knowing the law. He should know society, its problems, and its aspirations. The good judge does not just look at the language of the single clause of the constitution, statute, contract, or will which he must interpret. The judge looks at the text in its entirety. One who interprets a single clause of the constitution interprets the entire constitution. One who interprets a single clause of a statute interprets all the statutes in their entirety.

The quality of a judge is determined by examining his rulings. Each case is examined on the merits. All the cases are given a comprehensive evaluation. The good or worthy judge is the judge who, in this comprehensive evaluation, used the available tools to achieve the role of the judge optimally. Indeed, the quality of a judge does not depend on a single decision given. We all make mistakes, including the judges among us. A mistaken ruling does not tip the scales any more than a good ruling does. Examining the quality of a judge depends on evaluating the entirety of the judge's work. Of course, one should also consider the judge's development over the years.

Some judges fulfill their roles properly without giving thought to their roles. They act intuitively. The criteria for their actions are internalized, without them having articulated them. In my opinion, judges should try to develop their judicial philosophy. This philosophy is the most practical tool that judges have. It guarantees that the intuition undergoes a process of rationalization. Without intuition, it is difficult for a judge to act. But judges should not act on intuition alone.

Good judges therefore lay the basis for a judicial philosophy that allows them, using the tools at their disposal within their legal systems, to decide according to the law that best realizes their roles. They will therefore develop a theory of interpretation that will help them fulfill their roles. In my opinion, that theory is purposive interpretation. Good judges will develop the common law in their system in order to realize their roles. When necessary, they will deviate from precedent, providing that the considerations supporting the new rule outweigh those supporting the old rule when taken together with the harm caused by the very act of change.

There are degrees in the quality of judging. There are better and worse judges. All judges should aspire to attaining the highest level, without ever attaining it. To my mind, the good judge is not a person of extremes. His world is not divided into black and white. Good judges know to balance between the extremes. Good judges understand that even if law is everywhere, law is not everything; they are aware that law is not a closed framework that lives inside itself. Without society, law has no value, and social values nourish the law. Indeed, law is inseparably connected to society's values and principles. True, judges do not create these values and principles, but they help introduce them into the law and remove them from law. In the field of law, conflicting values must be balanced.

The law deals with people. Human complexity influences the complexity of law. There is no single, unique solution to the problems of the individual and of society; there is no one theory that explains law and its development. There is always a need for balance and awareness of the limitations of judges and their role in within the three branches of government.

In this book, I discussed the normative aspect of judicial work. This is not the forum to discuss additional aspects of judicial work and the qualities needed to actualize them. It suffices to note that at the core of judging is judicial temperament. That is the quality that allows the judge to listen to the parties' arguments with an open mind, without interrupting and without constantly seeking to educate them; that is the quality that allows the judge to restrain his power and to understand its limits; it is a quality of humility and the lack of arrogance that educates the judge to understand that he does not have a monopoly on wisdom; it is recognition of his capability of erring and the need to admit mistakes. In addition to judicial temperament, of course, other qualities such as personal and professional integrity are necessary, without which a person cannot be a judge.

REALITY

It is hard to be a judge. It is even harder to be a good and worthy judge. It is sevenfold harder to be a good and worthy judge in a democracy under terror. It is hard to be a judge because the judge is a loner. It is hard to be a good or worthy judge, because doing so requires the power to abstract, recognition of law in its entirety and the relationship between it and society's values and principles, the ability to balance conflicting demands and to give expression to what is fundamental and basic, disqualifying what is temporary and passing—and to do all that with maximal objectivity. It is hard to be a good and worthy judge in a democracy under terror, because when terror strikes a democracy, the tension between the needs of the community and the liberty of the individual reaches its peak.

THE FUTURE

Understanding the Judicial Role

What does the future hold for the role of the judge in a democracy? It is, of course, impossible to foretell the future. But we can make several suppositions. I believe that the view of the judicial role as I have described it will take root and deepen. The need to bridge law and society will become more pressing. Social changes are becoming more and more intensive. Changes that in the past took place over generations today take place in a matter of years. In the future, those periods of time will become even shorter. The legislature cannot always keep pace with these changes. Society will need courts more than ever to bridge the gaps between law and life. This is the case for gaps created by technological changes, such as the computer and Internet; it is the case for gaps created by social changes, such as attitudes toward religion, the institution of marriage, social rights, and other changes related to the ways in which people relate to their surroundings.

The role of the court in protecting the constitution and its values will certainly become strengthened as the essence of the constitution as a supreme norm and the judicial review that accompanies it become more deeply understood. Changes in the view of constitutional democracy—the daily bread of the world's important democracies (such as those of the United States, Canada, and Germany)—will become internalized. The man in the street will understand, better than he does today, that democracy is not just majority rule but also the rule of values, including human rights. Trends toward "popular constitutionalism"[2] will be, I believe, short-lived. They reflect a dissatisfaction with a specific court. They do not pose a satisfactory intellectual alternative to the role of the judge in a democracy, as provided in this book. Thus, the judicialization of politics will continue.[3] The non-justiciability of legal aspects of politics will decrease.

As in the past, so too in the future, the court will protect the state's democratic values. Judges come and go, but democracy and the need to protect it remain. I am convinced that in the future, too, judges in general, and Supreme Court judges in particular, will place the protection of the state's democratic values at the top of their agenda. They will protect both formal and substantive democracy. I do not expect that to change. The precedential foundation laid by generations of judges will serve them. They will construct their own buildings on that foundation.

---

[2] *See* Larry D. Kramer, *The People Themselves: Popular Constitutionalism and Judicial Review* (2004).

[3] *See* Alec Stone Sweet, *Governing with Judges: Constitutional Politics in Europe* (2000); Martin Shapiro and Alec Stone Sweet, *On Law, Politics and Judicialization* (2002); Alec Stone Sweet, *The Judicial Construction of Europe* (2000); Herbert Jacob et al., *Courts, Law and Politics in Comparative Perspective* (1996).

Developing Judicial Means

Judges have few tools at their disposal. I hope that the tools presently available will be developed. I am certain that new tools will be created. Indeed, interpretive theory should be developed. Modern purposive interpretation is at the start of its journey. The common law has developed nicely in the past; I am convinced that it will develop nicely in the future. The theory of balancing will continue to be the central means at judges' disposal. I also hope that jurisprudence will provide us with a better understanding of the tool of balancing and aid us in determining the weight of competing values. In the future, will the approach to judging and its role be as it is today? I do not know. The present situation may continue; there may be further liberalization or restriction of access to the court. I hope that the latter development does not take place. In modern democracies, claims of non-justiciability are becoming fewer; standing rules are becoming more and more liberal. The role of comparative law will expand. As the trend toward globalization continues, comparative law will become a natural means of interpreting and developing the law.

The Relationship with the Other Branches

What does the future hold for the relationship among the branches of the state? It is clear that the existing tension between the judicial and other branches will continue. Such tension is positive. I do hope that in the future, it will be based on a better understanding of the other branches and their functions.[4] The question is whether it will break the rules of the game. I hope that the answer is no. There is a myth that strong courts are needed when the other branches of the state are weak. The truth is, democracy needs strong courts *especially* when it has a strong legislature and a strong executive.

[4] *See Judges and Legislators: Toward Institutional Comity* (Robert A. Katzmann ed., 1988).

Further, it is a myth that courts become stronger because of weak governments and legislative bodies. The strength of the judicial branch and the judicialization of politics are not dependent on the weakness of the political branches. They are based on democracy itself. They assume strong and effective political branches.

Public Confidence in the Judiciary

Will public confidence in the court system be maintained or even grow? I am convinced that judges will do all they can to maintain this confidence. They will be guided by neither activism nor self-restraint, but rather will weigh claims on the merits. Sometimes that will mean activism; sometimes the result will be self-restraint. Whatever the result, judges will be subject to criticism. Such criticism is appropriate and desirable. Will it also be fair? I have no clear answer to that. Increasingly, people criticize court decisions without reading them; too many people criticize decisions they don't understand. I fear that the future does not hold positive developments in this area.

Judicial Independence

In the future, the independence of the court system will be put to the test. I hope this independence will be maintained; I hope that institutional independence—which is missing today in many democracies—will be established and preserved. I do hope that the judicialization of politics will not increase the politicization of judicial appointments. On the contrary: it should reduce such attempts. If politics is judicialized, what is needed is objective, professional, and independent judges. That calls for less politics in the appointment of judges. It seems to me that the trend is toward more professionalism and less politics.[5]

[5] See the powers and composition of the Judicial Service Commission in the appointment of judges in South Africa: Articles 174 and 178 of the Constitution of the Republic of South Africa. See also the United Kingdom proposals for the

A Role That Is a Mission

I regard myself as a judge who is sensitive to his role in a democracy. I take seriously the tasks imposed upon me; to bridge the gap between law and society and to protect the constitution and democracy. Despite frequent criticism—and it frequently descends to the level of personal attacks and threats of violence—I have continued on this path for the last twenty-six years. I hope that by doing so, I am serving my legal system properly. Indeed, as judges in our countries' highest courts, we must continue on our paths according to our consciences. We, as judges, have a North Star that guides us: the fundamental values and principles of constitutional democracy. A heavy responsibility rests on our shoulders. But even in hard times, we must remain true to ourselves. I discussed this duty in an opinion considering whether extraordinary methods of interrogation may be used on a terrorist in a "ticking bomb" situation:

> Deciding these applications has been difficult for us. True, from the legal perspective, the road before us is smooth. We are, however, part of Israeli society. We know its problems and we live its history. We are not in an ivory tower. We live the life of this country. We are aware of the harsh reality of terrorism in which we are, at times, immersed. The fear that our ruling will prevent us from properly dealing with terrorists troubles us. But we are judges. We demand that others act according to the law. This is also the demand that we make of ourselves. When we sit at trial, we stand on trial. In deciding the law, we must act according to our purest conscience.[6]

That is my approach to my role as a judge. I have taken this approach with me daily into the courtroom. It is my approach to writing decisions. It is an approach central to which are the values

---

creation of an independent statutory Judicial Appointment Commission to recommend judicial appointments: see The Constitutional Reform Bill: A Supreme Court for the United Kingdom and Judicial Appointments (Bill No. 18 of 2004–05).
[6] H.C. 4054/95, *Pub. Committee Against Torture in Isr. v. Gov't of Israel*, 43(4) P.D. 817, 845; [1998–9] IsrLR 567, 606.

of a democracy; it is an approach central to which is the human being, created in the image of God; it is the approach that views the judicial role as service and not as power.

As a judge, I do not have a political platform. I am not a political person. Right and left, religious and secular, rich and poor, man and woman, disabled and nondisabled—all are equal in my eyes. All are human beings, created in the image of the Creator. I will protect the human dignity of each. I do not aspire to power. I do not seek to rule. I am aware of the chains that bind me as a judge and as the president of the Supreme Court. I have repeatedly emphasized the rule of law and not of the judge. I am aware of the importance of the other branches of government—the legislative and executive—which give expression to democracy. Between those branches are connecting bridges and checks and balances.

I view my office as a mission. Judging is not a job. It is a way of life. Whenever I enter the courtroom, I do so with the deep sense that, as I sit at trial, I stand on trial.

Index